CHINA IN THE GLOBAL ECONOMY

Income Disparities in China An OECD Perspective

OECD

ORGANISATION FOR ECONOMIC CO-OPERATION AND DEVELOPMENT

ORGANISATION FOR ECONOMIC CO-OPERATION AND DEVELOPMENT

Pursuant to Article 1 of the Convention signed in Paris on 14th December 1960, and which came into force on 30th September 1961, the Organisation for Economic Co-operation and Development (OECD) shall promote policies designed:

- to achieve the highest sustainable economic growth and employment and a rising standard of living in member countries, while maintaining financial stability, and thus to contribute to the development of the world economy;
- to contribute to sound economic expansion in member as well as non-member countries in the process of economic development; and
- to contribute to the expansion of world trade on a multilateral, non-discriminatory basis in accordance with international obligations.

The original member countries of the OECD are Austria, Belgium, Canada, Denmark, France, Germany, Greece, Iceland, Ireland, Italy, Luxembourg, the Netherlands, Norway, Portugal, Spain, Sweden, Switzerland, Turkey, the United Kingdom and the United States. The following countries became members subsequently through accession at the dates indicated hereafter: Japan (28th April 1964), Finland (28th January 1969), Australia (7th June 1971), New Zealand (29th May 1973), Mexico (18th May 1994), the Czech Republic (21st December 1995), Hungary (7th May 1996), Poland (22nd November 1996), Korea (12th December 1996) and the Slovak Republic (14th December 2000). The Commission of the European Communities takes part in the work of the OECD (Article 13 of the OECD Convention).

OECD CENTRE FOR CO-OPERATION WITH NON-MEMBERS

The OECD Centre for Co-operation with Non-Members (CCNM) promotes and co-ordinates OECD's policy dialogue and co-operation with economies outside the OECD area. The OECD currently maintains policy co-operation with approximately 70 non-member economies.

The essence of CCNM co-operative programmes with non-members is to make the rich and varied assets of the OECD available beyond its current membership to interested non-members. For example, the OECD's unique co-operative working methods that have been developed over many years; a stock of best practices across all areas of public policy experiences among members; on-going policy dialogue among senior representatives from capitals, reinforced by reciprocal peer pressure; and the capacity to address interdisciplinary issues. All of this is supported by a rich historical database and strong analytical capacity within the Secretariat. Likewise, member countries benefit from the exchange of experience with experts and officials from non-member economies.

The CCNM's programmes cover the major policy areas of OECD expertise that are of mutual interest to non-members. These include: economic monitoring, statistics, structural adjustment through sectoral policies, trade policy, international investment, financial sector reform, international taxation, environment, agriculture, labour market, education and social policy, as well as innovation and technological policy development.

FOREWORD

China has experienced rapid economic growth since 1978, averaging 8 to 9% per year. As a result, average standards of living are far higher than ever before in China's history and absolute poverty has fallen significantly. However, economic inequality has also increased significantly, raising questions about the sustainability of existing policies. China's level of inequality appears to be lower than in countries such as Brazil, Mexico, Russia, South Africa and Turkey, but it is well above the average for most OECD countries. What is distinctive in the Chinese case is the speed at which inequality has apparently increased, with only some of the Central Asian Republics and Russia experiencing such an increase in the level of inequality in so short a period of time. This growth in inequality, particularly the widening gap between urban and rural dwellers, and different regions of the country, is widely discussed in China as a potential threat to social stability.

With the financial support of the government of Japan, the OECD's Directorate for Employment, Labour and Social Affairs, and the Department of National Economy of the National Development and Reform Commission of China (NDRC), organised a seminar on income inequality trends from Chinese and international perspectives held in Paris on 20 and 21 October 2003.

This publication includes the papers written by experts from the National Development and Reform Commission, as well as by the OECD Secretariat, and by experts from OECD member countries. This collection not only provides a detailed assessment of trends in income inequality in China, but also reviews trends in OECD countries, in terms of changes in household income inequality, earnings dispersion and regional disparities. The discussion at the seminar and this publication together provide a solid foundation for further co-operation between the OECD and the National Development and Reform Commission of China, which has also prepared the concrete groundwork for a Directorate on Employment and Income Distribution to carry out further work in this area.

This study is published under the responsibility of the Secretary-General of the OECD.

Eric Burgeat
Director
Centre for Co-operation
with Non-Members, OECD

John Martin
Director
Directorate for Employment,
Labour and Social Affairs, OECD

TABLE OF CONTENTS

PART I. ASSESSING INCOME DISPARITIES IN CHINA

PART II. INCOME DISPARITIES IN OECD MEMBER COUNTRIES

BASIC STATISTICS OF CHINA

LAND		
Area (thousand km²)		9 597
Agricultural area (thousand km²)		1 300
Forests (thousand km²)		2 633
PEOPLE		
Population, 2003 (million)		1 292
Annual rate of change of population, 2003		0.60
Inhabitants per km², 2003		135
Major cities, 2002 (million, non-agricultural and total inhabitants):	Shanghai	10.0
	Beijing	7.9
	Tianjin	5.1
	Guangzhou	4.7
	Wuhan	4.6
	Chongqing	4.2
Civilian labour force, 2002 (million)		754
Civilian employment, 2003 (million)	Total	744
	Agriculture, forestry, fishing	365
	Manufacturing, mining, utilities and construction	161
	Services	218
PRODUCTION		
GDP (2003, billion CNY)		11 690
GDP per head (2003, USD)		1 093
GDP per head (2002, USD PPP)		4 580
Origin of GDP (2003, % of total):	Agriculture, forestry, fishing	14.6
	Manufacturing, mining, utilities and construction	52.3
	Services	33.1
Gross fixed capital formation (2003, billion CNY)		5 188
	% of GDP	44
	Per head (USD)	485
GOVERNMENT		
Government final consumption (2003, % of GDP)		12.6
Government expenditure: central, local and social insurance (2003, % of GDP)		27.9
Government revenue: central, local and social insurance (2003, % of GDP)		26.6
FOREIGN TRADE		
Exports of goods and services (2003, % of GDP)		34.3
Main exports (% of total exports of goods):	Computers	14.3
	Clothing	11.9
	Telecommunications equipment	10.3
	Electrical machinery and semiconductors	9.7
Imports of goods and services, (2003, % of GDP)		31.8
Main imports (% of total imports of goods):	Electrical machinery and semiconductors	19.3
	Petroleum and petroleum products	6.5
	Computers	5.9
	Iron and steel	5.3
CURRENCY		
Monetary unit: CNY. Currency unit per USD, average of daily figures	2002	8.3
	2003	8.3
	May 2004	8.3

PART I.

ASSESSING INCOME DISPARITIES IN CHINA

Chapter 1

THE EVOLUTION OF INCOME DISTRIBUTION DISPARITIES IN CHINA SINCE THE REFORM AND OPENING-UP

by
Han Wenxiu,

Deputy Director General, Department of National Economy,
National Development and Reform Commission, China

Main changes in overall income distribution

Since the beginning of its open-door policy, China has carried out a series of market reforms which fundamentally improved the allocation of productive forces, resulting in sustained and rapid economic growth and a steady increase in household income. Thus, living conditions have improved greatly. During the 23 years between 1978 and 2001, the average annual growth rate of China's GDP was 9.4%, urban households per capita real disposable income increased by 6.4% annually, and the real per capita net income of rural households increased by 7.3% annually (Table 1.1). Engel coefficients for urban and rural households decreased from 57.5% and 67.7% in 1978, to 37.9% and 47.7% in 2001, respectively (Table 1.2).[1] Overall, this period witnessed the most substantial economic development in China's history, with the most rapid income increase for urban and rural households, and the greatest benefits obtained by the Chinese people. In general, China has reached a well-off standard of living.

However, a rapid increase in disparities in income distribution was observed during these 23 years. China has changed from a country with a fairly even income distribution into a country with wide income disparities. The Gini coefficient in 2000 reached 0.417 (Tables 1.3 and 1.4), surpassing many developed and developing countries (Table 1.5).[2] The coefficient may be even higher if factors such as statistical errors, due to unreported high incomes, and illegal incomes, are considered. The continuous increase in income disparities exerts more and more negative effects on economic and social development. The slow income growth in rural areas and the gradual enlargement of the low-income group in urban areas impede growth in consumption, and thus affect the growth of the economy as a whole. Increases in monopolistic income and illegal incomes are also damaging the population's enthusiasm and creativeness, which also impacts on economic efficiency.

1. The Engel coefficient is the share of total expenditure (or income) devoted to food, with lower coefficients implying higher living standards.

2. The Gini coefficient is a measure of inequality, varying between 0 and 1; the higher the coefficient, the higher the level of inequality.

Changes in income distribution patterns among social groups

Overall, income disparities between urban and rural areas, between regions, sectors, and among social groups, have increased to different degrees since 1978, although the problem of "dislocation of the brain and the body", *i.e.* a situation where intellectual labour was paid less than physical labour, has been remedied.

Urban and rural income disparities

The ratio of urban per capita disposable income to rural net per capita income increased from 2.57 in 1978 to 2.90 in 2001, and is expected to surpass 3 in 2002 (Table 1.6).

Regional income disparities

Increases in household income take place noticeably quicker in the coastal areas than in the central and western regions. The ratio of rural per capita net income in the eastern, central and western regions was 1.09/1/0.91 in 1978, and increased to 1.47/1/0.77 in 2000 (Table 1.7). During the same period, the ratio of urban per capita disposable income in the three regions also increased from 1.10/1/1.01 to 1.49/1/1.06 (Table 1.8).

Income disparities among sectors

Among 16 sectors of the economy, the incomes of workers and staff in monopolistic sectors increased much faster than in more competitive sectors. The ratio of these incomes in the sector with the highest wages, and that with the lowest, was about 1.764/1 in 1990, and increased to 2.493/1 in 1999 (Table 1.9). The disparity would be even greater if other incomes and fringe benefits were taken into consideration.

Income disparities among social groups

Income disparities among certain social groups widened rapidly, and became a source for concern. In 1996, the highest income decile of urban households had a per capita income 3.8 times as high as that of the lowest urban income decile. In 2001, the ratio of per capita incomes of the two groups rose to 5.4, and the living conditions of the low-income group were fairly difficult.

The causes of increasing income disparities

Imbalances in economic development

The main explanation for increasing income disparities is the imbalance in economic development. Due to differences in natural conditions, historical endowments, human resource disparities, ideological changes, as well as the fact that the reform process began in the coastal areas, the disparity of economic growth between the coastal areas and the inland provinces, and that between the eastern, central and western regions, gradually enlarged. At the same time, economic growth rates, labour productivity and the economic efficiency of diverse industries with different ownership also differed. In a market economy, economic development is inevitably uneven, which in turn causes income disparity among residents. The more imbalanced the economic development, the greater will be the income disparity.

Imperfections in the economic system

Historically, a dual-track economic structure separates the urban and rural economies. The current household registration system breaks the connection between the urban and rural labour markets. In particular, it affects the flow of productive factors between urban and rural areas, which again restricts opportunities for increasing incomes in rural areas, resulting in a wider income disparity between the urban and rural populations. Certain sectors and industries managed to gain high profits, based on monopolies which have not been efficiently controlled and regulated. Excessive administrative examination and approval led to universal rent-setting and rent-seeking. An incomplete state property management system, lack of standardised capital markets, and non-transparent firm, village and administration management, all caused widespread corruption, and conspicuously unfair income distribution.

The impact of market mechanisms on income distribution

Wages in private and foreign-funded enterprises are determined by the market directly, and this practice is beginning to extend to state-owned and collective enterprises. The fierce competition among enterprises also brings about differences in individual incomes. Differences between simple and complex labour are more obvious, and earnings for those participating in intellectual or managerial activities have actually become more related to effort. At the same time, the contribution of capital, technology and other production factors further enlarged disparities in income distribution. All of the above are the result of market mechanisms.

Insufficient income redistribution

China lacks a sound system for managing income redistribution. Individual incomes are not transparent, causing many practical problems for income taxation. Tax cheating is very common. In particular, high incomes are not well adjusted. Moreover, many unreasonable practices persist in the income distribution system. First, the individual income tax adjusts wage incomes effectively, but does not satisfactorily adjust the income components that are causing increasing income disparities, such as capital incomes. Second, the tax rate negatively affects low income individuals. Third, rural incomes are quite low, while taxes and fees are a fairly heavy burden. In comparison, urban incomes are higher, and real incomes are increased by various benefits and public services. Fourth, some irrational factors emerged in the course of the reform of the welfare system for workers and staff in urban areas. For example, in the reform of the public housing system, flawed reform plans in many localities led to an unbalanced distribution of both housing and monetary compensation, so that some families were left without housing, or with inadequate housing. In addition, low income groups lack effective social protection. Although various measures have been established, such as fighting poverty in rural areas, an urban minimum living standard subsidy, a minimum wage and salaries standard and the re-employment project for laid-off workers, the level of basic protection for the low-income population is inadequate, due to insufficient state financial resources and limited financial transfers.

Conclusions, trends and countermeasures

Overall, the current pressing issues in the income distribution system are all problems related to development and systemic transition, reflecting the incompleteness of the socialist market economy system for the time being, and thus are inevitable. Looking at income inequality as a whole, it may be the case that rational, and thus inevitable, disparities are more significant than irrational disparities. The widening of income disparities occurred, on the one hand, during a process when overall incomes increased steadily and, on the other, where economic efficiency has also been continuously improved. In this regard, the process has helped overall economic growth and social development. However, it should be clearly noted that, compared to the past, certain reform and development measures taken in recent years have direct effects on income distribution. In the past, people generally gained benefits from reform, and income distribution changed, with some people getting more and some less. By contrast, recent measures led to gains and losses as well, but involved more significant adjustments for vested interests. The widening income disparity and the inequitable distribution impose more and more negative effects in economic and social development. In particular, corruption and related phenomena have already caused detrimental social influence. Meanwhile, equalitarianism and the lack of effective incentives inside state-owned units have impacted on further improvements in efficiency. More determined and effective measures should be taken to resolve these problems.

There are several reasons why the trend of widening income disparities will continue during the 10th five-year period. First, the role of market mechanisms in adjusting income distribution will be enhanced. Equalitarianism in state-owned units will be disrupted further, and the implementation of the principle distribution according to work will be increased. The connotation of "work" will be enriched, so that each factor of production will contribute more broadly and deeply to the distribution process. Gradually, factor income will carry more weight in overall income. However, all these factors may cause an increase in income inequality. Second, unbalanced development between urban and rural areas, and at the regional level, will persist, and may even get worse. These disparities will not be eliminated in the short run. Third, the complete elimination of irrationally high incomes and illegal incomes takes time, although these incomes may be constrained to a certain degree with the deepening of reform and the enhancement of laws and regulations.

These problems of income distribution emerged, and gradually worsened, during the process of reform and development. In fact, only the acceleration of development and the deepening of reform will help to solve them. Procedures to reform the income distribution system and to adjust the structure should follow certain principles: first, maintain the combination of distribution according to work with distribution according to productive factors and fight against equalitarianism; second, take into consideration social equality and prevent polarisation; third, continue to encourage a part of the population and regions to become rich first, and achieve common prosperity step-by-step; and fourth, continuously improve living standards, on the basis of the development of production factors.

In the long term, China's overall objective for the adjustment of income distribution is to form a distribution structure with fairly small high and low-income groups, and a dominant middle-income group. In the short term, and as suggested in the 10th five-year plan, income distribution will be regulated by the strengthening of state taxation functions, protection of legal incomes, rectification of irrational incomes, regulation of high incomes, and prohibition of illegal incomes, so as to prevent the excessive enlargement of income disparities. As required by this proposal, the short-term objectives for adjustment of income distribution are:

- The trend towards the widening of overall income disparity will be constrained initially. As rational income disparities may rise, irrational income disparities should tend to decrease.

- High incomes will be efficiently adjusted, and the living standards of the low-income population in both urban and rural areas will be assured.

- Distribution will be normalised, to further improve efficiency and make it more equitable.

To accomplish these goals, the overall approaches to solving income distribution problems are as follows:

Rely on development. This means solving problems through economic development. First, this requires maintaining a fairly fast rate of economic growth, so as to increase urban and rural household incomes. Second, it entails simultaneously maintaining the trend of development in the eastern region, accelerating development in the central and western regions, and effectively implementing the western region's development strategy, to bring about co-ordinated development of regional economies. Third, it implies that, while pursuing urban economic development, it is also necessary to accelerate the growth of the rural economy, propel urbanisation actively and steadily, and try to achieve co-ordinated development of the urban and rural economies. Fourth, as high and new technology industries will be actively built up, tertiary industries and labour-intensive industries should be vigorously developed at the same time, in order to improve employment, so as to create 40 million urban jobs and transfer 40 million persons from the rural labour force within the next five years.

Rely on reform. This implies further deepening of the reform of the income distribution and related systems and a reduction in systemic impediments, so as to create the necessary means of solving income distribution problems. It first requires continuous adhesion to the market orientation of reforms, a full display of the fundamental role of market mechanisms in primary distribution, pushing forward the reform process of the productive factors, breaking-up of monopolies and support for competition. Second, it needs a further deepening of government organisational reforms, a substantial transformation of government responsibilities, a change in government economic management and acceleration of the reform of the systems of administrative examination and approval. Third, an improvement in the reforms of the state-owned management system, and its internal income distribution system, is required. Reforms in the distribution of goods and social benefits, and of collective consumption, need to be continuously promoted, simultaneously with an acceleration in the transformation of the wage system, monetarisation, and enhancement of the transparency and standardisation of labour remuneration.

Standardise primary distribution. Primary distribution is the origin and basis of the whole distribution process. Current income distribution problems arose mainly from primary distribution. Solutions to these problems must start from managing primary distribution in a more equitable way, which better embodies the principle of giving priority to efficiency. To achieve this, it is necessary to firmly follow the principle of working step-by-step. Thus, the first stage should be to protect legal incomes, and then continue to encourage part of the population to become rich through honest work and legal business management. Further steps should include eliminating equalitarian mechanisms in public-owned economic units, in order to increase income differences reasonably and match the earnings of labour to contribution. It is necessary to allow and encourage productive factors, including managerial expertise, technology and capital, to fully participate in income distribution. Another step should be to rectify unreasonable incomes, to outlaw illegal gains, and to adopt effective measures to adjust and standardise monopolistic and other unreasonable incomes from these monopolistic industries. Strong measures will need to be taken against unlawful practices and crimes, such as appropriation of public properties, tax evasion, smuggling, corruption, bribery and adulteration, in order to determinedly outlaw related illegal gains.

Enhance redistribution. The socialist income distribution policy should emphasise economic efficiency and also realise social justice through redistribution measures. Redistribution requires also a firm step-by-step approach. The first is to effectively adjust high incomes by improving and reinforcing the management of the taxation system. This process should encompass taxation of wages and salaries, as well as other incomes, and proper taxation of private property. It should also encourage high-income individuals to support charities and public welfare through tax credits, offsets, or tax deduction policies. A second step is to set up the necessary protection for the basic living standards of low-income individuals. This means to continue the policy of financing basic living needs first and then construction (first food, then construction). Other objectives are to keep increasing the ratio of fiscal revenue to GDP, to set up the framework for public finances, and to develop the government's ability to redistribute incomes and to provide public services. It is also necessary to secure the basic living standards of low-income individuals, by further improving the social security system, and to fight harder against poverty in both urban and rural areas.

The current major policies and measures to solve problems in the income distribution system are:

Taxation reform

- Enhance tax adjustment for high income groups.
- Improve the personal income tax system, by combining comprehensive taxation and categorised taxation, and moving to comprehensive taxation, when conditions permit.
- Accelerate the building-up of the personal credit system and improve the transparency of personal incomes, through the establishment of a comprehensive personal income reporting system.
- Further accelerate the control and management of the personal income taxes of high income groups, and prohibit illegal tax evasion.
- Introduce an inheritance tax as soon as possible, so as to bring about adjustments in other taxes on personal capital at a suitable time, and also through tax offsets or deductions and other preferential policies, to encourage high-income individuals to support charities and public welfare.
- Impose taxes on the consumption of luxuries, high-quality goods and services, and appropriately increase the coverage of the consumption tax.

Governance

Public administration and governance can be reformed in a number of ways:

- Improve income adjustments and inspections in monopolistic industries.
- Further implement the policy of separation between government administration and enterprises, so as to transfer a number of the administrative functions of some industries or enterprises, to related government agencies or industrial associations.
- Re-organise the various government funds and fees, so as to completely eliminate the basis of monopoly systems and introduce market competition in all spheres, in order to end monopolistic practices. For industries with non-natural monopoly, eliminate all sorts of barriers to market entry, and allow enterprises with different types of ownerships to participate and compete freely and fairly. For industries with natural monopolies, introduce competition, in order to separate out non-monopolistic business, and to encourage competition and the free movement of labour.

- Reform the system of administrative examination and approval. This is a fundamental measure to prevent rent-setting and rent-seeking, to limit illegal gains, and to improve government efficiency.

- Substantially reduce the areas submitted to administrative examination and approval.

- For the remaining fields, the examination and approval process should be open to the public, to improve administrative transparency.

- Implement a system of monitoring of administrative examinations and approvals. Investigate the responsibilities of those officials who do not act according to regulations and who do not make decisions in a scientific way, since these decisions often result in serious economic losses and have a negative influence on society. It will be necessary to legally and heavily punish actions such as seeking personal interest by jurisdiction, and bartering power for money.

Social security and social protection

Further reforms are needed in the following areas:

- Build up and improve the social security system, independent from enterprises or institutions. Gradually extend social security coverage to individuals without cover in urban areas, and pool management and services as much as possible.

- Set up stable mechanisms for social security funds. Gradually establish the tripartite system of funding, with suitable contributions from individuals, complemented by enterprises, and with government support as a last resort. Establish efficient management mechanisms. Apply specific management and specific accounts, and use funds in accordance with their functions; strengthen supervision of social security funds and, finally, organise the social security budget.

- Further improve reform of the old-age pension, basic health and unemployment insurance systems, and also progressively provide allowances to all those urban households with per capita incomes lower than the local minimum living guarantee level.

- Actively study effective ways to implement the old-age pension, health insurance and minimum living guarantee in rural areas, and appropriately tackle the problems of rural urbanisation and the access for migrants to social security.

Other

There are many other areas of administration and management where reforms need to be made:

- Strengthen fiscal transfer payments, to enable government to further improve the capacity and quality of public services. Make basic public services available to all.

- The government must pragmatically assume its responsibilities with regard to rural compulsory education. A new financing system should be established, to match the reform of the finance and taxation systems, and the reform of the tax and fee systems in rural areas. Financial administrations at all levels should legally increase their investment support for compulsory education, so as to guarantee funding and free compulsory education provision. Investment in educational infrastructure construction should be increased, in order to ensure fundamental schooling conditions and fully implement the project of compulsory education in poor areas.

- The development of a basic healthcare system in rural areas is a priority, in order to promote the efficient use of such facilities for rural dwellers. Full use should be made of fiscal transfer payments, to help poor areas to establish a co-operative medical care security system. Governmental investment in rural healthcare and disease prevention should be increased. Particular efforts should be made to guarantee poor areas and populations the minimum medical security and public healthcare.

- Relieve difficulties in the working and living conditions of low-income groups in urban and rural areas.

- Continue to fight poverty through development in rural areas. Combine this fight with the development of the western region, the restructuring of agriculture and the rural economy, and ecological environment improvement. Continue to strengthen the infrastructure of the poverty prevention project, including: water supply, power supply, transportation and communication systems, and improve local working and living conditions. Rigorously develop education, science and technology, culture and healthcare systems, to improve the quality of the population in poor areas. In those areas with the most adverse natural conditions, well-planned measures should be taken step-by-step to fight poverty with development by migration.

- Establish instruments to combat urban poverty and secure the basic living standards of urban low-income groups; adopt more effective policies and financial measures, to enhance structural transformation and restructuring of old industrial bases, and obsolete and unproductive industrial and mining regions, in order to avoid the formation of structural poverty among a large group in urban areas; continue to provide well-planned and supply-oriented training to laid-off workers, to improve their knowledge and professional skills in science and technology; carry out these preferential policies to promote employment of laid-off workers, encourage employment in community services, and improve the employment of groups in difficulty, so as to increase their incomes; establish a system to provide cheap or rental housing that secures the basic living conditions of low-income households; improve the schooling assistance system, guarantee the rights to education of children from low-income families; establish social protection tools to fight poverty and to assist the poor; look for new ways to fight poverty, including improved work incentives.

- Establish a mechanism for a regular increase in the wages of public servants. This could include establishing a system of social surveys, to investigate average incomes in society, and use this as a reference to establish and adjust these wages. Fix the ratio of these wages to the average income in society, and adjust them every year or other period accordingly. Due to the huge regional disparities, wages of public servants should be standardised at the local level, and be in line with local wages and administration standards. To encourage public servants to work in less-developed regions, the wages of public servants in these regions may be higher than in developed regions. The additional costs may be subsidised by governments at higher levels.

- Establish a unique wage system with normalised criteria for public servants. Overall, public servants can have special treatment, other than wages. These measures may include special housing standards, special social security treatment (such as old-age pension and medical insurance), but these systems should be set up by legislation.

- Reform the system of public car allocation in the government. Abolish the use of automobiles for business, and subsidise the costs saved as an "auto-subsidy" to public servants, according to their rank, and finally turn the subsidy into part of their wages.

- Deepen the reform of state-owned enterprises, based on further improvement in the current reform of company managerial structures, which is the key to improving the income distribution system in these enterprises. At the same time, the roles of the government and enterprises should be well defined, so as to solve the problems of "over-action" and "under-action". It is not the role of government to specify income distribution in state-owned enterprises. However, government should: *1)* ensure that the owners of state-owned properties really match their position; define the owner's responsibilities and obligations reasonably; establish a mechanism to maintain and increase the value of state-owned properties, and prevent the loss of the properties in the reform of income distribution; and *2)* establish a system of inspection of the minimum wage. Having been bound to the minimum wage system, enterprises can make decisions about income distribution, according to their own situation and the practices of other enterprises (including foreign enterprises). In such a framework, enterprises may decide: *1)* wage and treatment levels, and payment methods, such as annual wages, stock and term bills, and technological shares, for their managerial personnel and technicians, and *2)* wage and treatment levels and payment methods, including share-holding, for the staff and workers.

- Seek ways to increase farmers' incomes through the development of the economy as a whole and, in this perspective, attention should be paid to two aspects of the principle of "use both hands and both should be firm". The first aspect is to increase farmers' incomes from both agricultural and non-agricultural sources. The second is to find ways not only to increase farmers' incomes but also to reduce their burdens. To definitively resolve farmer's income problems requires the acceleration of "four transitions", "three reductions" and "two securities". The "four transitions" include: *1)* hastening the industrialisation of agriculture, *2)* normalising land management: *i.e.* the average rural per capita disposable area must be five times higher than currently, *3)* improve intensive management, *i.e.* raise the technological levels, quality and value-added of agricultural production, and *4)* promote urbanisation. From now and for a certain period, the degree of urbanisation should rise by 1% every year. Among the "three reductions", the first task is to reduce farmers' educational burdens by instituting free compulsory education. This can be started in rural areas, or can be implemented immediately in the central and western regions. To this end, financial support from the government to the rural compulsory education system should increase significantly. Correspondingly, financial support from the government to higher education may be reduced. The development of universities and colleges should rely on their own finances and other social donations. The second "reduction" is to lessen taxes and fees imposed on farmers, through comprehensive reform of the tax and fee systems in rural areas. The third is to set up the administrative organisation of counties and townships, proportionally to their population, and thus reduce the personnel involved. The "two securities" are: *1)* guarantee rural areas access to, and improve conditions of, basic public services; thus, the government should increase investments to improve water supply, electricity, roads, communication, and medical and healthcare, and *2)* set up a preliminary rural social security system with a low security standard level, but broad coverage. Most importantly, the problems of the old-age pension for one-child families, and also the basic living security and medical insurance for poor families in rural areas, should be tackled.

These goals are very difficult to achieve, but are of great significance, and thus must be studied and attained.

Table 1.1. **Growth rate of GDP and urban and rural household incomes since the reform era**

Year	GDP growth rate (%)	Per capita net income of rural households (CNY)	Per capita disposable income of urban households (CNY)	Ratio of incomes (urban/rural)
1978	1.7	133.6	343.4	2.57
1979	7.6	160.2	387.0	2.42
1980	7.8	191.3	477.6	2.50
1981	5.2	223.4	491.9	2.20
1982	9.1	270.1	526.6	1.95
1983	10.9	309.8	564.0	1.82
1984	15.2	355.3	651.2	1.83
1985	13.5	397.6	739.1	1.86
1986	8.8	423.8	899.6	2.12
1987	11.6	462.6	1 002.2	2.17
1988	11.3	544.9	1 181.4	2.17
1989	4.1	601.5	1 375.7	2.29
1990	3.8	686.3	1 510.2	2.20
1991	9.2	708.6	1 700.6	2.40
1992	14.2	784.0	2 026.6	2.58
1993	13.5	921.6	2 577.4	2.80
1994	12.6	1 221.0	3 496.2	2.86
1995	10.5	1 577.7	4 283.0	2.71
1996	9.6	1 926.1	4 838.9	2.51
1997	8.8	2 090.1	5 160.3	2.47
1998	7.8	2 162.0	5 425.1	2.51
1999	7.1	2 210.3	5 854.0	2.65
2000	8.0	2 253.0	6 280.0	2.79
2001	7.3	2 366.4	6 859.6	2.90

Source: *China Statistical Yearbook*, 2002, National Bureau of Statistics, China.

Table 1.2. **Engel coefficients for urban and rural households**

Year	Rural households (%)	Urban households (%)
1978	67.7	57.5
1979	64.0	57.2
1980	61.8	56.9
1981	59.9	56.7
1982	60.7	58.7
1983	59.4	59.2
1984	59.2	58.0
1985	57.8	53.3
1986	56.4	52.4
1987	55.8	53.5
1988	54.0	51.4
1989	54.8	54.5
1990	58.8	54.2
1991	57.6	53.8
1992	57.6	52.9
1993	58.1	50.1
1994	58.9	49.9
1995	58.6	49.9
1996	56.3	48.6
1997	55.1	46.4
1998	53.4	44.5
1999	52.6	41.0
2000	49.1	29.2
2001	47.7	37.9

Source: *China Statistical Yearbook,* 2002, National Bureau of Statistics, China.

Table 1.3. **Trend in the Gini coefficient, 1978-2000**

Year	Rural household Gini coefficient	Urban household Gini coefficient	Overall Gini coefficient
1978	0.2124	0.16	-
1980	0.2407	0.16	-
1981	0.2406	0.15	-
1982	0.2317	0.15	-
1983	0.2461	0.15	-
1984	0.2439	0.16	-
1985	0.2267	0.19	-
1986	0.3042	0.19	-
1987	0.3045	0.20	-
1988	0.3026	0.23	0.341
1989	0.3099	0.23	-
1990	0.3099	0.23	0.389
1991	0.3072	0.24	-
1992	0.3134	0.25	-
1993	0.3292	0.27	-
1994	0.3210	0.30	-
1995	0.3415	0.28	0.389
1996	0.3229	0.28	0.375
1997	0.3285	0.29	0.379
1998	0.3369	0.30	0.386
1999	0.3361	0.29	0.397
2000	0.3536	0.32	0.417

Source: Reports by the National Bureau of Statistics, China.

Table 1.4. **Estimates of the Gini coefficient by domestic and foreign experts**

Source	Year estimated	Gini coefficient
World Bank	1978	0.300
	1979	0.330
	1981	0.288
	1988	0.382
	1995	0.445
Institute of Economy, Chinese Academy of Social Science	1988	0.382
	1995	0.445
Li Qiang	1996	0.458

Source: Zhao Renwei *et al.* (1999), *Re-investigation of China's Income Distribution*, China Financial and Economic Publishing House.

Table 1.5. **Gini coefficients of major countries in the world**

Country	Year	Gini coefficient
Developed countries		
United States	1997	0.408
Japan	1993	0.249
Germany	1994	0.3
Canada	1994	0.315
United Kingdom	1991	0.361
France	1995	0.327
Italy	1995	0.273
Australia	1994	0.352
Developing countries		
Brazil	1996	0.6
Mexico	1995	0.537
South Africa	1993-1994	0.593
India	1997	0.378
Indonesia	1996	0.365
Transition countries		
Russia	1998	0.487
Ukraine	1996	0.325
Poland	1996	0.329
Romania	1994	0.282
Vietnam	1998	0.361

Source: *Development Report*, 2000/2001, World Bank.

Table 1.6. **Changes in urban and rural incomes, 1978-2001**

Year	Per capita net income of rural households		Per capita disposable income of urban households	
	Absolute value (CNY)	Index (1978=100)	Absolute value (CNY)	Index (1978=100)
1978	133.6	100.0	343.4	100.0
1979	160.2	119.2	387.0	112.7
1980	191.3	139.0	477.6	127.0
1981	223.4	160.4	491.9	127.6
1982	270.1	192.3	526.6	133.9
1983	309.8	219.6	564.0	140.6
1984	355.3	249.5	651.2	158.1
1985	397.6	268.9	739.1	160.4
1986	423.8	277.6	899.6	182.5
1987	462.6	292.0	1 002.2	186.9
1988	544.9	310.7	1 181.4	182.5
1989	601.5	305.7	1 375.7	182.8
1990	686.3	311.2	1 510.2	198.1
1991	708.6	317.4	1 700.6	212.4
1992	784.0	336.2	2 026.6	232.9
1993	921.6	346.9	2 577.4	255.1
1994	1 221.0	364.4	3 496.2	276.8
1995	1 577.7	383.7	4 283.0	290.3
1996	1 926.1	418.2	4 838.9	301.6
1997	2 090.1	437.4	5 160.3	311.9
1998	2 162.0	456.2	5 425.1	329.9
1999	2 210.3	473.5	5 854.0	360.6
2000	2 253.0	483.5	6 280.0	383.7
2001	2 366.4	503.8	6 859.6	416.3

Source: *China Statistical Yearbook,* 2002, National Bureau of Statistics, China.

Table 1.7. **Comparison of eastern, central and western regions: rural per capita net income**

Year	Eastern (CNY/person)	Central (CNY/person)	Western (CNY/person)	Eastern/Central (Central=1)	Eastern/Western (Western=1)	Eastern/Central/Western (Central=1)
1978	139	127	116	1.09	1.20	1.09:1:0.91
1980	218	181	172	1.20	1.27	1.20:1:0.83
1981	268	225	199	1.19	1.35	1.19:1:0.84
1982	306	264	235	1.16	1.30	1.16:1:0.86
1983	366	312	249	1.17	1.47	1.17:1:0.85
1984	397	357	274	1.11	1.45	1.11:1:0.90
1985	439	377	314	1.16	1.40	1.16:1:0.86
1986	482	417	329	1.16	1.47	1.16:1:0.87
1987	550	433	356	1.27	1.54	1.27:1:0.79
1988	685	490	424	1.40	1.62	1.40:1:0.72
1989	766	529	461	1.45	1.66	1.45:1:0.69
1990	848	633	534	1.34	1.59	1.34:1:0.75
1991	906	615	562	1.47	1.61	1.47:1:0.68
1992	1 002	698	605	1.44	1.66	1.44:1:0.70
1993	1 222	802	670	1.52	1.82	1.52:1:0.66
1994	1 617	1 087	850	1.49	1.90	1.49:1:0.67
1995	2 127	1 403	1 061	1.52	2.00	1.52:1:0.66
1997	2 549	1 763	1 281	1.45	1.99	1.45:1:0.69
1998	2 746	1 931	1 405	1.42	1.95	1.42:1:0.70
1999	2 933	2 005	1 503	1.46	1.95	1.46:1:0.75
2000	3 063	2 077	1 593	1.47	1.92	1.47:1:0.77

Source: Reports by the National Bureau of Statistics, China.

Table 1.8. **Comparison of eastern, central and western regions: urban per capita disposable income**

Year	Eastern (CNY/person)	Central (CNY/person)	Western (CNY/person)	Eastern/Central (Central=1)	Eastern/Western (Western=1)	Eastern/Central/Western (Central=1)
1978	372	337	341	1.10	1.09	1.10:1:1.10
1981	481	409	435	1.18	1.11	1.18:1:1.06
1985	803	647	708	1.24	1.13	1.24:1:1.09
1990	1 621	1 161	1 265	1.40	1.28	1.40:1:1.09
1995	4 471	2 108	2 445	2.12	1.83	2.12:1:1.16
1997	6 276	4 318	4 484	1.45	1.40	1.45:1:1.04
1999	7 146	4 837	5 124	1.48	1.39	1.48:1:1.06
2000	7 682	5 165	5 487	1.49	1.40	1.49:1:1.06

Source: Reports by the National Bureau of Statistics, China.

Table 1.9. **Income disparities among workers and staff of major sectors**

	1979		1990		1995		1999	
	Wage (CNY)	Rank	Wage (CNY)	Rank	Wage (CNY)	Rank	Wage (CNY)	Rank
Farming, forestry, animal husbandry and fishery	470.0	13	1 541	15	3 522	16	4 832	16
Mining and quarrying	676.0	5	2 718	1	5 757	11	7 521	14
Manufacturing	597.0	9	2 073	13	5 169	14	7 794	13
Production and supply of electricity gas and water	850.0	1	2 656	2	7 843	1	11 513	3
Construction	714.0	2	2 384	6	5 785	10	7 982	12
Geological prospecting and water conservancy	708.0	3	2 465	3	5 962	8	8 821	10
Transport, storage, post and telecommunication	694.0	4	2 426	4	6 948	4	10 991	5
Railway transport	866.8		3 014		9 098		12 639	
Aero transport	956.1		3 843		12 686		19 726	
Post and telecommunication	713.4		2 753		9 201		14 424	
Finance and insurance	610.0	8	2 097	12	7 376	2	12 046	1
Real estate	548.0	12	2 243	7	7 330	3	11 505	4
Social services	392.0	14	2 170	9	5 982	7	9 263	8
Healthcare, sports and social welfare	573.0	10	2 209	8	5 860	9	9 664	7
Education, culture and arts, radio, film and television	545.0	13	2 117	10	5 435	13	8 510	11
Scientific research and polytechnic services	669.0	6	2 403	5	6 846	5	11 601	2
Government agencies, party agencies and social organisation	655.0	7	2 113	11	5 526	12	8 978	9
Others					6 295	6	10 068	6
Highest/lowest	2 168.0		1 764		2 227		2 493	

Source: *China Statistical Yearbook,* various years, National Bureau of Statistics, China.

Chapter 2

INCOME DISPARITIES IN CHINA: A REVIEW OF CHINESE STUDIES

by
Feng Jianlin,

Programme Officer, Department of National Economy,
National Development and Reform Commission, China

China started its economic reform and opening-up in 1978. Since then, the economy has been growing rapidly, and the lives of the people have improved greatly. On the whole, the population has reached a well-off standard of living. During the 24 years between 1978 and 2002, GDP grew at an average annual rate of 9.4%, with the per capita disposable real income of urban households increasing by 6.7% annually, and the per capita net real income of rural households by 7.2% annually. However, with the transition and development of the economy, many problems emerged in the distribution of incomes among households. The main problem is the continuous increase in income inequality. China's scholars have paid a lot of attention to income disparities, and many insightful studies concerning the status of income disparity, its causes, its effects on China's economy and possible policies to reduce disparities, have been published, as reviewed in this chapter.

Present income inequality

Overall picture of China's household income disparities

Overall, if households were categorised into five groups according to their income levels, with each group containing 20% of the total population, the groups with the highest, higher, average, lower and lowest income, had 47%, 22%, 15%, 10%, and 6% of total household income, respectively, in the late 1990s. Compared with the pattern in the early 1990s, the proportion of the highest income group increased by about 5 percentage points, while the shares of the other groups decreased by small margins (Zeng, 2002). Less than one-third of the population have incomes about average or above, and the remaining more than two-thirds have incomes below the average. Therefore, the overall distribution of resident income in China takes the shape of a cone or a pyramid (Xia and Fan, 2002).

The Gini coefficient is widely used to describe the income distribution pattern. Change in the Gini coefficient indicates that income disparities have increased since the reform and opening-up, although different results were reported, due to differences in data collection and processing methods. Overall, results indicated that the Gini coefficient was less than 0.3 in the late 1970s and early 1980s. The coefficient exceeded 0.3 in the middle 1980s and continued to increase after 1990. It was about 0.40 and 0.45 in 1993 and 1995, respectively. Study groups from the World Bank and from China's Academy of Social Sciences believed the coefficient was 0.445 in 1995; Li Qiang reported it to be 0.457 in 1996 (Zhao, Li and Riskin, 1999), while the National Bureau of Statistics reported it to be

0.40 in 1990 and 0.417 in 2000 (Gong, 2001). Since the Gini coefficient is not sensitive to changes for the high and low income groups, Theil's entropy measurement (Niu, 2002) and the coefficient of variation (Bian and Zhang, 2002) were applied to study the evolution of income distribution, drawing similar conclusions that inequality has increased.

Different aspects of inequality

Income inequality can be attributed to the income disparities between urban and rural residents, within urban residents, within rural residents, among residents in different regions, among employees in different industries, and among employees of units with different ownerships.

Income disparities between urban and rural residents

Since the reform and opening-up, the income disparity between urban and rural residents first decreased, and then increased (Zeng, 2002). In the first stage, between 1978 and 1985, the disparity decreased. In 1978, the ratio of the annual per capita disposable income of urban residents to the annual per capita net income of rural residents was 2.57. During the period 1979-1985, the government increased the prices of agricultural products and reformed the agricultural system into the household contract management system. Farmers' income thus grew significantly, the gap between the incomes of rural and urban residents narrowed, and the above-mentioned annual per capita income ratio decreased to 1.86 in 1985. The second stage is the period since 1986. As early as 1984, urban economic reform was started. Enterprises obtained tax cuts and freedom in wage distribution, which led to a fast growth in the incomes of urban residents. The income ratio between urban and rural residents exceeded 2, and kept growing. Currently, the ratio is over 3.

Income disparities within urban and rural areas

The Gini coefficients for urban and rural residents showed a long-term upward trend (Zeng, 2002; Zhang and Xu, 2002). The Gini coefficients of urban and rural residents were 0.16 and 0.23 in 1978, and 0.23 and 0.3 in 1989, respectively. The Gini coefficient of urban residents exceeded 0.3 in 1999 and that of rural residents exceeded 0.35 in 2000. By comparison, the Gini coefficient of rural residents has always been higher than that of urban residents. Meanwhile, the Gini coefficient of rural residents increased almost linearly over the years, with fairly minor fluctuation.

Regional income disparities

Both rural and urban household incomes showed a growing regional disparity. Income disparity among residents in the eastern, central and western regions grew rather markedly. In 1978, among all the provinces, municipalities and ethnic autonomous areas, Shanghai had the highest rural resident net income, which was as much as 3.15 times of that in Hebei, the area with the lowest rural resident net income. In 2000, Shanghai still had the highest rural income, and Tibet the lowest, while the ratio between the incomes increased to 4.21. In 1990, Guangdong had the highest per capita urban resident disposable income, which was CNY1 154 higher than the lowest level, in Inner Mongolia. In 1995, the difference widened to CNY4 576 (the highest was Shanghai and the lowest Shanxi). The ratio of the highest urban resident per capita income over the lowest in 1990, 1995 and 2000 was 2.00, 2.60 and 2.48, respectively (Zeng, 2002).

Income disparities among industries

Since the late 1970s, employees in all industries have enjoyed continuing increases in their wages and salaries. However, the speed and magnitude of the increase differed a great deal among industries.

In 1978, the ratio of the wages of the best and the worst-paid industry was 1.81. The ratio decreased to 1.58 in 1987, and increased thereafter. It reached 1.86 in 1992, and has grown rapidly since then. In 2000, the ratio was 2.63 (Zeng, 2002). Overall, income disparities among industries have widened.

The industry list according to the income levels of employees has also changed since the late 1970s. In 1978, the industries with the highest incomes were the power industry, and the gas and water supply industries; those with lowest incomes were social services, grain planting, forestry, fishery, education, cultural and art undertakings, broadcasting, film and television undertakings, real estate, the wholesale and retail industry, and the catering industry. This pattern did not change significantly until the mid-1980s. Since then, banking, insurance and the real estate industries gradually turned from low-income into high-income industries, while mining and construction industries experienced the reverse (Zeng, 2002).

Income disparity among units with different ownerships

The relative gap between the wages and salaries of employees in public-owned units, and those of employees in non-public owned units, increased steadily during the early 1980s and the early 1990s. The gap decreased in the middle 1990s. Overall, the wages and salaries of non-public owned units were higher than those of public owned units, while state-owned units had higher wages and salaries than collective units (Zeng, 2002).

Evaluation of present income disparities

Economists hold different views about the current income disparities. Disagreements mainly include: *1)* Whether the disparity is such that there is an alarming value of the Gini coefficient, *2)* Whether polarisation exists, and *3)* Whether the disparity is acceptable or not.

Dispute on the alarming value of the Gini coefficient

According to common interpretation, income distribution is even if the Gini coefficient is below 0.2, fairly even if it is between 0.2 and 0.3, fairly reasonable if it is between 0.3 and 0.4, has fairly large disparities if it is between 0.4 and 0.5, and the income distribution disparity is very significant if the coefficient is above 0.5 (Gong, 2001). Since the Gini coefficient of China is now above 0.4, many scholars have warned that income inequality in China has gone beyond the range of "fairly reasonable" and has exceeded the alarming value of the Gini coefficient, *i.e.* 0.4. If inequality continues to grow unchecked, economic, social and political risks may be triggered. Therefore, close attention should be paid to the present income disparities (Zhang and Xu, 2002; Ye, 2002; Zhang Lei, 2002). However, it is also argued that, due to its dual economic structure, with separate rural and urban economies, and statistical errors, the alarming value for China should be more than 0.4, and 0.45 was suggested to be the suitable value for the alarming line. During the late 1990s, the Gini coefficient for China was more than 0.45, so that the trend of increasing disparity was a reason for concern (Liu Shaobin, 2002).

Yet it has also been pointed out that, due to differences in historical traditions, cultural and religious backgrounds, the development of the social security system, and international political and economic circumstances, the same level of inequality in different countries may have different influences on economic development and social stability. Therefore, to set a common international alarming value for the Gini coefficient is very difficult. Different countries, and even a country in different periods, may have different alarming values, and there is no absolutely applicable alarming value for all countries. Compared internationally, China's Gini coefficient in the late 1990s was intermediate. Evaluations of the present income disparity should be made with great care.

About polarisation

The argument about whether China's income distribution is polarised has focused on three questions, *i.e.* whether polarisation is a state or a trend; what the value is for the Gini coefficient that defines polarisation and how to define polarisation, if it is a trend.

Trend or state?

What on earth is polarisation? Scholars have provided different answers. Some have defined it as a trend, some as a state, and different conclusions drawn accordingly. First, polarisation. This view holds that polarisation signifies a trend, with increasing disparity in China meaning that polarisation is emerging. As the gap between high and low incomes grows, the rich become even better off, while some poor people can hardly secure subsistence level (Song, 1995). Second, non-polarisation. This view argues that what polarisation defines is a state of income distribution at certain points in time. It should not be interpreted as the process of a change in disparity. Only when the income disparity reaches a certain point can it be regarded as polarisation. It is argued that, while income inequality in China is currently increasing, it has not yet reached the state of polarisation (Liu Shaobin, 2002).

Critical value for the Gini coefficient

If polarisation is a state, a criterion should be set to define this state. Scholars thus suggested the Gini coefficient as an indicator, and many critical values of the Gini coefficient defining polarisation have been proposed. Arguments exist about whether the international standard applies to China, and how to modify the standard according to the real situation in China.

- International standards

According to the international standard set for market economies, polarisation happens if the Gini coefficient goes above 0.5. The Gini coefficient in China now is less than 0.5, and thus there is no polarisation (Chen, 1997).

- Modifications

Scholars have also argued that the Gini coefficient, as an internationally accepted indicator of income disparity, was developed and abstracted for the experiences of many countries. It provides general guidance only. However, consideration should be taken of the various capabilities of countries with different economic structures to withstand income disparities. Unlike western market economies, China's economy has a dual structure, with separate urban and rural economies. There is fairly small disparity, and thus the economy can handle income disparity rather well. The critical value of 0.5, which might work for other countries, should not be simply applied in the case of China (Zhou, 2002). Different views exist about how to modify the critical value for the Gini coefficient. Since a transitional economy has a higher level of state ownership than market economies, the critical Gini value for a transitional economy was believed to be lower than 0.5. Thus, it has been argued that the income distribution in a transitional economy would be in the state of polarisation if it has a Gini coefficient larger than 0.43. During the period from 1998 to 1997, only in one year (1994) was the Gini coefficient above 0.43. For all the other years, it was less than 0.43. Therefore, it is hard to conclude that the current disparity is polarisation (Chen and Zhou, 2002). On the other hand, some scholars held that the critical Gini coefficient value for China should be at least 0.5, since it has a large population with a typical dual economic structure. The present disparity in China has a certain tendency to polarisation. Nevertheless, it is not yet in this state (Luo, 2002).

From a sociological perspective, individual subjective acknowledgement of income disparities should be taken into account in defining the critical Gini coefficient value for polarisation. Income distribution disparities are not only an economic, but also a social problem. Economists often rely on economic analysis and ignore sociological perspectives in their research on income inequality. To comprehensively evaluate whether a disparity is reasonable or not, a relative deprivation index, as a subjective judgment of different individuals about the fairness of income disparities, should be combined with economic analysis. The index represents the subjective feelings of people when they compare their incomes with others, or with their own expectations. In the calculation of the national Gini coefficient, the index of a certain social group should be multiplied by the population share of that group. In the case of China, the dual economic structure results in different relative deprivation indexes in the urban and rural areas, since urban and rural residents have different reference systems. An overall relative deprivation index should be multiplied with the Gini coefficient, to show the overall deprivation acknowledged by all individuals. If 0.5 is a critical value indicating social instability economically, the sociologically critical value for the Gini coefficient should be higher than 0.5 (Liu Lei, 2002).

Relative and absolute polarisation

If polarisation can be defined as a trend, a criterion is also needed to define such a trend. Scholars have therefore suggested the concepts of relative and absolute polarisation. Study results indicated that the current disparity in China has a tendency towards relative polarisation, but cannot yet be treated as polarisation. Polarisation indicates the trend of income changes for different parts of the population. Accordingly, absolute income trend analysis and relative income trend analysis were introduced, to study the evolution of the income distribution pattern, and thus to define whether polarisation occurred. Absolute polarisation exists if the real income of the highest income group increases, while the real income of the lowest income group decreases. Relative polarisation exists if the ratio of the highest income to the mean income increases, while the ratio of the lowest income to the mean income decreases (Zhang and Xu, 2002). Absolute and relative polarisation analyses were used to study sample data of urban incomes in the years from 1986 to 1995. It was found that there was only one year (1988) out of the ten years that satisfied both absolute and relative polarisation tests. Therefore, there was no polarisation in China until the mid-1990s (Zhao, Li and Riskin, 1999).

Urban incomes in the 15 years from 1985 to 1999 were also studied, but with different categorising methods. When the sample was divided into ten even-sized groups, only the year 1988 passed the absolute polarisation criterion, and the nine years 1986, 1988-89, 1992-94 and 1997-99 passed the relative polarisation analysis, with only 1988 passing both. If the sample were divided into 20 even-sized groups, three years, 1988, 1989 and 1992, satisfied the absolute polarisation criterion, and the same nine years met the relative polarisation criterion. Three years, 1988, 1989 and 1992, passed both the absolute and relative polarisation tests. It can be seen clearly that the categorising method affects the results significantly. The greater the number of groups into which the population was divided, the wider was the gap between the highest and the lowest incomes, and the more prominent would be the polarisation. Neither the 10-group nor the 20-group categorisation method have indicated serious polarisation in urban household income distribution, according to the absolute criterion. However, if analysed by the relative polarisation criterion, there was fairly serious polarisation in urban resident income distribution in China (Zhang and Xu, 2002).

Scholars also noticed that the judgment as to whether polarisation existed depended upon the data sampling and collection. The results indicating the disparity as being fair usually came from analysis of the normal incomes of residents, and the results indicating polarisation often came from consideration of illegal and abnormal incomes. For instance, between 1988 and 1997, using 0.43 as the critical value for polarisation for the Gini coefficient, including illegal and abnormal incomes would imply that the national income distribution was polarised; if analysed by the absolute and relative polarisation methods, 40% of the years showed relative polarisation. Illegal and abnormal incomes worsened the trend of relative polarisation, though it was still hard to conclude that the degree of disparity implies polarisation (Chen and Zhou, 2001; Chen, 2000).

Is the present disparity acceptable?

Non-polarisationists can be further divided into two groups according to their final conclusions about the level of disparities:

Unacceptable inequalities

Many scholars believe that the present disparity is unacceptable. Some described the disparity as "too large" or "too significant", after comparing the present inequality level with that of other countries, and some felt that the disparity was worsening when compared with historical data. Zhao Renwei, and others, compared the Gini coefficient of China with other countries, and found that the Gini coefficient of China was lower than in some African and South American countries, but much higher than in many Asian and even developed countries in Europe (Zhao, Li and Riskin, 1999). Deng Yongpeng believes that the present disparities among different regions, among urban and rural areas, among industries and among social groups are very serious (Deng, 2000). Luo Shuming pointed out that with the reform and establishment of a market economy, household income inequality in China increased and worsened gradually (Luo, 2002). Zhang Lei argued that China was a country with highly even income distribution in 1978, and that after only 20 years it turned into a country with significant income disparity, and thus, income inequality is a serious problem (Zhang Lei, 2002).

Acceptable inequalities

Chen Zongshen believes that the present income disparity in China is acceptable. The reasons for this include: *1)* the Gini coefficient is still less than 0.5, *2)* the formation and existence of income inequality is a necessary result of the breakdown of the practice of equalitarianism, *3)* the real incomes of all social groups including the poor have increased, even though disparities have widened, *4)* the disparity is reasonable if improvement in the economic growth rate and efficiency are taken into account, and *5)* society is by and large fairly stable. Therefore, current disparities are acceptable (Lin and Zhang, 2001).

Zeng Guo'an studied income inequality since 1978, comparing the current level of disparity with income disparities in 112 countries in the 1990s, and concluded that by the end of the 1990s, income inequality in China was about average, and the disparities among urban residents and among rural residents were fairly low, although the disparities between urban and rural residents and among employees in different industries were a bit high. Income inequality in China was higher than that of developed countries and about average, if compared with that of developing countries (Zeng, 2002).

Causes of the formation of inequality

The process of the formation of income distribution disparity in China was very complicated. Scholars analysed the causes from many aspects, including the effects of resource endowments, the historical heritage, economic structure, government policy, marketisation, ownership, the institutional system, the legislative system, individual differences, wealth accumulation, economic development, and so on. Scholars have developed varying interpretations of these factors, putting the emphasis on different causes. Generally speaking, all the causes integrated with and affected each other, contributing to the present level of income disparity.

Resource endowments

The three economic zones, *i.e.* the eastern, central and western regions, have significantly uneven resource endowments, including natural resource endowments and social resource endowments. The eastern part lacks mines, but it is well located, with good river and land transportation systems, industrial and infrastructure facilities, and a good basis of science and technology. The central region is rich in energy resources, with fair transportation facilities, while the western region has a lot of resources, but with outdated transportation and information systems and a high population growth rate (Guo, 2002). These different endowments contribute significantly to the unbalanced development of the regions, affecting household income levels in different regions (Deng, 2000; Zhang and Gong, 2002).

The historical heritage

The current situation of growing income inequality has many historical causes. The disparity in regional development and the income gap between the urban and rural areas have existed for a long time. An important reason for the income disparity between urban and rural residents is that labour productivity and product commercialisation in rural areas are rather low, due to thousands of years of household operation traditions (Dai and Zhang, 2002). The collective system for agricultural products set up in the 1950s enabled the government to buy and sell agricultural products at relatively low prices. The prices of industrial products determined by the pricing system for these products were higher than for agricultural products. These two pricing systems built up the price differences between agricultural and industrial products, which made farmers' income fairly low.

Since 1978, the central government adopted a gradual opening-up policy, started from the east to the west, resulting in fast economic development and a rapid increase of household incomes in the south-eastern region. On the other hand, the reform and opening-up in the central and the western regions was relatively slow, and household income grew very slowly. The regional income disparity thus enlarged, gradually and steadily (Liu, Niu and Shi, 2002). Affected by the traditional planning system, some industries had excessive supply, while others had excessive demand. Those with excessive supply experienced overheated competition, and the income of their employees was low. Those industries with excessive demand made high profits, and the income of their employees was high (Lu, 2002).

The effects of the dual economic structure

As a huge developing country, China has a typical dual economic structure. The urban and rural economies differ dramatically, and this is reflected in different types of labour productivity, management systems and economic features. These differences worked together, contributing to the income gap between the urban and the rural areas. Compared with the urban area, the countryside relies heavily on manual work, and the marginal productivity of labour is very low. Meanwhile, the rural population is growing fairly rapidly. Therefore, hidden unemployment is very common in rural areas. On the other hand, cities harbour industries with modern machinery, and labour productivity in urban areas is high. Urban industries can use cheap labour forces supplied by the countryside and this supply seems almost endless. Urban industries thus gain extra profits, which are then re-invested to achieve capital accumulation, further enhancing economic growth in the urban areas (Ma, 2002). Therefore, the gap between the urban and rural economies grew continuously.

China's economy has been operating on the basis of separation of the labour and goods markets between urban and rural areas. Dual governance systems exist in the urban and rural areas, impeding circulation and optimisation of productive factors. This led to disparities between the rural and the urban areas in their development of capital, labour forces and technology, resulting in inequality of development opportunities and conditions (Dai and Zhang, 2002). The urban economy is basically a market economy, or is transforming into a market economy, while the rural economy is still mainly an agricultural economy, producing goods to satisfy its own needs. It is estimated that the self-supply ratio in rural areas is about 40%. The transformation of the dual economic structure is slow, which restricted population movement and migration. Allocation and use of the excessive labour supply in the rural areas could not be optimised, and labour productivity could not be improved quickly. This again contributed to the disparity between the urban and rural economies, impeding the growth of farmers' income (Ma, 2002).

The effects of policies

Most scholars believe that the development of income inequality was closely linked to the policies adopted by the government since the reform and opening-up. The effects of these policies on income distribution were summarised into two aspects, *i.e.* "policy preference" and "policy absence" (Huo, 2002). Policy preference refers to the fact that the government granted preferential policies to certain localities and enterprises, and allowed the monopolistic operation of some industries. Due to policy preferences, different localities, enterprises and industries operated in an unfair competitive environment, which increased income disparities. The first and most commonly mentioned policy preference is that during the early years since the reform and opening-up, the government set preferential policies for the eastern region, investing heavily, and allowing the region to lead the reform and opening-up. Preferential policies were developed in foreign investment, taxation and banking for the eastern region. These beneficial policies significantly expedited economic growth and the technological improvement of the industries in the coastal regions. By comparison, it was not until 1991 that the government opened up inland border cities, cities along rivers and capital cities of provinces. However, these late-opened cities had already lost the necessary capability to compete fairly with coastal areas in many aspects, including infrastructure conditions, capital use, technology, and so on.

Private businesses were also the subject of policy preferences. The government introduced many preferential measures for the development of the private sector. For example, start-up private enterprises could obtain tax cuts and preferential loan treatment, foreign enterprises that were exporting products or applying high technology might enjoy income tax exemptions or reductions, foreign enterprises were granted tax exemption in land use. At the same time, private enterprises are mostly new enterprises with low social burdens, such as pensions for retired personnel. This gave them more advantages in their competition with public-owned enterprises, which usually have heavy inherited social burdens. Therefore, the labour costs of enterprises differ, leading to differences in competitive capability and income disparity between the private sector and publicly-owned enterprises. Certain specific industries also enjoyed preferential policies. In recent years, administrative measures were taken to exclude privately-owned enterprises from entering sectors such as telecommunications, electricity generation, banking, insurance and the aviation industry, among others. The implementation of this institutional monopoly enabled these industries to make monopolistic profits, and the income of their employees accordingly was high. This is an important reason for the growth of income inequality among urban residents.

Policy absence has three main sources: flawed policies, the absence of necessary compensation measures, and distortion and exaggeration of policies in practice. The reform and opening-up broke down the approach of equalitarianism in income distribution, by implementing a system under which distribution according to work is dominant, and various modes of distribution coexist. Enterprises link their wages and salaries to profits. The wages and salaries of government and institutional employees are financed from government revenues, but governmental and institutional units are responsible for financing bonus and other fringe benefits for their employees. The initial intention of such institutional reform was to relieve the financing burden on the government, and to stimulate all units to be creative. Nevertheless, since those governmental and institutional units are among public service sectors, they usually do not directly control productive resources and therefore cannot make profits to finance themselves. Many of them started to seek rents, set rents, impose unreasonable charges, or even set up companies and enterprises to monopolise markets. These so-called "revenue-making" activities brought huge profits to some units. However, the government did not develop effective measures to regulate these activities, which disturbed the order of income distribution and the market economy, and also worsened disparities.

The effects of marketisation

Since the reform and opening-up, and particularly since 1992, the socialist market economy has developed gradually and steadily. Markets play a more and more important role in the allocation of productive resources. The effects of markets on income distribution have been enhanced accordingly. These effects mainly have two aspects, *i.e.* direct effects on individual income, and on regional economic development. The market mechanism has replaced the traditional planning system in income distribution in China (Dai and Zhang, 2002). The market pricing system differentiates simple and complex labour, skilled and unskilled labour, creative and non-creative labour, and pays different wages accordingly. Meanwhile, other productive factors, including capital, technology and management expertise, started to participate in the process of income distribution. To date, the coexistence of a supply shortage of capital and technology, and an excessive supply of cheap labour, is rather conspicuous in China. The marginal productivity of capital and technology is much higher than that of ordinary labour (Yu, 2002). Either to distribute according to marginal contribution, or to distribute according to factors possessing status, would worsen income disparities (Zhou, 2002). At the same time, economic restructuring and job market competition inevitably brought about lay-offs and unemployment, and thus directly increased income disparities (Bi and Jian, 2002). Therefore, increasing income disparity among individuals is an unavoidable result of the transformation from a planned economy to a socialist market economy (Yu, 2002).

Institutional effects

Many institutional factors affect household income distribution. The most direct effects of social and economic institutions on income distribution include unsatisfactory protection for the poor and ineffective adjustment of high incomes. The unsatisfactory protection for the poor resulted from the less developed social security system (Liu, Niu and Shi, 2002; Cao, 2002; Lu, Wang and Zhu, 2002). Income inequality among residents due to marketisation requires the government to take measures to re-adjust incomes, to promote fairness and to provide the poor with the necessary protection. So far, in China, the social security system, including livelihood protection for laid-off workers of state-owned enterprises (SOEs), unemployment protection, subsistence allowances for urban residents, basic old-age pension, unemployment insurance, medical insurance, working injury insurance and birth insurance for females, has been established only partially. However, being incomplete, the system does not have a unified management mechanism; it has problems in collecting funds, and the coverage is very limited. As a result, the current social security system cannot fully meet the requirements of economic growth.

The adjustment of high incomes is not effective, because the taxation adjustment of high incomes is unsatisfactory. The current tax system has many flaws, which affect the efficiency of taxation on high incomes and significantly weaken the capability of the government to make transfer payments (Dai and Zhang, 2002). Among these flaws, the most important might be that the only taxable incomes are now wages and salaries, and taxation on other incomes is fairly weak; therefore, the impact of personal income tax on income distribution is not as effective as expected (Wu, 2002). Imperfect policies cannot reduce income inequality satisfactorily. First, a heavy burden of taxes and fees is imposed on rural residents, while little is imposed on urban residents (Yi, 2002). Second, a large portion of individual income tax is collected from average workers and employees, while high-income individuals find all sorts of ways to avoid taxes. Third, there are no comprehensive and sound policies to re-distribute incomes. Taxes levied are not diversified, the tax rates are fairly low and tax cheating is very common. Due to the ineffectiveness of the tax system, some people earn a lot and pay little, while some earn little but pay a lot.

The effects of the legal system

The legal system in China is still not complete and sound. Many laws and regulations need to be further established and perfected. The incomplete legal system and the loose implementation of laws and regulations result in the fairly common occurrence of illegal and abnormal incomes (Yang Yiyong, 2002a). A few have managed to achieve high incomes through illegal actions such as bribery, corruption, trading power for money, smuggling, or tax cheating. Some took advantage of enterprise transformation and occupied state-owned properties. With a less-developed legal system, supervision of these illegal and abnormal incomes does not have enough legal support and is very difficult (Li and Li, 2002; He and Wang, 1999). According to a recent study, illegal and abnormal incomes increase the Gini coefficient, and are a fundamental reason for the present large income disparity (Chen and Zhou, 2001). The underground economy was also investigated. Since these activities are fairly common, and usually return an unbelievably high profit, the underground economy contributes significantly to income disparities (Zhang Xiangda, 2002).

Differences among individuals

In the transition to a market economy, the effects of the human capital of each individual's income are growing. Scholars have studied the effect of education on individual incomes, and found that the average return to education in 1995 was much higher than in 1988. Among enterprises, the average income return to education in foreign enterprises was the highest, and that in SOEs was the lowest. Among different regions, those with well-developed labour markets have higher returns to education. The effect of education on individual incomes and on income distribution is growing in importance (Zhao, Li and Riskin, 1999).

A regression analysis was made on data collected from 55 cities, in order to reveal the relationship between individual characteristics and income. The results showed that individual income was affected by education, age, sex, political status and other characteristics. The more education received and the higher the age, the higher would be the average income. Males had higher average incomes than females. Individuals holding communist party membership had higher incomes than non-members (Bian and Zhang, 2002). A study on the income of Tianjin residents in 1988 and 1998 also showed a positive correlation between individual incomes and age and education, and that males had higher average incomes than females (Chen and Zhou, 2002).

The role of wealth

Since the reform and opening-up, incomes have increased continuously while wealth disparities among people have been growing gradually. In the mid-1990s, the 20% of residents holding the highest financial assets owned 48% of all financial assets owned by urban residents, while the 20% of residents with the lowest financial assets only held 4% of the total. Disparity due to ownership of financial assets was very high, which contributed much more significantly to total income inequality than other factors. In addition, there is a large disparity in ownership of real estate among urban residents. Differences in the adjusted rent from real estate also increase urban income disparity (Zhao, Li and Riskin, 1999). Meanwhile, the "Matthew effect" of the market also contributes to the increase in income disparity (Zheng Rongqi, 2002). The eastern region has already acquired physical and human capital, technology, and the good market reputation necessary for further development. Regional disparities will grow, even if the western region could achieve the same growth rate as the eastern region. Moreover, due to a sound economic environment and a high yield rate for productive forces, the eastern region obtains large inflows of productive factors, which further accelerates economic growth in the east. In contrast, the backward central and western regions have a lower inflow of productive factors, and the economy grows slowly.

Unbalanced regional development generates diffusion and feedback effects. The diffusion effect means that developed regions can then promote development of poor areas, through technology and capital transfer. In the early stage of economic development, along with the diffusion effect, a feedback effect also occurs, which means that productive factors, such as labour, capital, technology and resources of the undeveloped regions would migrate to the developed regions, due to differences in rates of return. As such feedback happens, regional development will be further imbalanced, and income distribution will widen (Hang, 2002).

The effects of income inequality on economic development

The discussion of the effects of income inequality on economic development is mainly focused on its effects on consumption, investment and economic structure. Some believe that a suitable increase in income inequality is a necessary outcome of market competition, and is somehow reasonable and positive (Yu, 2002). Most people believe that excessive income inequality has many negative effects on economic development.

Effects on consumption

With increasing income inequality, the consumption of people with rapid income growth also grows, but at a rate less than the growth rate of their income. Their marginal consumption rate decreases. On the other hand, people with little income growth may have a high marginal consumption rate, but they simply cannot consume as much as they wish, due to their low incomes. Increasing income inequality restrains the growth of total consumption and effective demand (Cao, 2002; Dai, 2002). It is also believed that income disparities affect total consumption through their effects on savings. The higher the income, the more an individual tends to make savings for bequests and donations: the lesser the income, the more an individual tends to make savings to guard against emergencies. Therefore, the overall consumption propensity curves look like a saddle, with the increase of income. At present, because of excessive income inequality and the high proportion of residents with middle and low incomes, the consumption propensity in China is fairly low, causing a shortage of consumption demand (Zhu, Fan and Yan, 2002). From the view of economic dynamics, income inequality leads to the worsening of expectations of future income. The economy would then be trapped into a vicious cycle of "worsening of income expectation-consumption decrease-investment decrease". Therefore, income inequality is a key reason for a shortage of consumption demand (Sha, 2000). Nevertheless, it is also argued that, according to consumption data for middle and low-income urban residents, the excessive supply in the market at present is mainly caused by the mismatched supply structure, but has no significant relation to income inequality (Li, Chang and Yang, 2002).

Effects on investment

As consumption is restrained, the sale of goods slows down, which decreases the expected marginal return on investment, and thus reduces investment demand (Zheng Rongqi, 2002).

Specifically, increasing income disparities decrease consumption demand; the decrease of consumption demand sends a market signal through industrial chains back to those related industries, demanding production adjustment. Theoretically, excessive investment demand would not exist as long as the signal channels function correctly and in a timely manner. However, due to the coexistence of complicated credit links, the market still creates many artificial demands, even at a time when consumer goods are not being sold well. In this case, the investment goods producer would not reduce the production at the right time, leading to an excessive supply of investment goods and a relative lack in investment demand (Yang Tianyu, 2002). Due to low expectations of returns on investment and low marginal consumption, many high-income residents are not sensitive to changes in interest rates. The effects of their savings on economic development are uncertain. These savings may further push the economy to an overheated state when the economy is booming, and may not function actively to restore the economy when it is in a downturn (Zhang, 2000).

However, some people believe that increasing income disparities help the accumulation of financial assets, which facilitates investment in securities and private enterprises, and thus helps to increase tax, create employment and develop the economy. However, growing income inequality will result in further differences in household investment in education, which may start a cycle between low education investment and low income, leading to the formation of low-income groups in the future (Li, Chang and Yang, 2002). It is also believed by some that the effects of income disparities on investment depend on how large these disparities are. An appropriate level of income inequality is good for capital accumulation, investment in human capital, optimisation of economic structure, and thus for economic development. Excessive income disparities (especially caused by illegal incomes) exert negative effects on social stability, domestic consumption and the improvement of social welfare, impeding economic development (Liu and Li, 2002).

Effects on economic structure

Scholars believe that increases in income disparities negatively affect the upgrading of the economic structure. With excessive income inequality, there is a gap in consumption demand between the low income group and the high income group, trapping industries in a dilemma. On the one hand, the majority of the population still have significant demand for consumption goods popular in the 1980s, such as colour televisions, refrigerators and motorcycles. On the other, the small high-income group wants to buy cars and villas, but the demand is not sufficient to achieve a marketable scale. Therefore, with excessive production capacity, some industries, such as television manufacturing, cannot leave the market, and price competition results, while other industries, such as the automobile industry, cannot develop into strong industries. The restructuring and upgrading of the secondary industry is impeded, which in turn affects the development of the primary and tertiary industries (Qu, 2001). It has been pointed out that increasing income disparities bring a range of economic risks, such as restraining consumption, worsening development disparities between urban and rural economies and among regions, disturbing the economic order, and affecting social stability. Therefore, the growth in income inequality severely restrains the sustainable development of the economy and society (Ye, 2002).

Policy proposals to reduce income disparities

Scholars have made many policy suggestions to reduce income inequality. As regards the overall approach, some believe that China should reduce income disparities through development, while others suggest adjusting income distribution before further development. The argument is related to the discussion of the inverted-U theory of Kuznets. This theory suggests that changes in income inequality are related to changes in economic structure. In the early stage of economic growth, income inequality may increase due to uneven opportunities. A period with relatively stable income disparities will follow. Finally, inequality will reduce gradually. This means that with economic growth, income inequality among individuals tends to increase at first, and then decrease, following an inverted U-shaped curve. This whole process, including the worsening and then reduction in income inequality, may last for 50 to 100 years. Many scholars have studied the relationship between economic growth and income disparity development in China, but no generally accepted view has been formed about whether the inverted-U theory can be applied to China's economy. Some people believe that the inverted-U theory still works for the socialist market economy, in that changes in income disparities were related to the processes of economic reform. At present, China's income disparity lies in the first part of the inverted-U curve. According to this view, further increases in income disparities are inevitable during the present stage of economic growth in China (Xu and Chen, 2000). It has been argued, however, that some unfair income disparities would be corrected and reduced with the deepening of reform, and the improvement in market mechanisms and the judicial system.

Others have argued that the inverted-U theory has yet not been proven by economic facts. On the contrary, experiences in Chinese Tapei, Korea, Sri Lanka and other developing economies and countries, have shown stable and even reduced income inequality, when their economies grew rapidly (Zheng Jianren, 2002). Other research has found that provincial data on household incomes in different years in China did not support the inverted-U theory (Zhao, Li and Riskin, 1999). Therefore, it was believed that the theory may not be a general rule for developing countries and should not be applied to China's economy directly. The theory should not be treated as a theoretical basis for the current increase in income disparities. It has also been argued that it should never be believed that increasing income inequality is a necessary price for the development of the economy (Li, 2000). Others argue that, at present, China should further develop the economy as always, proceed to the next stage of economic development, and thus reduce income disparities. In this view, only accelerating economic development can create a material basis for common prosperity (Wu, 2002). Only when the size of the cake grows can it be distributed well, and thus the problem of income inequality can only be solved through development (Chen, 2002; Zhao, 2002).

It has been further pointed out that the inverted-U theory has not analysed the endogenous dynamics and nature of income inequality in depth, and that the theory only touches lightly on the development of trends in income inequality and thus needs further proof. Furthermore, the theory cannot explain why income disparities in the United States and the United Kingdom have witnessed increases rather than decreases, and thus the theory cannot be treated as a general rule for economic development. Two important factors affecting income disparity are market competition and government macro-economic policies. Whether income inequality would develop following the inverted-U curve as an economy grows depends on the trade-off between these two factors. To ignore the influence of income distribution policies and claim that an increase in income disparity in China is inevitable, simply according to the inverted-U theory, is not scientific thinking (Yan and Tang, 2002). Therefore, some scholars have warned against following the "grow and then distribute" strategy taken by Europe and the United States by emphasising the costs of polarisation, the worsening of social conflicts, and elongation of the industrialisation process paid by European countries and the United States. Alternatively, China should take the "distribute and then develop" strategy as did Chinese Tapei, Japan, Korea and Singapore. This means to achieve continuous improvement in income distribution through redistribution of physical and human capital, and structuring and developing the economy in accordance with China's resource endowments (Sun and Zhong, 2002).

It has been suggested that the experience of Chinese Tapei shows that income distribution and economic growth can be co-ordinated. For the time being, however, through the combination of market competition, institutional reform and refined macro-economic adjustment, China should set up a model of economic growth which improves income distribution, and an income distribution model which accelerates economic growth, so as to accomplish mutual motivation between improving income distribution and economic growth (Quan, 2002). Most scholars believe that China should reduce income inequality, and they have made many suggestions on how to achieve this.

Accelerate and improve the building of markets

China should accelerate economic reforms and set up market mechanisms for fair competition (Liu, Niu and Shi, 2002), build and improve markets for capital, labour, technology and information, allow productive forces to move freely according to the rules of the market economy, and finally set up national markets. Legal and rational income disparities would further stimulate and enhance the speed and efficiency of economic growth, and illegal and irrational income disparities should be gradually cleared away with the development of the market economy (Zhang Meixia, 2002). At the present time, institutional monopolies should be eliminated according to the requirements of the World Trade Organization (WTO), so that competition can be introduced as far as possible, and a fair and competitive market environment can form (Zhang and Gong, 2002). In the meantime, laws and regulations should be improved to regulate market activities. This should include: strengthening market regulation; strictly executing laws; heavily restricting production of artificial, fake, counterfeited and inferior products; punishing dupery and cheating; combating unfair competition practices, and protecting the interests of consumers and business operators (Song, 1995; Yang Yiyong 2002).

Break down monopolies and eliminate unfair competition

Other proposals include: restricting and breaking down monopolies by the formulation of anti-monopoly laws to encourage market competition; other laws and regulations to increase new entries to certain industries; to encourage capital to circulate rationally, and compete in an orderly way among industries and reduce income disparity among industries (Ye, 2002; Zhang and Gong, 2002). Control of income distribution should be enhanced for specific monopolistic industries, so as to prevent an excessive increase in income disparities. The excessive profits of monopolistic industries should be collected by the state through taxes, such as a resource tax and a compensation tax (Yang Yiyong, 2002a and 2002b; Zhang, 2002).

Build a national labour market to facilitate rational movement of labour

The building of a nationwide labour market would enable workers to move according to their own comparative advantages. Different levels of human resources would receive different payments. A national labour market would also bring intensive competition to high-income jobs, and reduce irrational income disparities. Therefore, it is necessary to break down institutional obstacles to the movement of workers, including in the household registration, the social welfare and the employment systems. Options include to gradually abolish the household registration system, which separates the urban and the rural populations, to incite redundant rural workers to migrate to other industries (Xia and Fan, 2002), and to increase the flexibility for residents to migrate and work in cities of different sizes, and between the urban and rural areas (Chen, 1997; Liu, Niu and Shi, 2002). Reforms to the social welfare system would include reducing the scope of benefits in-kind and paying welfare in cash transparently.

Make education universal

Each citizen should enjoy equal rights and opportunities of access to education. The country, the society, and individuals should co-operate in the drive to make nine years of compulsory education universal, enlarge the scale of higher education, develop various vocational education and training options, and improve the professional skills of the labour force. Also, free training should be provided to laid-off workers; general, adult, and training on-the-job should be improved, and the right to education gradually equalised (Zhang Meixia, 2002; Wang Jialin, 2002).

Enhance tax adjustments

The personal income tax system should be improved, the minimum income level for taxation increased, a tax on luxury consumption imposed, and income adjustments for high income individuals strengthened (Xia and Fan, 2002). An inheritance tax and a wealth tax should be introduced, to prevent wealth accumulation, reduce disparity of individual wealth, and generate more wealth owned by society (Zhang Meixia, 2002). Meanwhile, in order to make individual incomes transparent, all incomes should be transformed into the form of wages and be paid in money; bank accounts should be registered with the real names of the individuals, and an income reporting system should be set up and implemented (Liu, Niu and Shi, 2002), so that the negative impact on taxation of hidden incomes and benefits in-kind can be eliminated (Zhao, 2002).

Increase farmers' incomes

To increase farmers' income is most important for the economic growth of China. Urbanisation should be strengthened, farmers transferred to cities, and the problem of farmers' income solved in the long term (Huang, 2002). Different localities should adjust the structure of local agriculture, and improve industrialisation of agriculture, according to their comparative advantages. Redundant rural labour should transfer to non-agricultural industries and cities in an orderly way. Emphasis should be placed on the development of township enterprises, combining the development of such enterprises with the processes of urbanisation and the industrialisation of agriculture. The necessary public services should be provided to farmers. Efforts should be made to increase support to infrastructure building, make compulsory education universal, and invest more in medical and healthcare facilities in rural areas. At the same time, effective measures should be taken to reduce farmers' financial burdens. and to give tax credits and reductions to low-income farmers (Xia and Fan, 2002).

Advance the development of the western region, and reduce regional disparities in economic development

To reduce the disparity in economic development between the eastern, central and western regions, the country should increase transfer payments to the western region, strengthen infrastructure construction in the central and western regions, encourage investment in the regions, direct capital, technology and talents to the central and western regions, increase the economic strength of the regions by various means, and accelerate economic development in the regions. These policies could increase residents' incomes in the central and western regions through economic development, and finally reduce income disparities between the east, central and western regions (Xia and Fan, 2002; Zhang and Gong, 2002).

Other policies are designed to bring about co-ordinated development of the urban and rural economies, and reduce disparities between the urban and rural areas. Agricultural and industrial products should be exchanged according to their real values, and mechanisms should be set up to guarantee the steady increase of farmers' incomes. The prices of agricultural products should be stabilised, grain storage improved, the circulation system updated, investment in agriculture increased, and agricultural production conditions improved. The current income distribution system, which is preferentially biased towards cities, should be changed, to gradually reduce income differences between rural and urban areas, due to differences in benefits not included in wages and salaries. Equal opportunities and an environment for the development of rural and urban residents should be provided (Deng, Yi and Zhou, 2000).

Increase employment

An increase in employment is a fundamental measure to reduce income disparities among urban residents. The principle of "employment first" should be applied, and a serious attempt made to create equal opportunities for employment (Wang Hongyan, 2002). The re-employment project should be strengthened, to control the unemployment rate (Xia and Fan, 2002). Service industries should be vigorously developed (Zhang and Gong, 2002), tax reductions or exemptions should be granted to labour-intensive medium and small enterprises, and enterprises induced to hire more laid-off workers.

Enhance the social security system

The goal should be to build up a social security system covering the entire society, to secure the basic living standards of the low-income groups, and to prevent the worsening of poverty. Improvements in the urban social security system could include emphasis on old-age pensions, unemployment assistance and medical insurance, with further improvements to the subsistence security system with "low security standards and broad coverage". In the rural area, measures should be taken to enhance the fight against poverty in both impoverished and other areas. The subsistence security system should be set up and implemented in areas where conditions permit, and the fight against poverty in rural areas standardised step-by-step. In addition, effective social relief and assistance systems and methods should be explored (Xia and Fan, 2002; Sun and Zhong, 2002). A social security tax should be initiated as soon as possible, and funding methods for social security should be standardised (Lu, Wang and Zhu, 2002). It is also important to work hard to develop charity undertakings, to encourage all of society to provide material and monetary help to groups and individuals in difficulties (Zeng, 2000).

Reform the wage and salary system

The current wage and salary system combining monetary and in-kind incomes should be reformed to make payments in the form of wages and salaries only (Zhao and Li, 2002). Other proposals are to establish and enact laws against discrimination in employment and wage payments, introduce fair competition in labour markets, equalise the incomes of workers providing the same work, improve economic efficiency, and set up a minimum wage system.

Enhance the legal system, severely penalise corruption

At present, income disparities due to corruption are of a vicious character and have caused social discontent. It is now extremely urgent to punish corruption. Determined legal measures should be taken to penalise embezzlement, tax cheating and bribery, among other types of corruption. A property reporting system for civil servants should be set up, transparency in government operations increased, tax laws further improved, tax collection enhanced, and conditions which allow illegal incomes gradually eliminated. Random pricing activities should be punished (Han, 2000; Zhang and Tang, 2000).

BIBLIOGRAPHY[1]

Bi Xianping and Jian Xinhua (2002), "Relationship between Economic Restructuring and Income Distribution Disparity in China", *Economic Review*, Vol. 4.

Bian Yanjie and Zhang Zhanxin (2002), "Marketization and Income Distribution: Analyzing the 1988 and 1995 Urban Household Income Surveys", *China Social Sciences*, Vol. 5.

Cao Ming (2002), "The Reasons for the Increasing Gap among Income Distributions and their Restrictions on Economic Development", *Journal of Yunnan Normal University,* Vol. 4.

Chen Deren (2002), "Thoughts about Income Distribution Disparity", *Hubei Social Sciences,* Vol. 9.

Chen Zongsheng (1997), "Income Distribution Disparity in China's Urban Residents, its Determinants and Trend – A Study Based on Tianjin", *Economic Research*, Vol. 3.

Chen Zongsheng (2000), "Further Study on Income Distribution Disparity among Residents in China", *Economic Research*, Vol. 7.

Chen Zongsheng and Zhou Yunbo (2001), "Effects of Illegal and Abnormal Incomes on Resident Income Disparity and the Economic Explanation", *Economic Research*, Vol. 4.

Chen Zongsheng and Zhou Yunbo (2002), "Income Inequality of Chinese Urban Residents and its Determinants – Evidence from Tianjin", *China Economic Quarterly,* April.

Dai Jinfa and Zhang Xianwei (2002), "Consideration of Some Problems of Income Distribution in Our Country at Present", *Journal of Shangrao Normal College*, Vol. 1.

Dai Yuanchen (2002), "The Stimulating Effect and its Limitation of Income Allocation Regulation", *Economic Survey*, Vol. 4.

Deng Hong, Yi Wentao and Zhou Xinyu (2000), "To Adjust Policies on Income Distribution, a Key to Stimulate the Current Economy", *Education and Research of Finance,* Vol. 2.

Deng Yongpeng (2000), "Reasons and Countermeasures for Excessive Income Disparity", *Gansu Social Sciences*, Vol. 1.

Gong Hong'e (2001), "Gini Coefficient and its Application", *Reference Data for Research*, Vol. 91.

1. All references are in Chinese and are published in Chinese journals.

Guo Junshan (2002), "Experimental Analysis of Regional Income Disparity in China", *Statistics and Decision Making*, Vol. 3.

Han Fuyong (2000), "Thoughts on Further Improvement of China's Income Distribution", *Journal of Jinan University*, Vol. 4.

Hang Xing (2002), "Disparity of Chinese Resident Income Allotment: Reasons and Countermeasures", *Fudan Journal (Social Sciences),* Vol. 2.

He Wei and Wang Huanchen (1999), "Analysis of Rent Seeking in Market Economies and in Transitional Economies", *Economic Science*, Vol. 6.

Huang Yantai (2002), "Examination of Resident Income Distribution in the New Framework of Economic Growth", in Gao Peiyong (ed.), *Income Distribution, Voices from Economists,* Economic Science Press, Beijing, pp. 14-36.

Huo Haiyan (2002), "Limitations of Income Distribution Policies in China at Present and Their Modification", *Journal of Zhengzhou University*, Vol. 1.

Li Shi (2000), "Further Explanation for Several Questions in the Study about Income Distribution", *Economic Research*, Vol. 7.

Li Suang, Chang Xinghua and Yang Yiyong (2002), *Studies on Income Disparity Among China's Urban Residents,* China Press of Planning, Beijing.

Li Yiming and Li Fuxin (2002), "Analysis on Income Distribution Disparity in Today's China", *Statistics and Decision Making*, Vol. 9.

Lin Youping and Zhang Shu (2001), "Review of Studies on Income Distribution in China since the 1990s", *Economic Review*, Vol. 4.

Liu Hongkai, Niu Jiangwei, and Shi Hongfei (2002), "Study on Resident Income Distribution in Today's China", *Journal of Social Science of Jiamusi University,* Vol. 2.

Liu Lei (2002), "Sociological Judgment on Income Distribution Disparity", *Tianjin Social Sciences*, Vol. 5.

Liu Shaobin (2002), "The Analyses and Adjustment and Control of the Gap between Incomes Distribution", *Journal of Hubei University (Philosophy and Social Science)*, Vol. 9.

Liu Xiaoying and Li Li (2002), "Effects of Income Disparity on Economic Development", *Journal of Jianghan Petroleum Institute (Social Science Edition*), September.

Lu Jiefen, Wang Hongling and Zhu Yulin (2002), "Social Security Policies to Promote Fairness in Income Distribution", *Reform of Economic System*, Vol. 5.

Lu Renfa (2002), "Examine Income Distribution and Improve Adjustment of the Income Distribution", in Gao Peiyong (ed.), *Income Distribution, Voices from Economists,* Economic Science Press, Beijing, pp. 137-150.

Luo Suming (2002), "Strengthen Government Adjustment to Prevent Polarisation in Personal Income Distribution", *Journal of Yunnan University of Finance and Economics*, Vol. 10.

Ma Yanjun (2002), *Reduce the Income Disparity Between the Urban and The Rural Areas,* Luxing Institute of Economy, Vol. 1.

Niu Feiliang (2002), "An Overall Analysis of Chinese Urban Residents' Income Gap", *Journal of Northwest Sci-Tech University of Agriculture and Forestry*, Vol. 8.

Qu Yaohui (2001), "Analysis on the Effects of Income Disparity on Industrial Restructuring in China", *Economist,* Vol. 2.

Quan Heng (2002), "Mutual Motivation Between Income Distribution and Economic Growth", *Academic Quarterly of Shanghai Institute of Social Sciences*, Vol. 1.

Sha Yuying (2000), "Uneven Income Distribution Is the Key of Consumption Demand Shortage", *Business Research*, Vol. 8.

Song Donglin (1995), "Analysis and Theoretical Thoughts about Income Distribution in Today's China", *Research on Financial and Economic Issues*, Vol. 8.

Sun Jiangming and Zhong Funing (2002), "Evaluation and Reflection on the Strategies of China's Economic Growth and Income Distribution", *Journal of Nanjing University of Economics*, Vol. 1.

Wang Hongyan (2002), "Income Disparity among Urban Residents in China, Its Causation and Countermeasures", *Economics of Technology*, Vol. 2.

Wang Jialin (2002), "Adjustment Measures for Income Disparity in China", *Research on Coal Economy*, Vol. 7.

Wu Demin (2002), "Reconsideration of Income Disparity Among Urban Residents in China", *Reform of Economic System*, Vol. 1.

Xia Xingyuan and Fan Gang (2002), "Towards China's Present Receipts Distribution Pattern", *Contemporary Finance and Economics*, Vol. 5.

Xu Zongling and Chen Juan (2000), "Analysis on Economic Growth and Income Distribution Changes", *Journal of Shantou University*, Vol. 1.

Yan Pengfei and Tang Yi'ang (2002), "Research on Income Disparity among China's Residents", *Fujian Forum (Economic and Social Edition),* Vol. 3.

Yang Tianyu (2002), "Analysis of the Influence of Income Distribution and Credit Relation on Investment Demand in China", *Contemporary Economic Research*, Vol. 9.

Yang Yiyong (2002a), "The General Situation and Trends of China's Income Distribution Pattern and its Countermeasures", *Journal of Hangzhou Teachers College (Social Science Edition)*, Vol. 9.

Yang Yiyong (2002b), "Pattern and Problems of Income Distribution in China and Policy Proposals", *Prices in China*, Vol. 5.

Ye Hansheng (2002), "Adjust Income Distribution and Prevent Polarization", *Finance, Trade and Economy*, Vol. 10.

Yi Qiuhong (2002), "Four Factors Affecting Increase of Farmers' Income in China", *Reform of Economic System*, Vol. 4.

Yu Limin (2002), "Preliminary Analysis of Income Distribution Disparity in China", *Contemporary Economic Research*, Vol. 9.

Zeng Guo'an (2000), "Necessity of Income Disparity Adjustment by the Government in Market Economies", *Economic Review*, Vol. 2.

Zeng Guo'an (2002), "China's Resident Income Difference Since the End of 1970s: Trend, Appraisal of Its Status Quo, and Choices of Adjustment Policies", *Economic Review*, Vol. 5.

Zhang Donghui and Xu Qifu (2002), "Experimental Research on Income Distribution Disparity in Urban Residents in China", *Contemporary Economic Research*, Vol. 1.

Zhang Lei (2002), "Status and Countermeasures of the Income Distribution in China", *Journal of Zhenyang University*, Vol. 3.

Zhang Meixia (2002), "Income Distribution Disparity and Income Distribution Order", *Journal of Wuhan Communication and Management Institute*, Vol. 6.

Zhang Xiangda (2002), "Relationship Between Underground Economy and Income Distribution", *Statistical Research*, Vol. 11.

Zhang Yatao (2000), "About Negative Effects of Excessive Income Disparity", *Economist*, Vol. 9.

Zhang Yi and Gong De'en (2002), "A Study on the Distribution Pattern of the Size-Income Enjoyed by Chinese Urban Inhabitants", *Journal of Huaqiao University (Philosophy and Social Science)*, Vol. 3.

Zhang Ying and Tang Ren (2000), "Basic Policies to Solve Problems with Income Distribution in Today's China", *Socialism Research*, Vol. 2.

Zhao Renwei (2002), "Changes in Income Distribution During the Transitional Period and Countermeasures", *Journal of National College of Administration*, Vol. 3.

Zhao Renwei, Li Shi and C. Riskin (1999), *Re-study of Income Distribution Among Residents in China*, China Financial and Economic Press.

Zhao Yaohui and Li Shi (2002), "The Decline of In-Kind Wage Payments in Urban China", *China Economic Quarterly*, April.

Zheng Jianren (2002), "Income Distribution: Whether We Can Own Both Efficiency and Equity", *Journal of Radio and TV, University (Philosophy and Social Sciences),* Vol. 2.

Zheng Rongqi (2002), "Reasons and Countermeasures for the Increase of Regional Disparity of Resident Income in China", *Journal of Henan College of Financial Management Cadres*, Vol. 1.

Zhou Zhenhua (2002), "Connotation, Structure and Trend of Income Distribution Patterns in China", *Reform*, Vol. 3.

Zhu Guolin, Fan Jianyong and Yan Yan (2002), "Theory and Data About Tepid Consumption and Income Distribution in China", *Economic Research*, Vol. 5.

Chapter 3

DISPARITIES BETWEEN URBAN AND RURAL AREAS AND AMONG DIFFERENT REGIONS IN CHINA

by
Yin Yanlin,

Director, Division of Income Distribution,
National Development and Reform Commission, China

In China, urban, rural and regional disparities in economic development and household income have a great bearing, not only on the growth of the national economy, but also on social stability. Since the beginning of the reform and opening-up, these disparities have undergone changes in different directions, and recent years have seen a general trend toward enlargement. At present, urban-rural and regional disparities in China are greater than in many other countries, and have had negative effects on economic development and social stability. In the years following China's entry into the World Trade Organization (WTO), such disparities could continue to grow. It is therefore necessary to consider this as an issue of great importance, and to adopt effective measures to solve the problem.

Disparities between urban and rural areas

Main characteristics of the growing urban-rural disparities

The urban-rural disparity is a chronic historical issue in China. Following the beginning of the reform, the income gap between urban and rural residents actually diminished in the 1980s. For instance, in 1978, the per capita disposable income of urban residents was 2.57 times the per capita net income of farmers, and this figure decreased to 1.86 in 1985 and to 2.12 in 1988. Starting from 1989, the income gap between urban and rural residents has been fluctuating, with a general trend toward widening. In 2002, the per capita disposable income of urban residents was 3.11 times the per capita net income of farmers, reaching a record high in the past 20 years. Taking into consideration monetary income only, the income of urban residents would be four times that of farmers; taking also into account the fact that urban residents enjoy various welfare allowances, while farmers do not, then the real income of urban residents should be equivalent to five or six times that of farmers.

In terms of the Gini coefficient, it is important to note that the Gini coefficients for both rural and urban China are less than the national Gini coefficient, which covers both the urban and rural populations. According to the National Bureau of Statistics (NBS), in 1988, the rural Gini coefficient stood at 0.30, the urban 0.23, while the national coefficient was 0.341; in 2000, the rural Gini coefficient reached 0.35, the urban 0.32, while the national coefficient was 0.417. Due to the growing disparities between urban and rural areas, the national coefficient, based on the national population combining urban and rural residents, is higher than both the urban and rural Gini coefficients.

Main factors contributing to the growth of urban-rural disparities

Many factors affect urban-rural disparities. A prominent feature of the Chinese economy in its modern history has been a dualistic structure; for a very long time, urban areas have been superior to rural areas in China, in terms of economic development and individual income. This is the basic starting point for studying the disparities between urban and rural areas. By 1978, when the reform was initiated, total agricultural output had grown by 106.2% over that of 1952, with an average annual growth of 2.82%. However, during the same period, China's total industrial output had increased by a factor of 15.576, growing at an average rate of 11.4% annually. Hence, the growth rate of industrial output was four times that of agricultural output, which laid the economic foundation for the income gap between urban and rural residents. In 1957, only eight years after the founding of New China, the per capita disposable income of urban residents amounted to CNY235, while the per capita net income of farmers was only CNY73; that is, the income gap was as large as 3.2.

In the past two decades, the urban economy has maintained more rapid growth than the rural economy, and industry has grown more quickly than agriculture; the gap between urban labour productivity and that of rural areas has been enlarging, which is the fundamental cause of the widening of the income gap between urban and rural areas. By 2001, China's agricultural output had grown by 184.8% over that of 1978, an average annual increase of 4.66%; during the same period, industrial output surged by 1 075.9%, with an annual growth of 11.3%, 2.4 times the growth rate of agriculture. In 1978, the agricultural output (added value) per farmer stood at CNY360, while industrial output per worker reached CNY2 513, so that agricultural productivity was only 14% of industrial productivity. In 2001, agricultural output (added value) per farmer was CNY4 001, while industrial output per worker rose to CNY30 133, which means that agricultural per capita output only amounted to 13% of that of industry. This enormous difference in productivity leads to the income gap between urban and rural areas.

Great disparities exist between urban and rural areas in terms of the resources used in production. On the one hand, an abundant labour force works on very limited arable land in the Chinese countryside, with each farmer possessing on average only 0.29 hectare of arable land. In consequence, the level of land per farmer is far below the world average. On the other hand, urban labour utilises much more in terms of fixed assets per person than do farmers. The total fixed assets used by farmers for agricultural production amounted to CNY60 334 billion in original value in 1985, with each farmer taking CNY194, on average; this total reached CNY354 409 billion in 2001, with each farmer using an average of CNY971. In 2001, each industrial worker used CNY68 405 of fixed assets in original value and CNY43 945 in net fixed assets, 70 and 45 times that used by farmers, respectively.

The long-term artificial partition of urban and rural labour markets, and price differences between agricultural and industrial products, also lead to disparities between the urban and rural population in income and consumption. First, the household registration system restricts the migration of the rural population to cities, confines farmers to production and living on limited land resources, and prevents them from enjoying the benefits of urban development. Second, the price index of farm produce purchase has a direct bearing on the pace of farmer's income growth. Purchase prices for farm produce increased by 22.1% and 7.1%, respectively, in 1979 and 1980, by 12 to 23% in the period 1987-1989 and by 13 to 40% in 1993-1995, and in these years, farmer's income grew rapidly. Since 1997, there have occurred both a temporary and a structural surplus of farm produce, and a continuous decline in farm produce prices. At present, prices have still not recovered and the government is unable to provide farmers with effective protection and subsidies. Therefore, there has been a scenario of slow growth for farmer's income.

Trends in disparities between urban and rural areas

Despite the fact that enormous disparities exist between urban and rural areas, with various negative effects on economic and social development, it is likely that such disparities will continue to grow in the future, due to the influence of various factors. The productivity of agriculture and rural areas is still growing at a lower rate than that of industry and urban areas, and the proportion of agricultural output in total output will further shrink. Primary industry accounted for 50.5% of GDP in 1952, but this figure dropped to 28.1% in 1978 and to 15.2% in 2001. Due to the fact that the share of agricultural output is in steady decline, farm income, which is based on agricultural activities, is unlikely to grow rapidly.

China's WTO membership will prevent farm produce prices from rising to the level of previous years, which constitutes a negative factor for the growth of farmers' incomes. In 2003, the Chinese government issued tariff rate quotas (TRQs) for the import of 8.652 million tons of wheat, 6.325 million tons of corn and 3.78 million tons of rice, which accounts for 9.2%, 5.5% and 2.1% of the national output in 2001, respectively. The total of the TRQ import of the above three kinds of grain is equivalent to nearly 5% of China's total grain production in the past two years, and 13% of the national total of marketable grain. The TRQ import of grain actually functions as a constraint on domestic grain prices. Once these prices rise to a level higher than international prices, or international grain prices decrease to a level lower than domestic prices, grain imports will rocket, impacting directly on Chinese farmers' incomes.

The migration of rural labour to urban areas is confronted by many obstacles, and it will take a long time for China to achieve complete urbanisation. In 2002, the urban population accounted for 39.1% of the national total. If the urbanisation rate goes up by 1 percentage point annually on average in the future, the urban population will make up 47% of the national total by 2010. However, the rural population will still be in the majority, and this huge rural population has to live on the agricultural output, which is shrinking in relation to industrial output. The government's financial strength is limited. Priority will have to be given to the urban population in the allocation of budgetary expenditures on social security and social relief to people in difficulty for a very long period of time.

The negative impact of expanding urban-rural disparities and countermeasures

From an economic perspective, the growing disparities between urban and rural areas will result in a break in the connection between the urban and rural economies. In recent years, sales of consumer goods have been growing at a lower rate in rural areas than in urban areas. Although farmers have a higher propensity to consume than urban residents, farmers' purchasing power is weak, due to their low income. This fact has become the most prominent constraint on the development of rural markets. From the social or political point of view, the growing gap between urban and rural areas will lead to social instability. Urban-rural disparities should be eliminated, not through controlling urban development and the income of urban residents, but through the economic and social development of rural areas and increased support for rural development from the government. Efforts should be made to develop the rural economy and improve agricultural productivity by strategic restructuring of agriculture and the rural economy, so as to promote industrialised agriculture and link farmers scattered across the country to a unified national market, through leading enterprises and intermediaries. The food industry should be developed and the added value of agricultural products increased. Rational rural land transfers should be pushed forward, by more large-scale operations, with the precondition of protecting farmers' interests and increasing agricultural production. Attempts also should be made to accelerate the process of urbanisation and reduce the proportion of the rural population. The household registration system should be reformed, so as to eliminate the partition of urban and rural areas, and build a unified nationwide labour market. To facilitate the rational and orderly movement of labour between urban and rural areas and among different regions, efforts should be made to promote more even payments through the movement of the labour force, and to bring market forces into play in curbing the expansion of the income gap between urban and rural areas.

The government should increase transfer payments to rural areas, and set up and improve the rural social security network and relief mechanisms for the poverty-stricken rural population. Analyses show that the government does not grant subsidies to agriculture, but collects taxes and fees from agriculture and farmers. Some of the taxes and fees collected from farmers, such as the Agriculture Tax, are turned over to the central government; the remainder are used to support rural elementary and secondary education, and the operation of township and village authorities. Therefore, it is extremely important to carry out rural tax and fee reform, reduce farmers' tax burden, streamline the organisation and personnel of township and village authorities, and cut expenditure. The administrative system for rural compulsory education should be reformed, and educational funding should not be raised directly from farmers, but appropriated by governments at the central, provincial and local levels. Meanwhile, the central and provincial governments should increase transfer payment to rural areas to support rural education, health care, dissemination of agricultural technologies and rural infrastructure development such as water, power, road, telecommunications, etc. The establishment of the minimum living allowance system should be accelerated, and social security provisions such as pensions and health care for rural residents be put in place.

Regional disparities in China

Main characteristics of growing regional disparities

The income gap between farmers in the eastern and western regions is widening. In 1978, the per capita annual net income of eastern farmers amounted to CNY139, 120% of that of western farmers, and the income gap was not large. In 1995, the per capita annual net income of eastern farmers reached CNY2 127, twice that of western farmers, which was CNY1 061. In recent years, the per capita annual net income of eastern farmers has remained at more than 1.9 times that of western farmers. In terms of absolute amounts, the gap in per capita annual net income between eastern and western farmers amounted to CNY23 in 1978 and CNY1 470 in 2000.

The income gap between urban residents in the eastern and western regions is also expanding. In 1978, when the reform and opening-up was initiated, urban residents in the eastern region had a per capita annual disposable income of CNY372, 110% of that of the middle region, and 109% of that of the western region. In 2000, the per capita annual disposal income of eastern urban residents reached CNY7 682, 140% of that of the western region and 149% of the middle region. The absolute amount of the income gap grew by a large margin over that of 1978. One noticeable fact is that the income gap between eastern and middle urban residents is larger than that between eastern and western urban residents, and this scenario is the opposite to that of the farmers' income gap. The following three factors contribute to the relatively high income of western households: the western region does not lag much behind the middle region in terms of urban economic development; western cities are less populated than those of the middle region; and residents of western cities have been given favourable policy support from the central government.

The per capita GDP gap is growing between the eastern and western regions (Table 3.1). The per capita GDP of Guizhou province accounted for 13% of that of Shanghai in 1952, 7% in 1978 and 7.7% in 2001. The per capita GDP of Gansu province was nearly as much as that of Jiangsu province in 1952, amounting to 95% of the per capita GDP of Jiangsu; the figure fell to 81% in 1978, which means the gap had enlarged, but not significantly; however the figure dropped to 32% in 2001, indicating a huge gap between the two provinces in terms of per capita GDP. The contrast between

Qinghai province, located in the north-western region, and Guangdong province, in the eastern region, is also food for thought. The two provinces had the same per capita GDP at CNY101 in 1952; Qinghai's per capita GDP was higher than that of Guangdong by 17% in 1978; but in 2001, Qinghai's GDP was only equivalent to 42% that of Guangdong. The per capita GDP of a region reflects the local level of economic development, and differences in economic development and their changes determine the income gap between regions and the direction of changes.

Main factors contributing to the expansion of regional disparities

The increase in regional income disparities should be attributed to the differences in economic development and the enlargement of such differences. Economic development is subject to human resources, natural resources, capital, technology and other factors:

Differences in economic growth rates. Since the beginning of reform and opening-up, the eastern coastal region has maintained an average economic growth rate of over 10%, while western provinces have been growing relatively rapidly, but at a rate less than 10% (Table 3.2). The differences between the eastern and western region in economic growth rates and level of economic development are the main factors that directly lead to the regional income gap.

Differences in human capital. First, in terms of the educated population per 100 000 people in 2000, the eastern region had 5 982 people with college or higher degrees, while there were only 2 965 in the western region, 3 017 less than the eastern region; the eastern region had 11 146 people with secondary education, while there were 9 218 in the western region, 1 928 persons less than the eastern region; the eastern region had 33 961 people with junior middle school education, while there were 25 659 in the western region, 8 302 less than the eastern region; the eastern region had 35 701 people with elementary education, while there were 37 557 in the western region, 1 856 more than the eastern region (Table 3.3). This shows that western people are less educated than eastern people. Second, the illiteracy ratio in the eastern region stood at 5.98% in 2000, 0.74 percentage point lower than the national ratio, but the ratio in the western region was 11.99%, 5.27 percentage points higher than the national ratio and 6.01 percentage points higher than the eastern ratio (Table 3.4).

The above data illustrate the fact that it is a tremendous task to carry out the Nine-Year Compulsory Education Programme across the western region and eliminate the illiteracy of young adults there. The completion of the task in the next five to ten years has a bearing on the realisation of the objectives of the Western Region Development Programme and the pace of China's modernisation drive. The national statistics show that the illiterate population is concentrated in rural areas, and regional data demonstrate that the illiterate population mainly live in the western region, particularly western rural areas, which have an illiteracy ratio higher than the national ratio by 6.09 percentage points (Table 3.5). It is clear that it has become urgent to develop education in western rural areas. Third, in terms of the education of employees, 7.4% of them were illiterate in the eastern region in 1999, while this ratio reached 23.14% in the western region, nearly 16 percentage points higher. Among the employed population, 16.25% had senior middle school education in the eastern region, compared with only 9.52% in the western region, 6.73 percentage points lower. Employees with college and higher education accounted for 7.04% of the employed population in the eastern region, and only 3.66% in the western region, leaving a gap of 3.38 percentage points (Table 3.6).

Fourth, in terms of the student population in higher learning institutes and technical secondary schools, graduates from colleges and universities based in the eastern region made up 48.02% of the total college graduates nationwide in 2000, while the western region only took 21.27%. Colleges and universities based in the eastern region enrolled 46.19% of the national college enrolment in 2000, while the western region accounted for 21.82%, nearly 7 percentage points lower than 28.5%, which is the same as the ratio of western people in the national total population. Despite the fact that the central government declared education to be a priority of the Western Region Development Programme in 1999, the enrolment of western students in colleges and universities did not expand by a substantial margin in 2000. Statistics show that the student population of colleges and universities based in the eastern region accounted for 47.10% of the national college student population in 2000, while western colleges and universities took up only 21.36% (Table 3.7). There are similar gaps between the eastern and western regions in terms of number of graduates, enrolments and the student population of technical secondary schools.

Natural resources, mainly land and mineral resources

First, in relation to land resources, the western region of China boasts a vast territory, making up 70% of China's total area, but only a very limited amount of the land can be used for agricultural production. Statistics show that desertification has affected nearly one-third of China's territory, and most of this takes place in the north-western region. Due to adverse physical, chemical, temperature and rain conditions, the productivity of arable land in the western region is inferior to that of the eastern region in terms of either total yield per hectare or marginal output. At present, 20 million western people live a poverty-stricken life, due to the lack of water or suitable agricultural conditions. Western agriculture enjoys some comparative advantages over other regions of China, but from the perspective of global agricultural development, the comparative advantages of the western region are not obvious. For instance, a US farmer cultivates more than 1 000 mu of land on average, and a Chinese farmer works on average over four mu of land. Although the average amount of land farmed by a farmer in the western region is higher than the national average, it is far less than the average amount in the United States. In addition, Chinese farmers are engaged in agriculture under very poor natural conditions and with out-of-date production facilities.

The western region boasts richer mineral resources than the eastern region. For example, the natural gas reserve in the western region constitutes over 80% of the national total; 97% of China's rare earth deposit is located in Baotou city. The nickel, vermiculite, bauxite, and gypsum reserves in Gansu Corridor account for 68%, 95.7%, 86.2% and 85.7% of the national total, respectively. The sylvite and magnesium chloride deposits in Caidam Basin account for 98% and 100% of the national total, respectively. To sum up, the rich mineral deposits of the north-western region, worth CNY33.7 trillion, provide very favourable conditions for the economic growth of the western region. However, the advantage of the western region in resources has not yet been fully transformed into economic advantages. On the one hand, the efficiency of resource development is low. For instance, rare earth is not fully processed and has low added value, and moreover, Chinese enterprises of rare earth compete against each other with low prices in the international market. On the other hand, mineral resources in the western region to some extent lack comparative advantages. For example, the quality of western iron ore is quite low, and considering the cost of transportion over a long distance from the western region, many iron-ore-consuming domestic enterprises prefer to import ore from other countries.

Capital formation

Material capital is the basis for a country, region or an enterprise to be engaged in economic activities such as production and distribution, and also the basis of economic growth. The possession of material capital has a great bearing on economic development. Statistics show that the per capita capital formation of the eastern region amounted to CNY5 013.72 while that of the western region was only CNY1 953.68, 38.97% of that of the eastern region. The per capita fixed capital of the eastern region reached CNY4 169.76, while that of the western region only CNY1 795.92, 43.07% of the eastern region. The gap between the eastern and western region is much larger in terms of capital stock (Table 3.8). In 2000, computer ownership in urban households reached 9.72 computers per 100 households nationwide, 14.83 computers per 100 households in the eastern region and 6.09 in the western region, only 41.07% of the eastern region and 62.65% of the national average. This fact demonstrates that the western region lags much behind the eastern region in information technology (IT) development. If no efforts are made to control the situation, the gaps in economic growth and social development between the eastern and western regions will further expand.

Technological progress

It is very difficult calculate the level of technological advance of different regions and their contribution to economic growth. Regional disparities are studied under only a few indicators related to technological advance. First, the volume of trade of the technology market of the western region accounted for 13.21% of the national total in 1994 and 20.56% of the eastern region in 1994; 13.20% of the national total in 2000, at the same level as 1994, but only 19.02% of the eastern region, 2 percentage points down from 1994 (Table 3.9). Second, statistics show that 11 299 patent claims in three categories filed from the western region were approved in 2000, making up 11.86% of the national total of 95 236 and equivalent to 19.08% of that of the eastern region. In the category of invention, the western region had 1 045 patent claims approved, 16.92% of the national total and 30.05% of the eastern region; in the category of practical new technology, the western region had 6 679 claims approved, accounting for only 12.26% of the national total and 22.06% of the eastern region; in the category of industrial design, the western region's claims were equivalent to 10.32% and 14.04% of the eastern region (Table 3.10).

The third indicator is the construction of high technology (hi-tech) development zones. High technology can be a strong motor for modern economic development, in developed countries such as the United States, as well as in China. The development of hi-tech has an important bearing on regional economic development. It is a Chinese characteristic that the high technology industries are concentrated in hi-tech development zones across the country. Therefore, a study of these zones can lead to findings about hi-tech development. It can be seen that 66.25% of all the hi-tech enterprises were based in the eleven provinces of the eastern region in 2000, while there were only 16.64% in the western region. In terms of the employee population, the eastern region had 55.22%, while the western region reached 18.57%. Just over 70% of total output and 70.68% of total income of hi-tech enterprises were concentrated in the eastern region, and only 11.93% and 12.04% in the western region, respectively. Around 90% of total exports were from the eastern region, but only 3.58% were from the western region (Table 3.11). In the western region, cities such as Lanzhou, Chengdu and Xi'an boast comparatively advanced science and technology resources, and substantial progress needs to be made in institution building, attitude changes and administrative innovation, to really transform science and technology resources into tangible productivity.

The level of opening up to the outside world

Areas which are economically more developed are also more open to the outside world. In 1999, the degree of opening of the eleven eastern coastal provinces/municipalities was 64.47%, but this ratio was under 10% in the middle eight provinces and the twelve western provinces, autonomous regions and municipalities, equivalent to less than one-sixth of that of the coastal provinces. Three southern coastal provinces are the most open, at 127.68%, and Guangdong province, at 163.32%, is the most open province (Table 3.12). If inter-provincial domestic trade is not taken into account, Guangdong's ratio of opening up is still higher than that of some developed countries. In contrast, the ratio of opening up of Henan province and Ningxia Autonomous Region is less than 7%, at the bottom level among the 31 provinces, autonomous regions and municipalities.

Both geographical and policy factors have contributed to the formation of the above-mentioned gaps. The opening process was carried out in geographical order. At the end of 1970s and the early 1980s, four special economic zones were set up as pilot programmes in Shenzhen, Zhuhai, Shantou and Xiamen; in the middle 1980s, another fourteen coastal or port cities were opened; in the late 1980s and early 1990s, the opening-up programme was extended to Hainan province, the Pudong area of Shanghai, and more port and border cities, and inland major cities, arriving at the phase of an all-round opening nationwide. Due to constraints in natural conditions, economic base and order of initiation, the opening-up of the middle and central regions has not been as successful as that of the eastern region. In terms of sectors, the manufacturing sector, which mainly concentrates in the eastern region, was opened earlier and more thoroughly than other sectors. China's regional disparities should be mainly attributed to the above factors.

Development trend of regional disparities

In the near future, some underdeveloped areas may develop in leaps and bounds, and catch up with other developed areas to some extent, but the general trend is that regional disparities will further grow, mainly for the following reasons: developed areas enjoy better basic conditions for accelerating development. For instance, talented people, capital and advanced technologies, which represent the direction of advanced productivity, will continue to move to the eastern region, which is developed, more open, and more attractive to foreign investors, with a better investment climate. Developed areas can better respond to the changes in domestic and international markets, and the government agencies continue to improve their efficiency. In a word, the developed eastern coastal region is acquiring a new mechanism of rapid economic growth. In contrast, underdeveloped areas are confronted with various difficulties and constraints to accelerating development, such as brain drain, lack of capital, out-of-date technologies and mindsets, over-dependence on the central government, an incomplete modern corporate system, inexperienced local governments and an inferior investment climate.

Lack of financial resources impedes the central government's ability to support underdeveloped areas. In 1998-2002, the central government's transfer payment to local governments totalled CNY1 231.9 billion, among which CNY177.7 billion were channelled to local social security and CNY175.5 billion were used to pay the salaries of employees of local government agencies and public organisations. In recent years, along with the rapid growth of fiscal revenue, the fiscal deficit is increasing. It is estimated that fiscal revenue will grow in the near future as rapidly as in the past; therefore the support of the central government will not be as strong as in the past.

The negative impact of enlarging regional disparities and main countermeasures

There are two aspects of the negative impact of enlarging regional disparities. One is economic and the other political, or social. If agriculture-centred regions and post-industrial regions coexist in one country or economy, it will be difficult to achieve a virtuous economic cycle. If great gaps exist between regions in economic development and income, there will be corresponding gaps in production equipment, management systems and consumption structure. It will be impossible to develop a smooth and logical transition, links and upgrading among different regions, and institutional friction and waste of resources will be inevitable. In addition, regional disparities could lead to an imbalance of social psychology and instability, as could urban-rural disparities. In the near future, it will be unrealistic to expect and demand that the eastern region should halt its growth and wait until the underdeveloped western region catches up, or to develop the poor regions at the expense of rich regions, so as to eliminate the economic and income gaps, and promote co-ordinated development of regional economies. A correct approach would be to promote the further development of the eastern region, and at the same time accelerate the development of the middle and western regions.

Further implement the Western Region Development Programme. The western region development programme, launched in 1999, has yielded good results, but the programme cannot be completed in a short period of time. A long-term development approach should be adopted and the efforts of several generations will be needed to change the outlook of the western region. More efforts should be made to strengthen infrastructure development in transport, telecommunications, energy, irrigation and water conservancy in the middle and western regions, and to change the investment climate of the western region. In the process of implementing the programme, the central government should increase its support to the western region.

Adjust and optimise the industrial and employment structure. Agriculture has been the major part of the economy of the middle and western regions. These regions should make a full display of their comparative advantages, such as vast land, smaller population and rich mineral resources, and turn their potential advantages into reality. Apart from the development of basic industries such as agriculture and mining, active efforts should be made to develop the processing industry, transport, post and telecommunications and commerce, and other parts of the service sector, so as to realise rapid economic growth and increase incomes. Additional efforts should also be made to protect the environment and prevent pollution.

Restructure the ownership system. Great efforts should be made to promote the private sector and strengthen the vitality of economic development. The experience of reform and opening-up in the past two decades shows that the rapid economic growth of the eastern region is closely associated with the development of the private sector. Eastern provinces, such as Jiangsu and Zhejiang, lead other provinces in various indicators of economic development, and their leading position may be attributed to the large-scale development of the private sector in these two provinces. The state sector still accounts for a major share of the economy in the middle and western regions, and efforts should be made to reform and restructure the state sector in these regions.

Allow and regulate the transfer of rural surplus labour from the middle and western regions to the eastern region. It is an inevitable trend to transfer labour from underdeveloped areas to more developed areas. On the one hand, labour emigration can help part of the population in underdeveloped areas to access the benefits of economic development in the developed areas; on the other, with the emigration of labour, the per capita resource of underdeveloped areas will increase, bringing in more investors. Additional efforts should be made to maintain an orderly and regulated emigration of labour and take account of the east region's ability to accept immigrant workers.

Improve the stock and quality of human capital. The human capital situation of different regions in China is positively correlated to their per capita GDP. A noticeable trend in recent years is that the impact of preferential policies on the expansion of regional economic disparities is diminishing, while the impact of human capital is growing. In the implementation of the western region development programme, if efforts are not made to improve human capital, economic development will lack driving forces. Therefore, the middle and western regions need to develop education, accelerate the development of science and technology and educational reform, and further change mindsets to meet the needs of development.

Table 3.1. **Per capita GDP of different regions**

	1952	1978	1990	2001
Eastern region				
Shanghai	436	2 498	5 190	37 382
Jiangsu	131	430	2 016	12 922
Zhejiang	112	331	2 122	14 655
Guangdong	101	367	2 397	13 730
Western region				
Guizhou	58	175	810	2 895
Sichuan	67	253	1 105	5 250
Gansu	125	348	1 099	4 163
Qinghai	101	428	1 558	5 735

Source: Fifty Years of New China, 1999; *China Statistical Yearbook*, 2002, China Statistics Press.

Table 3.2. **Average annual economic growth, 1980-1995**

Region	%
Eastern region	
Shanghai	9.2
Jiangsu	12.8
Zhejiang	13.9
Guangdong	14.6
Western region	
Guizhou	8.9
Sichuan	8.9
Gansu	9.1
Qinghai	7.9

Source: China Statistical Yearbook, 2002, China Statistics Press.

Table 3.3. **Educated persons, 1990 and 2000**

Per 100 000 persons

	College and higher	Secondary education	Junior middle school	Elementary education
National				
1990	1 422	8 039	23 344	37 057
2000	3 611	11 146	33 961	35 701
Eastern				
1990	2 862	11 076	26 029	34 087
2000	5 982	14 704	35 835	30 233
Middle				
1990	1 388	8 665	24 386	36 640
2000	3 440	11 462	36 105	34 975
Western				
1990	1 178	6 836	18 410	34 439
2000	2 965	9 218	25 659	37 577

Note:
The 1990 data are abstracted from *Main Data of the Fourth National Census of China* (manual collection) compiled by the Census Office of the State Council; the 2000 data are based on the quick collection of the Fifth National Census by 0:00 of 1 November.

National data include soldiers in active service in the People's Liberation Army, while provincial data do not.

Source: *China Statistical Yearbook,* 2001, China Statistics Press.

Table 3.4. **Illiterate population in eastern, middle and western regions, 2000**

Per 1 000 persons

	Illiterate population		Illiteracy ratio	
	1990	**2000**	**1990**	**2000**
National	180 030	85 070	15.88	6.72
Eastern	61 170	30 520	13.12	5.98
Middle	59 180	25 410	14.67	5.84
Western	59 680	32 070	21.61	11.99

Source: *China Statistical Yearbook,* 2001, China Statistics Press.

Table 3.5. **Urban and rural illiterate population in eastern, middle and western regions, 2000**

Per 1 000 persons

	Illiterate population			**Illiteracy ratio**	
	Total	**Urban**	**Rural**	**Urban**	**Rural**
National	85 070	18 420	66 650	4.04	8.25
Eastern	30 520	9 010	21 520	4.06	8.35
Middle	25 410	5 440	19 960	3.89	6.89
Western	32 070	4 660	2 7410	6.05	14.34

Note:

The data are based on the quick collection of the Fifth National Census by 0:00 of 1 November.

Soldiers in active service with the People's Liberation Army are not counted in the figures of the urban and rural illiterate population.

Source: *China Statistical Yearbook,* 2001, China Statistics Press.

Table 3.6. **Levels of education of employees in eastern, middle and western regions, 1999**

Percentage

	Illiterate	**Elementary**	**Junior middle**	**Senior middle**	**College and higher**
National	11.00	33.30	39.90	11.90	3.80
Eastern	7.94	27.64	41.67	16.25	7.04
Middle	8.99	31.84	41.97	13.20	4.00
Western	23.14	35.13	28.34	9.52	3.66

Note: The data are based on the sample survey of population change in 1999.

Source: China Statistical Yearbook of Regional Economy, 2000, Ocean Press.

Table 3.7. **Student data of colleges, universities and technical secondary schools in eastern, middle and western regions, 2000**

Number of persons

	Colleges and Universities			Technical secondary schools		
	Graduates	**Enrolment**	**Students**	**Graduates**	**Enrolment**	**Students**
National	949 767	2 206 072	5 560 900	1 507 237	1 325 870	4 895 159
Eastern	456 033	1 018 954	2 619 302	622 492	519 568	2 046 019
Middle	291 751	705 700	1 753 582	539 432	446 343	1 653 868
Western	201 983	481 418	1 188 016	345 313	359 959	1 195 272

Source: China Statistical Yearbook, 2001, China Statistics Press.

Table 3.8. **Total amount of capital formation in eastern, middle and western regions, 2000**

Billion CNY

	Total Capital formation	**Stock increase**	**Per capita fixed capital formation**	**Per capita stock**
Eastern	2 048 727	414 662	416 976	84 396
Middle	793 910	169 685	191 019	40 825
Western	638 107	56 054	179 592	15 775

Note: The data are calculated at current prices.

Source: *China Statistical Yearbook,* 2001, China Statistics Press.

Table 3.9. **Trade volumes of national and regional technology markets**

Billion CNY

	1994	1995	1996	1997	1998	1999	2000
National	2 288 69.6	268 344.7	300 204.5	351 371.8	435 822.8	523 412.3	650 751.9
Eastern	147 001.8	169 798.2	196 167.2	229 484.2	286 391.5	335 195.3	451 504.7
Middle	50 903.9	57 774.5	64 005.3	76 736.3	9 1764.8	104 298.9	113 379.5
Western	30 224.1	40 772	40 032	45 151.3	576 66.5	83 918.1	85 867.7

Source: *China Statistical Yearbook,* 2001, China Statistics Press.

Table 3.10. **Patent claims in three categories and approvals, 2000**

	Total approvals	Inventions	Practical new technology	Industrial design
National	95 236	6 177	54 407	34 652
Eastern	59 231	3 477	30 282	25 472
Middle	14 943	1 268	10 461	3 214
Western	11 299	1 045	6 679	3 575

Source: China Statistical Yearbook, 2001, China Statistics Press.

Table 3.11. **Main business indicators of hi-tech enterprises based in development zones, 2000**

	Enterprises (No.)	Employees (No.)	Total output (CNY1 000)	Total income (CNY1 000)	Total exports (USD1 000)
National	20 796	2 350 679	794 198 520	920 926 310	18 581 751
Eastern	13 777	1 298 085	556 290 270	650 930 590	16 816 240
Middle	3 557	615 983	143 134 800	159 146 950	1 100 643
Western	3 461	436 611	94 473 450	110 848 770	664 868

Source: *China Statistical Yearbook*, 2001, China Statistics Press.

Table 3.12. **Ratio of openness, 1999**

Percentage

Region and number of provinces	Commodity imports and exports/GDP	Foreign investment/GDP	Openness ratio
Coastal (11)	58.08	6.39	64.47
Northern coastal (5)	31.69	3.67	35.36
Middle coastal (3)	47.17	5.25	52.42
Southern coastal (3)	115.36	12.33	127.68
Middle (8)	7.76	1.46	9.22
Western (12)	8.62	1.06	9.68
National (31)	36.38	4.28	40.67

Note: The GDP data of three regions have been adjusted according to national data, and the data for foreign investment (FDI) are the sum of FDI and other kinds of foreign investment.

Source: *China Statistical Yearbook*, 2000, China Statistics Press.

Chapter 4

THE URBAN AND RURAL POOR IN CHINA AND THEIR INCOME-EARNING POTENTIAL

by
Huang Yanfen,

Associate Professor, Renmin University of China

and

Yang Yiyong,

Professor, National Development and Reform Commission, China

The government of China has announced that, on the whole, the Chinese people have reached a well-off standard of living, which is a good step towards the goal for the period between 2001 and 2020, to build a well-off society in an all-round way. However, farmers' incomes grew slowly in recent years and the fight against poverty in rural areas faces many problems. In cities, the population receiving subsistence allowances has increased from around 2 million to more than 20 million. Therefore, there are two views about China's economic development abroad, *i.e.* a "threatening view" and a "collapsing view". The "threatening view" says that China's economic growth brings threats to others. The "collapsing view" warns that there are potential risks for the Chinese economy to collapse. To appreciate the impact of China's economic growth on the poverty problem during the transition period, this chapter, by using solid data, studies China's poor population and its income-earning potential.

Urban and rural poverty in today's China

For historical reasons, China has a typical dual economy with the urban and rural economies clearly separated. Accordingly, the poverty problems in the urban and the rural areas have been considered and treated separately.

Urban poverty

The minimum living guarantee

In 1999, two steps were taken to set up a subsistence security system for urban residents – the minimum living guarantee (MLG). The first step was that the State Council issued the Regulation of Subsistence Security System for Urban Residents (referred to as the regulation), which took effect from 1 October 1999. According to the regulation "all urban residents with non-agricultural registered permanent residence should have the right to receive a subsistence allowance from the local government when family members cannot meet the local minimum living standard: those without any income, unable to work and without family support are entitled to receive the full subsistence allowance; those with some income are entitled to receive allowances so as to meet the minimum living standard" (Jiang Zemin, 1997; *China Society,* Beijing, 20 October 1999). The second step was that various localities raised the standard of subsistence security by 30% at the time of the 50th anniversary of the People's Republic of China (PRC). Eighty per cent of costs incurred were subsidised by the central government. All provinces, municipalities and ethnic autonomous areas, except Beijing, Shanghai, Shangdong, Jiangsu, Zhejiang, Fujian and Guangdong received fiscal subsidies from the central government. The amount of the subsidy made during the period July to December 1999 was CNY400 million (Table 4.1).[1]

In order to understand the living conditions of the urban poor, the Ministry of Civil Affairs launched a survey sampling 10 000 households in 100 cities nationwide in the period 23 September to 23 October 2002. The results showed that among households receiving the subsistence allowance, over 60% received less than CNY100 per month, about 30% received between CNY101 and CNY200, and only 8.4% received over CNY200. According to the results of the survey, the average per capita allowance was only CNY61 per month. The most extreme example was that in some areas, the allowance was just CNY10 per month, and a family with three members relied on CNY30 every month.[2]

Scale of the subsistence allowance

In 1997, the government initiated the subsistence allowance system in urban areas. At that time, there were no accurate statistical data on the number of recipients. According to an estimate of the Ministry of Civil Affairs, the number was less than 1.2 million. However, by the end of the years 1997, 1998, 1999, 2000, 2001 and June of 2002, there were 1.84 million, 2.81 million, 4.02 million, 4.58 million, 11.70 million and 19.31 million recipients, respectively. From 1998 to 2000, the average annual increase in the number of recipients was 762 700, *i.e.* a 39.5% increase each year. The number of recipients increased by 14.7 million from June 2001 to June 2002, up 321.57%, which is as much as 8.14 times the increase during 1998 and 2000. Such a rapid increase is abnormal (Figure 4.1).

The rapid increase in the number of MLG recipients does not necessarily mean that the impoverished population was increasing rapidly, but that more and more of the existing poor had their basic living subsistence secured more effectively. In the meeting of the State Council concerning the improvement of the social security system in September 2000, the Ministry of Civil Affairs reported in background reports that, in June 2000, there were 13.8 million urban residents living under subsistence level, and only 3 million of them were allowance recipients at that time. Why did a huge number of people receive nothing? The ministry explained that with limited funding, they could only help a limited number of people.

In the survey, it was found that: *1)* Some cities ruled that only the unemployed working population (males between 16 and 60, females between 16 and 55) could benefit from the local minimum income, *2)* Some cities required work unit/enterprises to take responsibility for the unpaid and laid off-workers, and then assumed that these groups had been paid already, *3)* Some localities set

1. Fan Baojun, speech at the national meeting of subsistence security for urban residents, 26 November 1999

2. On current fixed exchange rates, CNY1 is approximately USD0.12.

rules that families with women who had gold jewellery were not qualified for the subsistence allowance, *4)* Some localities set rules that families who had a television set, refrigerator or other electrical equipment, were not qualified for the subsistence allowance, *5)* Rules in some localities stated that families eating meat often were not qualified to receive an allowance, *6)* Local governments did not distribute subsistence allowances to employees of enterprises belonging to the central government, *7)* Families with members working in collective enterprises had difficulty in getting the allowance, *8)* Families in towns not under a county government were not covered by the subsistence allowance system. The above-mentioned restrictions were fairly common, and there were even more restrictions in practice. In some areas, people called the local restrictions "12 disqualifications", or "16 disqualifications". In fact, the MLG standard was strictly controlled in practice, which excluded many who should have received allowances from being assisted.

Another reason for the underestimation of China's urban poverty was that the established poverty line was low, and could not meet the requirements of needy families to develop and regain the mainstream of society by their own efforts. How many people are living in poverty? The lowest estimate of the poor urban population in China was reported to be about 13.8 million, but what would be the highest estimate? According to a survey of 50 000 urban workers and staff in 1992 by the National Union of Workers, there were more than 20 million people then living in poverty. According to a 1994 survey by the Social Survey Centre of the People's University, there were then about 50 million impoverished urban residents (Hong Dayong, 1997). The number would be even larger if the estimate were based on the actual place of residence of individuals, rather than their registered permanent residence. By the end of 2000, the MLG system was reported to have covered all those qualified. Yet there were only 3.2 million recipients, or only about 0.8% of the total urban population. Coverage was obviously very limited. In the last 10 years, residents receiving assistance in the United States amounted to about 12.7% of the population, while those in India to about 6% of the population. According to the specific situation in a developing country such as China, at least 6% of the urban population should have been receiving subsistence allowances, *i.e.* about 24 million (population with registered permanent residence in urban areas) to 30 million (population with residence in urban areas for a long time).

There are two main reasons for the rapid increase in the recipients of subsistence allowances in recent years. First, governments at all levels have a great responsibility for the people. General Secretary Jiang Zemin's important theory of the "Three Represents"[3] emphasises that the communist party of China should always represent the fundamental interests of the broadest masses of the Chinese people. Social assistance is closely related to the interests of the people. To implement this important theory, the work of the MLG should be carefully and completely carried out in urban areas. By updating understanding and concepts, and enhancing leadership, party commissions and governments at all levels treated the task of improving the subsistence security system in urban areas as an imperative duty, and made it a link between cadres and the masses, so as to create a stable social environment. Governments at all levels also increased financial support for people living in poverty. Second, the understanding of poverty has been improved. With development, people's understanding and attitudes toward poverty also develop. Because productive forces determine the production relations, the authors believe that to eliminate poverty in the first stage of socialist society is impossible. Therefore, it is necessary to confront the problem directly, and understand that the social

---

3. "To always represent: the requirements of the development of China's advanced productive forces, the orientation of China's advanced culture, and the basic interests of the broadest masses of the Chinese people, is the foundation for building our Party, the cornerstone for governing and the source of its strength."

assistance system should cover those in severe poverty, in basic poverty, and those in relative poverty as well.

Regional distribution of subsistence allowance recipients

As of June 2002, both Heilongjiang and Hunan have more than 1.5 million subsistence allowance recipients; the numbers of recipients in Liaoning, Jilin, Jiangxi, Henan, Hubei and Sichuan were between 1 million to 1.5 million; in Hebei, Shanxi, Inner Mongolia, Anhui, Shandong, Chongqing, Yunnan and Shaanxi between 500 000 and 1 million; in Shanghai, Tianjin, Jiangsu, Fujian, Guangdong, Guangxi, Guizhou, Gansu, Qinghai, Ningxia, and Xinjiang between 100-500 000; and the numbers of recipients in Beijing, Zhejiang, Hainan, Tibet and the Xinjiang construction corps amounted to less than 100 000 (Table 4.2).

According to the study by Wang Youjuan of the Urban Survey team of the National Bureau of Statistics of China, in 2000, the poor population in the eastern region was 2.72 million, in the central region, 5.82 million, and in the western region, 1.96 million. The total urban population in the central and western regions is about 53% of the total urban population of the country, while the poor population in the central and western regions accounted for three-quarters of the total poor population of the whole country, respectively. The National Union of Workers undertook a survey in 2002, and the results showed that the poor population in the eastern, central, and western regions accounted for 21.9%, 52.9% and 25.2% of the total poor population of the country. A study group of the Asian Development Bank found a similar result, which showed that the areas with a low poverty ratio were all the richest provinces along the coast, with Beijing an exception, and the areas with a high poverty ratio were all inland provinces in the west, with Henan an exception. However, there were some other exceptions when looking at the relationship between per capita GDP and the poverty population. Some of the poorest provinces, such as Guizhou and Qinghai, had fairly low poverty rates, while some rich areas, such as Liaoning and Tianjin, had relatively high poverty rates (Table 4.3).

Rural poverty

In 1978, the government of China launched a well-planned and organised programme to combat poverty through development, so as to solve the subsistence problems of the poor. After persistent efforts in three stages, *i.e.* fighting poverty by establishment of the household contract management system from 1978 to 1985, the large-scale fight against poverty through development from 1986 to 1993, and targeting poverty reduction from 1994 to 2000, the government's goal of solving poverty problems in rural areas by the end of the 20th century was basically met.

The poverty line in rural areas

In 1986, China started a large-scale programme to fight poverty through development. At that time, the poverty line in rural areas was a per capita annual income of CNY206, of which the proportion of food consumption, *i.e.* the Engel coefficient, was over 60%. The poverty line was then adjusted according to the price index every year. In 1990, it was CNY300, and in 1999 CNY625. At that time, the poor population in rural areas was very large and the degree of poverty was very serious; therefore, the focus of the fight against poverty was to guarantee subsistence. To establish a poverty line barely meeting the requirement of survival was in accordance with the situation at that time. Poverty fighting in rural areas mainly targeted absolute poverty, in order to secure subsistence. The main task of the poverty fighting office of the State Council was to help the most impoverished areas to develop, so that local people could live and develop in a normal way. With the continuous growth of China's economy and improvement in the people's lives, the poverty line should increase accordingly, and the issue of rural residents living in relative poverty should be considered. With this progress, the poverty situation would be examined more accurately, and the poverty line should be raised, so that development of the impoverished areas and the lives of the impoverished people can be further improved. Adjusting by the rural consumer price index (CPI), the absolute poverty line in the rural area changed from CNY630 in 2001 to CNY627 in 2002, and the income standard for the low-income population was adjusted from CNY872 in 2001 to CNY869 in 2002.

The scale of poverty in rural areas

During the 20 or more years since the reform and opening-up, poverty fighting in rural areas in China has made great achievements. The seven-year programme to help 80 million people out of poverty has in the main been fulfilled. However, it should be noted that the subsistence problem for some groups has not yet been solved. In bad years with natural disasters, some of those who had solved their subsistence problems may become impoverished again. More importantly, China is a developing country, the productive forces are still at low levels, and the chronology of the initial stage of socialism determines that rural poverty will exist for a long time. According to the Bureau of Forecasts and Surveys for National Rural Poverty of the National Bureau of Statistics, by the end of 2002, there was an impoverished population of 28.2 million in rural areas, decreasing by 1.07 million from the previous year, and the ratio of impoverished population was 3%, down by 0.1% from 2001. The population just above the subsistence level were about 58.25 million, decreasing by 2.77 million from 2001, and the ratio of the low income population to the whole rural population was 6.2%. The numbers of low income residents in the western, central and eastern regions amounted 29.45 million, 18.29 million, and 10.51 million, respectively, accounting for 50.6%, 31.4% and 18.0% of the population in each region.

The regional distribution of rural poverty

A large fall in poverty in the central and western regions. Due to the support of the government and good weather conditions for agriculture, poverty in the central and western regions fell. In 2002, a total of 1.08 million people in the central region escaped from poverty, as did a total of 700 000 in the western region. On the other hand, the impoverished population in the eastern region increased by 710 000 because of serious natural disasters, such as those in Hebei and Shandong.

Remaining poverty is mainly concentrated in the western region and the grain-producing areas. In 2002, the 12 provinces under the project of the western region development had 17.42 million people in poverty, which was 61.8% of the national poverty population in rural areas. Grain-producing areas had 15.54 million people in poverty, *i.e.* 55.1% of the total poor population in rural areas.

The situation of different provinces. The poverty rate in eight provinces, including Beijing, Tianjin, Shanghai, Jiangsu, Zhejiang, Fujiang, Shangdong and Guangdong, was less than 1%, while that in 13 provinces and areas, including Hebei, Liaoning, Jilin, Heilongjiang, Anhui, Jiangxi, Henan, Hubei, Hunan, Guangxi, Hainan, Chongqing and Sichuan, was between 1% and 5%, and in four provinces and districts, Inner Mongolia, Guizhou, Tibet and Qinghai, more than 10%.

The depth of rural poverty. The authors analysed a sample of 26 counties in Gansu province. At the end of 1999, these counties had a population of 8.71 million, with an average annual per capita GDP of CNY988, and a per capita income of farmers of CNY586. In comparison, the 587 national poverty counties had an average per capita GDP of CNY2 573 and an average per capita income of farmers of CNY1 427. Thus, in these 26 counties, the per capita GDP and the average income of farmers were about 38.4% and 41.1% of their counterparts in the 587 national impoverished counties, respectively. These comparisons clearly show that the rural economy of those 26 counties of Gansu stayed at a very low level, and that most of the rural population lived in serious poverty (Table 4.4).

Reasons for urban and rural poverty in China

Urban poverty

By the end of 2002, China had 20.53 million urban poor, whose standard of living did not reach the MLG standard. Only 5% of them were traditional "three-without" residents, *i.e.* those without income, working ability and family support. The new urban poor were mainly laid-off workers and the unemployed, due to restructuring, plus a certain number of on-post workers, retired personnel and their dependants.

Lay-offs and unemployment

Workers not in service were brought under the coverage of the MLG system in 2002. At the end of the year, there were 4.42 million workers not in service receiving an MLG allowance, about 22.9% of the total number of recipients. Other growing groups include dependants of the poor and others (mainly dependent on workers living in difficulty, laid-off workers, and the unemployed), the unemployed, laid-off workers, workers in service, the retired and the "three-without" personnel. In June 2002, there were 19.308 million MLG recipients, among whom 50.8% were workers living in serious difficulty (including workers in service, laid-off, not in service, and retired workers). The traditional "three-without" individuals assisted by the Department of Civil Affairs only accounted for 5% of the total. Among workers living in serious difficulties, 5.76 million were from state-owned enterprises (SOEs) (59%), and 4.05 million were from collective enterprises (41%). If categorised by their administrative relationship, 2.12 million were from enterprises supervised directly by the central government (22%) and 7.69 million were from enterprises supervised by local governments (78%) (Table 4.5).

According to the survey by the Ministry of Civil Affairs conducted from 23 September to 23 October 2002, 28.7% of families receiving assistance considered that job-hunting was their biggest difficulty, 25.9% said that medical costs were high, 17.3% considered the burden of education of children to be heavy, 12.8% of families lived with a per capita housing of less than 5 m^2, and 33.7% of families had disabled members. In recent years, groups of laid-off workers and unemployed formed in urban areas. Their incomes decreased significantly due to unemployment, which sometimes trapped their families into poverty. The investigation also showed that two-thirds of the families of unskilled laid-off workers had an average per capita monthly income of less than CNY300, 43.1% of them had not been re-employed for three years, and almost all the savings of the families were then used up. Since the average age of the laid-off workers is about 40, and one-third of them are laid-off couples, and the costs to support their parents, and feed and educate their children are increasing, it may be concluded that the incomes of many of these families are at less than the local subsistence level (Table 4.6).

In the period 1998-1999, 11.02 million laid-off workers were re-employed. In 1998, 6.099 million were re-employed and the re-employment rate was 50%. In 1999, 4.92 million were re-employed and the re-employment rate was 42%, down by 8% compared with 1998. Re-employment of laid-off workers became more difficult. However, hidden employment of laid-off workers is common. According to a sample survey of 10 000 laid-off workers in ten large and central-sized cities in July 1999, carried out by the Ministry of Labor and Social Security, 82% of the laid-off workers held paid jobs at least once, 32.29% had worked for over 6 months (17.26% had worked more than one year), 27.81% had worked for a period of three to six months, and 39.9% had worked for less than three months. As for monthly payments, 49.06% were paid less then CNY300; the remaining 50.94% were paid over CNY300, of whom 12.63% were paid over CNY500. Therefore, further attention should be paid to the issue of the hidden employment of laid-off workers.

Box 4.1. **Mr. Chen**

It is not easy to find Mr. Chen. He lives in a little shabby apartment-yard along a big street, about 100 metres away from a crossroads. The gate of the yard is parallel to the street and looks like a workshop with low houses where you never raise your eyes. Mr. Chen's employer did not provide housing and he lives in an apartment provided to his mother by the enterprise for which she had worked.

Mr. Chen, aged 52, high-school educated, healthy, was workshop manager of a printing factory before being laid off. He started in the job in 1974 and was laid off in April 1998. His monthly income before being laid off was about CNY300-700. He stated that the factory did not pay basic old-age pension insurance and unemployment insurance for the workers. The factory used to have more than 200 workers and now only has dozens. There is a re-employment service centre at the factory, distributing the basic living subsidy and occasionally providing vocational training. The basic living subsidy in September 1999 was CNY280. Mr. Chen has a happy family. His wife still works; his daughter is in the Normal University of Central China. But his mother-in-law has difficulties, with eight out of nine children (including sons and daughters-in-law) laid off.

After being laid off, Mr. Chen worked twice. First, from November 1998 to February 1999, he worked for a private enterprise as a salesman with a monthly income of CNY700, with free lunch. Second, from February to June 1999, he worked for a private printing factory with a monthly income of CNY700-800. There were no labour contracts for those jobs. He is now looking for a new job.

Note: The survey concluded that being laid-off is a "contagious disease". Often, the laying off of one member of a family affects other members and even leads to the laying off of others. Being laid-off causes major difficulties for a lot of people. Many workers of SOEs have married other SOE workers, with some even marrying workers at the same enterprise. With the current restructuring of SOEs, such a "marriage with parity" thus causes a correlation between laid-off family members. Therefore, the security of the basic living of the laid-off should not be weakened in any way. Otherwise, serious social problems will arise.

Abstracted from interviews conducted in 1999 with laid-off workers by Mo Rong, Director of the Office of Labor Force of China's Institute of Labor Science.

Incompleteness of the social security system

The social security system in China is still incomplete, and as such, it may contribute to poverty. For example, some enterprises and workers have not participated in the pooling fund for basic old-age pension insurance. Retired workers from such enterprises have to solve their living problems with the aid of the enterprises, or by themselves. Retired workers of enterprises in difficulty, and who have not contributed to the pooling fund, cannot obtain pensions. Other factors contributing to family poverty are those affected by sudden increases in costs. The medical insurance system has not been fully set up in China. Chronic diseases or diseases occurring suddenly often result in high expenditures and may push families into poverty. The heavy costs of educating children in college or university, plus the costs of purchasing housing and other abrupt increases in family expenditures, could possibly trap those poor families into poverty. A survey conducted between September and October 2002 showed that 64.9% of the families receiving MLG allowances have at least one member with a chronic or serious disease. Families with subsistence allowance face a vicious cycle of "diseases cause poverty, and poverty causes more disease".

Lack of human capital

Lack of human capital is another reason for urban and rural poverty in a market economy. According to a survey by the urban household survey team of the National Bureau of Statistics in 1995, families with heads educated to high school or lower levels accounted for 80.3% of the total families in poverty in 1995. Compared with 1990, the ratios of the families with heads with junior school education and primary school education among all poor families increased by 14.1% and

11.3%, respectively. The development of high-tech industries and the restructuring of traditional industries require continuous improvement in worker quality. Industrial transformation and accelerated mobility of workers demand timely vocational training for laid-off workers. Millions of redundant workers released from agriculture in future years will have to be trained so as to become qualified workers for industry. Further expansion of international labour markets generates new requirements for labour force training. All of the above calls for complete and sound vocational training systems and life-long learning education systems. In the transition period, preferential measures should be introduced to help disadvantaged groups to develop their human resources. Who are these weak groups in the labour market? Obviously, laid-off workers, the unemployed, farm workers, the disabled and women are groups with a disadvantaged status. Therefore, special measures should be taken in the training of these groups, to assist them to make effective progress.

Rural poverty

Natural conditions

Rural poverty in China is mainly located in the remote inland countryside with difficulties in transportation, production and living conditions, especially in mountainous areas. In 1994, almost all of the 592 national key poor counties were in the mountains, highlands and other areas with an adverse natural environment, particularly minority ethnic groups. These groups account for less than 10% of the national population, but make up 40% of the rural poor.[4] Poor natural environment conditions account for even more of the poverty problem in China, if all types of natural disasters are considered. These poor areas usually lie in remote regions, with complicated landforms, adverse climate, imbalanced ecology, serious and frequent natural calamities, and occluded transportation and information systems. Some areas suffer from a severe lack of water resources, with difficulties for both human beings and animals, some lack natural resources, and some suffer from serious regional diseases.

Adverse natural conditions significantly impede economic development in these areas. The various measures taken so far have not been able to overcome these adverse natural conditions. These poor areas have to produce goods and feed themselves under poor weather conditions. Generally speaking, they are able to feed and clothe themselves in the good years but fall back into poverty in years with natural disasters. In 1999, the ratios of the population falling back into poverty to the population escaping poverty in Hebei, Shanxi, Inner Mongolia, Henan and Hubei was 31.7%, 35.8%, 65.7%, 43.2%, and 27.6%, respectively. The population falling back into poverty in each of the areas of Anhui, Hebei and Henan was more than 1 million. In these areas, the cycle of "poverty – meeting basic needs – re-impoverishment" is as natural as the changing seasons. A wide of range of poverty fighting measures have not made effective changes to this cycle.

Family size

The family planning programme is implemented very well in cities, but faces fairly stubborn resistance in the countryside. The intention of the programme in rural areas is to improve the living standards of farmers, through population control and improvement of population quality. However, a farmer is likely to behave according to his own interests, paying no attention to the policies from which he cannot benefit. Many poor farmers disregard the family planning policy in order to try and have a male child. Their motivation may be that boys are preferred, but it is also true that they are driven by the expectation of future benefits. Heavy physical labour and strong men are demanded by

4. Office of Poverty Fighting of the State Council: statistical data of national key poor counties.

the outdated farm production styles. Parents in old age also need male children to provide support under Chinese traditions.

With rapid population growth, more poverty leads to more births and more births reinforce poverty. In some areas, the population density has far exceeded the capacity of available resources, resulting in a destructive over-use of natural resources. The so-called rule of "more poverty leads to more birth" is not a natural one. It is the desire of poor farmers to shake off poverty by increasing labour, since labour is the most important productive factor and more labour would bring more wealth. However, these farmers may not be aware that, with the development of society, the availability of labour is not sufficient to end poverty. Poverty will not change unless labour is combined with other productive factors, such as technology and capital. Therefore, the actual outcome of the desire to shake off poverty through larger families is probably to trap people into more severe poverty.

Educational opportunity

In relation to financial inputs to education, the policy adopted by the government is obviously in favour of cities. To implement the compulsory nine-year of education required by the government, the state provides financial support to the cities, while rural areas are required to collect funding from farmers. "To take a heavy financial burden with a small amount of income is social unfairness itself." For years, farmers have borne this unfairness in silence. As a result, only 30% of college students are from rural areas, with 70% of them coming from urban areas (*Today's Morning Paper,* 4 March 2002). Due to unfair allocation of educational resources, farmers are generally not well-educated, and this becomes a barrier for rural areas in seeking to shake off poverty.

On one hand, there are serious problems with the basic rural education system. Currently, the most important problems include the following: the junior school-age population will reach a peak in the 10th five-year period, while the development of a rural education system cannot match a sharp increase in admissions to junior school. Educational funding is in serious shortage, and the wages and salaries of teachers are often delayed. Dropout rates in rural primary and secondary schools are still high, being more than 10% in some localities. To enhance rural compulsory education is a strategic task for overall social and economic development in rural areas. With a weak foundation, it is very difficult for the rural compulsory education system to accommodate the large proportion of the population in these areas. Therefore, implementation of rural compulsory education is the most important and difficult part of the compulsory education programme. The Hope project is a social welfare programme based on charity, but basic rural education should not rely on the Hope project alone. The government should increase financial support to basic education. According to the authors' analysis, CNY78 billion will be needed to reconstruct classrooms and school houses which are in a dangerous condition. Moreover, taking into consideration the problem that many students cannot afford tuition and school fees, CNY1 trillion will be needed. The highest funding the Hope project has collected in a year was just over CNY100 million, and a substantial part of the funding raised provided allowances for students: this is "using a glass of water to put out a fire on a cart". The figures obviously tell us that the Hope project cannot finance basic education for all, not to mention the wage shortages for teachers. Accordingly, while encouraging charity through this project, the government should take the responsibility of financing basic education. In this regard, objectives should be established, and implemented concretely by government at all levels.

On the other hand, the problem of the dropout of the children of farm workers is very serious. Since the late 1990s, the number of children of those farmers who move and work has increased sharply. Some children were born in their parents' hometown and then taken to cities by their parents, while some were born in cities and continued to live there. According to a study by a workgroup on the issue of education for children of migrant workers, migrants' children are marginalised, due to the fact that they are excluded from both urban and rural education systems, and many families have to solve the problem by resorting to private education which, being outside the orthodox educational system, has many defects. Three objective factors are responsible for this problem. First, more and more household migration occurs and many school-age children come to cities with their parents. Second, the existence of the urban household registration system does not leave room for the education of children of migrant workers, and these children do not enjoy the same right to receive education as children with registered permanent residence in cities. Third, the poor economic conditions of the migrant workers means that they cannot pay the additional costs imposed by the urban public schools. The problem of child migration demands not only adjustment of the compulsory education system, but also system innovation in many aspects. More flexible and practical management practices are needed to widen access for migrant children. This requires: *1)* to make public schools the dominant way of absorbing migrant children, *2)* to regulate those schools which are set up specifically for migrant children, and *3)* the help of social groups and scholars to play an active and beneficial role to promote the education of migrant children.

In poor areas, the length of schooling has a tendency to increase with the increase in household incomes, but no such relation seems to exist in rural areas with a good economic situation. The reason may be that in the poor areas, educational opportunities for farmers with different economic backgrounds differ and lead to differences in their working ability. In well-developed rural areas, many farmers can afford the necessary education and thus are educated to similar levels. Their income level is then not determined mainly by their education, and there is no significant correlation between income and education. In poor rural areas, there is coexistence of material poverty and spiritual poverty. Due to reasons such as adverse natural conditions, out-dated education, culture, thinking and concepts, the impoverished population in China is still in a state of lack of education. Most of the poor have received very little education, and have scarce knowledge of science and technology, which can contribute to increasing their poverty. As an important investment in human resources, technological training has not yet received enough attention. Poverty means not only low income and low consumption. Amartya Sen viewed real poverty as the deprivation of basic abilities (income is a means for the realisation of basic abilities), including health, educational opportunity, social justice and others. In poor areas, the education system is underdeveloped, medical care conditions are poor, and human resources are low. In the meantime, the transformation and updating of the ways of thinking of the cadres and the masses lags seriously behind, due to inadequate transportation and information dissemination systems.

Fighting poverty in urban and rural areas, and the income-earning ability of the poor

The fight against poverty can be classified into two categories. The first approach is to fight poverty actively, *i.e.* to create the sorts of conditions necessary to help the poor to enhance their ability to earn incomes and thus to shake off poverty as soon as possible. The second approach is to fight poverty passively, *i.e.* to provide the conditions and environment for the poor to subsist. These two sorts of efforts should be combined, without any preference for one or the other, as the second approach is the basis for keeping a society stable, and the former is of utmost importance.

Fighting poverty in cities

First of all, economic development oriented to job creation should be rigorously promoted. For a rather long period of time in the future, the labour market in China will have excessive labour supply, and the unemployment problem may worsen. Thus, planning for economic development should consider this situation, rather than placing emphasis on development of "modern industries" or "high-tech and new sectors", or a unique model of enterprises. Economic development should be oriented towards creating employment, promoting the growth of small and middle-sized enterprises, leaving room for traditional industries to develop, and creating an environment to accommodate informal employment. Appropriate policy supports are needed to facilitate employment of low-skilled labour, particularly the unemployed poor, so as to increase their earnings.

Second, attention should be paid to innovative anti-poverty policies in cities. Social policies are always related to their social circumstances, and can only be effective if they change in accordance with changes in social circumstances. Since the reform and opening-up, the social, economic and institutional bases of China have changed significantly. The traditional economic planning system and the work unit (*danwei*) system are slowly breaking down; the socialist market economic system and its related social system are gradually taking shape. With these fundamental social changes, social policies, including anti-poverty policies, should be actively renovated. To stick to the old system and to make small amendments now and then may not work.

Third, vigorous efforts should be made to improve the social security system. Because the social security system is now in a process of reform and transformation, people face many social risks outside their control, and may be trapped in poverty as unforeseen incidents happen. Therefore, in order to provide basic security for people's life and to prevent the occurrence of poverty, it is necessary to accomplish the reform and transformation of the social security system as early as possible. The MLG system for urban residents should be further implemented and improved. At present, the system is the core anti-poverty programme in urban areas, contributing significantly to the fight against poverty in cities. Further steps are to secure the supply of funding, to make organisational innovations, to regulate the dynamic adjustment of allowance recipients, and to enlarge the coverage of the allowance so that the different demands of various households can be met.

Fourth, the social participation and input of the poor should be promoted. The poor should be encouraged through different formal channels to express their interests and concerns. Poverty fighting is not a unilateral action of the government, but should involve the co-ordinated co-operation of the government, the poor and society. The poor are not merely passive recipients of allowances and assistance, but also an active part of the fight again poverty. Experience shows that emphasis on the input of the poor should lead to a better result in the fight against poverty. Attention should be paid to foster the social capital of the poor, such as to encourage self-organisation, to help them to set up a mutual support network and to enhance their own ability to shake off poverty. Efforts should be made to encourage mutual assistance between family members and neighbours, to continuously promote community building and social work, to encourage non-governmental organisations to fight urban poverty, and to enlarge the social networks of the poor.

Fighting poverty in rural areas

To fight poverty through development is the key to fighting poverty in rural areas:

First, support should continue for the development of agricultural and breeding industries, to actively promote the industrialised operation of agriculture. Efforts should be concentrated on helping the population in poverty to develop planting and breeding programmes with market potential. To focus on increasing incomes of poor farmers, efforts should be made to improve quality and efficiency through technical progress, specialisation and variety optimisation. To improve the environment, protection and building up of the ecological system should be enhanced so as to achieve sustainable development. Based on market trends, suitable products and projects should be selected and related services of information, technology and marketing should be effectively implemented, to ensure growth in production. As needed in the process and requirements of industrialisation, the production of agricultural products with resource advantages and market demand should be planned and established, to form regionalised leading industries. The format of "company plus farmers" should be actively developed. Middle and large-sized agricultural product processing enterprises with good market orientation capacities should be encouraged to set up their supply bases in poor areas, providing services to farmers before, during, and after the whole production process, in order to form an industrialised management system combining commerce, industry and agriculture.

Second, government funding and loans for fighting poverty should be increased, to improve basic living and production conditions in poor areas. The government should further enlarge the scale of "subsidy through work", increase transfer payments according to the actual financial situation of poor areas, and implement special accounting management for the allocation of funding for financial poverty. Anti-poverty loans should be increased, to support agricultural and breeding industries, labour-intensive enterprises, agricultural product processing enterprises, and distribution companies with the capability to increase the incomes of poor people. Loans should also be increased to support infrastructure construction. Loans of small amounts to individual farmers should be increased to support poor farmers to further develop production. Basic land for plantation, infrastructure facilities, environmental transformation projects, and public service facilities should be established, based in poor villages and towns. By 2010, in the national key poor areas, water supply problems for people and animals should be solved, most villages should have access to electricity, transportation and roads, postal services, telephones, and radio and television signals; most poor towns should have a hospital and most poor villages should have a healthcare office, so that those regional diseases affecting production and life can be controlled.

Third, the technological and cultural knowledge of the population in poor areas should be improved. This would include combining agriculture, science and education, managing general education, vocational education and adult education systems collectively, and improving farmers' grasp of advanced and practical techniques through various vocational technical schools and short periods of training. The implementation of nine years of compulsory education in poor areas should be ensured, to further improve the admission rate for school-age children, and transform customs, and encourage scientific and civilized life styles.

Fourth, it is necessary to motivate the whole society to help the poor areas to develop. The Chinese government will foster good policy and investment environments to attract businesses to organise and participate in the economic development of poor areas. The government will provide necessary support to enterprises, including agricultural product processing enterprises, and improve the industrial structure, to bring benefits to farmers, and promote labour-intensive enterprises with the ability to increase employment of redundant labour in poor areas, enterprises that can promote the distribution of agricultural products produced by poor farmers. Besides using governmental resources to fight poverty, the country will further motivate social groups to participate so as to increase the resources to fight against poverty. In accordance with the anti-poverty programme, the coastal areas will be organised to support poverty fighting in the western region, and the scale of co-operation will be enlarged. Exchange and co-operation will be encouraged in all forms at all levels, especially the co-operation of enterprises. Opportunities should be given to various social groups in the fight against poverty, to actively create conditions to induce non-governmental organisations to participate in or carry out governmental anti-poverty projects.

Fifth, ordered anti-poverty policies promoted through development of the "responsibility system" for anti-poverty policy should be implemented – sticking to the principle that provincial governments take full responsibility, county governments carry out policies, work needs to reach villages, and the fight needs to reach individual households. The building of cadre teams and democratic organisation at the grass root level should be enhanced; the ability of the cadres and organisations to lead the masses to shake off poverty should be continuously improved. Supervision of anti-poverty funding and statistical work should be enhanced, and a system built up and sustained. Organisations fighting against poverty through development should be stabilised, and their abilities to lead, organise, co-ordinate, and manage the fight strengthened. With the deepening of the fight, China's combat against poverty through development will be further systematised and regulated, and finally co-ordinated according to laws and regulations. Following continuous social development and economic growth, the development of the fight against poverty will need further study of the extension of programmes to secure the subsistence of rural residents.

Strategic restructuring

To implement anti-poverty measures and policies to increase incomes, China should think of the problem of poverty as a whole, rather than considering rural and urban poverty separately.

First, poverty fighting should be one of government's long-term strategic tasks. It should be included in the state and regions' medium and long-term economic and social development programmes, with a special focus on the medium term. Balanced social and economic development strategies should be formulated, to turn the imbalanced growth between the coastal areas and the western region into co-ordinated development, in order to reduce the regional development gap and alleviate the national poverty problem in the next twenty years. Apart from the strategies and policies already applied to western region development, there are also other important measures to adopt. The first is to concretely carry out state investments to promote infrastructure construction in the central and western regions. Second, according to the comparative advantages of the eastern and western regions, it is important to implement regional specialisation policy, for instance, in developing specialised industries, agriculture and tourism in the western region. Co-ordinated regional development should be promoted, based on the motivation and market potential brought about by the continuous development of the eastern region. Third, poverty fighting should be further enhanced and its achievements consolidated. Poverty fighting measures should be further advanced in those areas which have shaken off the title of "poor county" in recent years. The transition from simple capital injection to investment in education, technology and culture should be confirmed as a necessary measure to consolidate anti-poverty results.

Second, it is important to enhance government intervention in income distribution, and adjust and regulate income distribution policies. One of the most important reasons for the formation of the present poverty problems in China is the disorder of income distribution and existence of unfairness. Therefore, under market mechanisms, importance should be attached to the usefulness of the government's intervention in regulating income distribution. The following policies may be adopted: First, in accordance with common practice in western countries, improve income distribution through the taxation system as soon as possible, for instance, by starting to tax inheritance and endowments, increase tax on personal incomes, interest, and certain consumption taxes. Meanwhile, combat tax cheating to prevent a part of society getting rich illegally. To convert a part of the incomes of these rich individuals into financial resources to alleviate poverty by the above-mentioned measures is an important and obvious embodiment of the government's function and responsibility. Second, in regard the role of the government in the field of wages and salary, set up authorised and categorised wage and salary standards, adjust the unfair income distribution in certain industries, properly restrict wage differences among industries, and strictly define and implement minimum wage standards and vigorously protect the incomes of the unemployed and low-income groups. Third, the government should increase its investments in agriculture to reduce the income disparity between the rural and the urban areas, and to reduce farmers' burdens substantially. The government should promote the development of efficient agriculture and agricultural product-processing through economic and technological means, so as to increase farmers' income. The reduction in income disparities between urban and rural areas will not only stabilise the income of the rural population, but will also absorb redundant rural labour, and alleviate the pressure on urban unemployment and poverty.

Third, the vocational education system should be vigorously developed. China should make innovations in seven aspects of the vocational education system. First, the vocational education system should be oriented to market demand rather than administrative orders. Supply and demand in the labour market should be the most important signal to adjust the activities of vocational and technical training agents. Second, it is necessary transfer the direct management of vocational training by the government to indirect management. The government should not supervise vocational training agents directly. Legal and economic measures should replace administrative measures as the macro-adjustment mechanism of the government. Third, implement the principle of "benefit those who invested" and dismantle the old system with monopoly by the government, so as to solve the funding shortage problem in vocational education. Fourth, introduce competition and motivation mechanisms. Let training agents compete in the market, judge their work according to social standards and social selection, and put forward a group of famous schools and certificates with concrete values. Fifth, implement a national certificate system to attach equal importance to diplomas and vocational qualifyication certificates. Sixth, transfer the present vocational training system only serving city residents and public-owned enterprises into a comprehensive vocational education system covering both urban and rural areas, and enterprises with various forms of ownership. Seventh, enhance training of farm workers, especially young farm workers.

Fourth, the social security system needs to be improved as soon as possible. Currently, a suitable policy orientation has been established to enable the social insurance system to cover all workers in urban areas, and the minimum living guarantee has also been established. It is necessary to promote the development of rural medical and healthcare, and build up an effective national living security network. Special consideration should be given to the migrant population when different localities develop anti-poverty programmes and assistance policies for local residents. With due respect to population migration in a market economy and the trend of China's migrant population, a subsistence security system for migrants should be developed, and the system should differ from the subsistence security systems for the urban and rural residents. Such a triple assistance system is necessary and proper given current circumstances. At the same time, the government should put emphasis on assistance to the social groups with the most vulnerable status, including the aged, women and children. In addition to setting up a minimum old-age pension standard, it is important to guarantee timely and full payment of pensions, improve maternity insurance, protect the employment rights of women, and provide appropriate subsidy systems for the aged, women and children, in order to alleviate the poverty problem in China.

Fifth, to improve other related measures, it is necessary to call for and set up concepts of enterprise and work effort, further implement the family planning policy to help the poor achieve lower birth rates, reform the traditional household registration system, and allow part of the poor population to shake off poverty through migration, promote the development of charity and all sorts of non-government mutual assistance, and provide help to impoverished groups through socialised, non-institutional arrangements.

BIBLIOGRAPHY

Bake, U. *et al.* (2000), *Globalization and Politics* (Chinese edition), Central Transition Press.

Deacon, B., M. Hulse and P. Stubbs (1997), *Global Social Policy: International Organizations and the Future of Welfare*, SAGE Publications.

Devine, J.A. and J. Wright (1993), *The Greatest of Evils: Urban Poverty and the American Underclass*, Aldine de Gruyter, New York.

Dixon, J. (1981), *The Chinese Welfare System: 1949-1979*, Praegar Publishers.

Foster, J. (1999), "Neo-liberalism and comments", *Foreign Theoretical Trends*, Vol. 12.

Geremek, B. (1994), *Poverty: A History*, translated by A. Kolakowska, Blackwell.

Guan Xinping (2001), "Globalization, Inequality and Social Policy: Social Protection in China on the Threshold of the WTO", *Social Policy & Administration*, Vol. 35, No. 3, Blackwell.

Jiang Zemin (1997), "Motivate the Whole Party and the Whole Society to Seize The Victory in Implementation of 'The Seven-Year Programme to Help 80 Millions Out of Poverty'", *Yangtze Daily,* 21 July 1997.

Kang Xiaoguang (1995), *Poverty and Poverty Fighting Theory in China*, Nanning, Guangxi People's Press.

Kroger, A. (1995), *Trade and Employment in Developing Countries* (Chinese edition), Shanghai People's Press.

Li Shi (1998), "Economic Transition and Changes of Income Distribution in China", *Economic Research*, Vol. 4.

Li Peilin (1995), *Report on Social Classes and Layers in Today's China*, Liaoning People's Press.

Li Qiang (1993), *Social Stratification and Circulation in Modern China*, China Economic Press.

State Council, Leading Group Office for Poverty Reduction (various years), *Statistical Data of National Key Impoverished Counties,* State Council, Beijing.

Study Group of the Ministry of Labor (1994), *Establishment and Improvement of Social Security System in China,* China Economic Press.

Xu Dianqing, *et al.* (1999), *Reform of China's Social Security System*, Economic Science Press.

Zheng Gongcheng (1997), *About Social Security System with Chinese Characteristics,* University of Wuhan Press, Wuhan.

Zhong Ming and Wang Yi (1999), *Polarization Gap, the Rich and the Poor in Today's China*, China Economic Press.

Zhou Binbin (1991), *Fight Against Poverty, Theories and Practices of Poverty Alleviation in Foreign Countries*, People's Press, Beijing.

Zhou Tianyong (1994), *Labor and Economic Growth*, Shanghai People's Press.

Zhu Ling (1992), "Poverty Fighting Theory in China and Review of Policy Studies", *Management World*, Vol. 4, Beijing.

Zou Zhizhuang (1984), *China's Economy*, Press of Nankai University.

Table 4.1. **Standard of subsistence security of the municipalities directly under the central government and the capitals of provinces and ethnic autonomous areas, September 1999**

CNY

Beijing	273	Shanghai	280	Wuhan	195	Kunming	182
Tianjin	241	Nanjing	180	Changsha	169	Lasa	169
Shijiazhuang	182	Hangzhou	215	Guangzhou	281	Xi'an	156
Taiyuan	155	Hefei	195	Nanning	195	Lanzhou	156
Huhehaote	143	Fuzhou	200	Haikou	221	Xining	156
Shenyang	195	Nanchang	143	Chengdu	156	Yinchuan	143
Changchun	169	Jinan	208	Chongqing	169	Urumchi	156
Harbin	182	Zhengzhou	169	Guiyang	156		

Source: Department of Calamity Relief and Social Assistance, Ministry of Civil Affairs.

Table 4.2. **Number of minimum living guarantee (MLG) recipients, June 2001 and June 2002**

Locality	Number of recipients June 2001	Number of recipients June 2002	Increase	Growth rate (%)
Beijing	76 757	88 454	11 697	15.2
Tianjin	32 072	256 326	224 254	699.2
Hebei	110 082	670 172	560 090	508.8
Shanxi	33 512	584 486	550 974	1 644.1
Inner Mongolia	118 985	620 769	501 784	421.7
Liaoning	732 605	129 700	564 395	77.0
Jilin	85 139	1 493 938	1 408 799	1 654.7
Heilongjiang	178 155	1 530 973	1 352 818	759.3
Shanghai	276 411	360 300	83 889	30.3
Jiangsu	90 794	223 734	132 940	146.4
Zhejiang	26 603	42 500	15 897	59.8
Anhui	133 556	904 127	770 571	577.0
Fujian	41 677	153 000	111 323	267.1
Jiangxi	120 358	1 079 876	959 518	797.2
Shandong	189 336	631 231	441 895	233.4
Henan	72 235	1 116 173	1 043 938	1 445.2
Hubei	417 721	1 220 906	803 185	192.3
Hunan	312 082	1 507 931	1 1958 49	383.2
Guangdong	153 050	230 836	77 786	50.8
Guangxi	83 589	448 306	364 717	436.3
Hainan	19 540	79 134	59 594	305.0
Chongqing	239 327	647 902	408 575	170.7
Sichuan	245 247	1 258 737	1 013 490	413.3
Guizhou	48 088	361 964	313 876	652.7
Yunnan	133 347	550 027	416 680	312.5
Tibet	5 354	37 612	32 258	602.5
Shaanxi	170 570	591 324	420 754	246.7
Gansu	127 709	466 823	339 114	265.5
Qinghai	53 500	167 866	114 366	213.8
Ningxia	86 432	131 820	45 388	52.5
Xinjiang	160 906	454 000	293 094	182.2
Xingjiang construction corps	-	99 628	99 628	-
National total	**4 574 739**	**19 307 875**	**14 733 136**	**322.1**

Source: China Statistical Yearbooks, National Bureau of Statistics, China

Table 4.3. **Poverty rates in different provinces**

Ratio of impoverished population				
0-2%	***2-4%***	***4-6%***	***6-8%***	*>8%*
Beijing Jiangsu Zhejiang Guangdong	Shanghai Fujian Hunan Guangxi Yunnan Anhui Jiangxi	Hebei Hubei Guizhou Chongqing Qinghai Shandong Sichuan	Tianjin Inner Mongolia Liaoning Jilin Hainan Xinjiang Shanxi Heilongjiang Gansu	Henan Shaanxi Ningxia Tibet

Source: *Study on Urban Poverty in China*, provided by experts of the Asia Development Bank.

Table 4.4. **Preliminary report on undertakings of Civil Affairs, 2002**

	Unit	**Number**
Disaster relief and assistance		
Urban MLG beneficiaries[1]	10 000 persons	2 053.6
Number of urban households receiving MLG	10 000 households	809
Rural MLG beneficiaries[2]	10 000 persons	404.7
Rural residents receiving traditional assistances[3]	10 000 persons	1 158.2
Expenditure of Civil Affairs		
Total expenditure on civil affairs	Billion CNY	35.45
Expenditure on urban MLG	Billion CNY	11.26
Average per capita monthly expenditure on urban MLG	CNY/person/month	54

1. Number of urban residents receiving MLG refers to the number of urban residents receiving MLG in those areas with the MLG system, including the "three-without" individuals, unemployed individuals, laid-off workers, retired personnel, and others.

2. Number of rural MLG recipients refers to the number of rural households receiving a subsistence allowance from local governments or collectives in those areas with the MLG system established by the time of reporting.

3. Number of rural residents receiving traditional assistance refers to the number of households receiving this assistance in rural areas without the MLG system, such as those households that cannot secure basic living and work in simple production activities, due to loss of main labour force or lack of work ability, natural calamities, or other incidents (including herdsmen, fishermen and salt-producers).

Source: Department of Finance and Logistics, Ministry of Civil Affairs, until 31 December 2002.

Table 4.5. **Categorisation of urban MLG recipients, October 2002**

Types of allowance recipients	10 000 persons	Share (%)
Workers in service	190.8	9.7
Laid-off workers	240.7	12.3
Workers not in service	401.9	20.5
Retired personnel	86.8	4.4
Unemployed	332.1	16.9
"Three withouts"	85.4	4.3
Others	625.8	31.9
Total	**1 963.5**	**100.0**

Source: Statistical Report of the Department of Calamity Relief and Assistance, Ministry of Civil Affairs, 15 October 2002.

Table 4.6. **Urban registered unemployment rate**

	1996	1997	1998	1999	2000	2001	2002
Registered urban unemployment rate	3.0	3.1	3.1	3.1	3.1	3.6	4.0

Source: China Statistical Yearbooks, National Bureau of Statistics, China

Chart 4.1. **Increase in allowance recipients, 1998-2002**

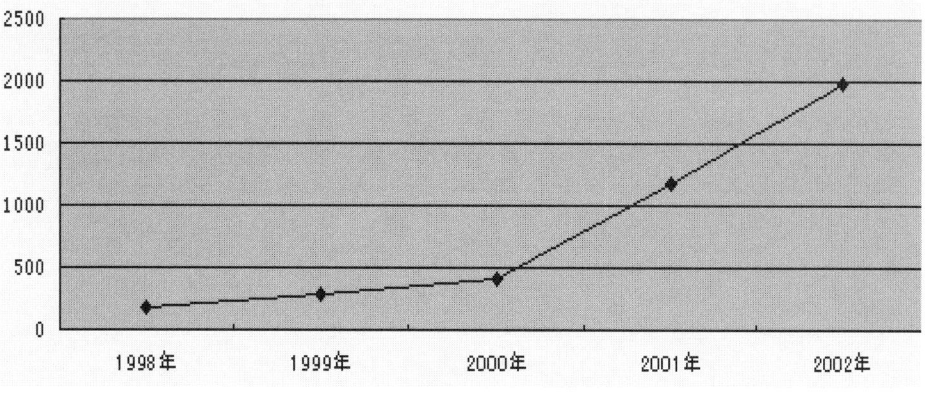

Source: China Statistical Yearbooks, National Bureau of Statistics, China

Chapter 5

ANALYSIS OF INCOME DISTRIBUTION IN CHINA'S POVERTY-STRICKEN COUNTIES: A CASE STUDY OF QINGLONG COUNTY OF HEBEI PROVINCE

by
Zhao Kun,

Programme Officer, Department of National Economy,
National Development and Reform Commission, China

Introduction

The absolute poverty line in China's rural region in 2002 was CNY625 per capita annual income, which is USD76 (with the exchange rate of CNY8.28 to the dollar). According to this standard, the population in absolute poverty in rural regions in China numbered 28.2 million, about 3% of the total population. About 54% of the population in absolute poverty is concentrated in the 592 key poverty-stricken counties, or state impoverished counties: there are 2 860 counties in China. All these 592 counties, located in 21 provinces of the central and western regions (31 provinces in total), are ethnic minority areas, old revolutionary base areas, border areas or destitute areas. Qinglong county of Hubei province is one of these impoverished counties. In this chapter, Qinglong county is taken as an example to analyse the problems of income distribution in China's poor counties.

Qinglong Manchu autonomous county is located about 300 km to the northeast of Beijing. Mountains cover most of the county's area, as the saying goes "eighty per cent hill, ten per cent water and ten per cent farmland". The population of the county amounts to 504 000 and 93% of them are farmers. In 2002, the per capita GDP of the county was USD393, equal to 40.6% of the national average. The shares of primary, secondary and tertiary industries were 28.2%, 36% and 35.8%, respectively. The share of primary industry is 13.7 points higher than the national average, while that of secondary industry is 15.8 points lower. The economic development level and structure determine the low income of Qinglong county residents and the large income disparity between urban and rural households. To analyse the income distribution of Qinglong county will help to learn about the typical problems of rural households, and the income disparities between urban and rural residents in the poor counties.

Overall income distribution

Low income levels. In 2002, the per capita income of urban residents was USD558 (CNY4 620), equivalent to 60% of the national average; the per capita income of rural residents was USD130 (CNY1 075), equivalent to 43.4% of the national average. As can be seen, it is the rural income that has the greater disparity between the county and the national average. The low-income level of rural residents is not only an important problem in the nation, but also the most prominent problem in poor counties.

Uneven growth rate of the income of rural residents. From 1997 to 2002, the per capita net income of rural residents fluctuated around USD121 (CNY1 000). In 2002, the amount was USD129 (CNY1 075.1). From 1998 to 2002, the growth rate of per capita net income for rural residents was 11%, -4%, -12.8%, 13.8%, and 11.7% respectively, which shows a wide fluctuation range. This is mainly due to the influence of such external factors as natural calamities and climate. On the other hand, the growth rate of per capita disposable income of urban residents was relatively steady. From 1998 to 2002, the growth rate of per capita disposable income of urban residents was 6.8%, 8.7%, 6.5%, 6.1%, and 9.6%, respectively.

Single income source. Analysing income sources, it can be seen that family business income is the principal part of the rural income. From 1998 to 2002, the ratio of family business income to the gross income of rural residents of the county was 55.6%, 47.8%, 62.1%, 57.6% and 62.3%, respectively. The ratio of wage income declined, being 40.2%, 46.6%, 33.0%, 35.9% and 35%, respectively, from 1998 to 2002. In 2002, the per capita net income of rural residents of the county grew at the rate of 11.7%. The growth rate of wage income was 5.7%, while that of family business income was 17%. The condition of the whole nation is distinctively different. In 2002, the real per capita net income of rural residents grew at the rate of 4.8%, of which income from wages grew by 11.6%, and that from agricultural business income only grew by 0.8%. In 2002, the per capita net income of rural residents of the whole nation was USD299 (CNY2 476), of which family agricultural business income was USD137 (CNY1 135), accounting for 46% of the total, which is 12 percentage points lower than that in Qinglong county. The difference shows that in China, relying only or excessively on agriculture, will not make rural residents well off.

The main part of the income of urban residents of Qinglong county is the wages of employees of state-owned and collective units (*i.e.* public-owned units), and the share of wages is rising. From 1998 to 2001, the share of wages in the real income of urban residents was 74.8%, 72.6%, 74.7% and 75.7%, respectively. In contrast, the share for China as a whole was 55%, in Shanghai 42% and in Zhejiang 48%. Among the county's urban residents, the share of income from the employees of publicly-owned units is 20 percentage points higher than the national average, and much higher than that of advanced areas such as Shanghai.

Widening income disparities among residents. In the first place, in the county, the income gap between urban and rural residents is widening. From 1998 to 2002, the ratio of the income of urban residents to that of rural residents increased from 3.4 to 4.3. On the other hand, income disparities between rural residents in different villages are also growing. In 2002, among the 396 administrative villages, the highest village per capita annual income was USD465 (CNY3 850), which is three times the average, while the lowest was USD24 (CNY200), less than one-fifth of the average. Second, compared with the situation for China as a whole, the incomes of Qinglong county's urban and rural residents are much lower, and the degree of impoverishment of the poor rural residents is greater. In addition, the income gap between urban and rural residents is larger than the national average. In 2002, for China as a whole, the per capita disposable income of urban residents was 3.1 times the per capita disposable income of rural residents. This disparity is already significant, but the income disparity between the Qinglong county's urban and rural residents is obviously even greater.

Reasons for low income levels and wider disparities

Single form of employment. In Qinglong county, 73% of the employed in the rural areas work on crop plantations *i.e.* the main income source is from crop planting. For the nation as a whole, farmers seeking jobs in cities and non-agricultural business focus on secondary and tertiary industries, which are becoming the main income sources of rural residents. Yet, in Qinglong county, these have not developed sufficiently. In 2002, the migrating labour force accounts for 5.8% of the total population, while for China as a whole, the ratio is 16%. The employees of township enterprises correspond to 10% of the total rural employed.

Single economic structure. Farming and animal husbandry income provide the major share of family business income. In 2001, farming and animal husbandry income provided 73% of the county's family business income for Qinglong county's rural households, with planting income at 99% of total farming income. The main farming crops are corn, tubers and beans. Plantation of mulberry and fruit cultivation, which is more economically beneficial, is limited, and contributes little to the growth of the economy and rural income. Animal husbandry focuses on raising livestock, just to produce meat, while the meat-processing industry is very weak. Most state-owned and collectively-owned enterprises depend on local resources, such as iron ore and marble, in order to develop mining. With this pattern of development, the county has to face significant problems, including high energy consumption, heavy pollution and resource exhaustion.

Downward trend in agricultural product prices. In recent years, continuous drought has caused a reduction in grain output in Qinglong county; at the same time, the price level for agricultural products in the market is declining. In 2000, the local retail price index was 97.1; the price index of grain was 83.1. In 2002, the local consumer price index was 100.9, the price index of grain was 93, of starches and tubers 96.3, and of bean and its products 92.9. The main reason for the price decline is the temporary oversupply of agricultural products in China.

Simple ownership structure. In 2002, for China as a whole, among the total gross industry output value of enterprises with an annual sales income over CNY5 million, the share of state-owned industry was 41.7%, while in Qinglong county the output of state-owned industry was 88% of the local industry output. This is one of the important reasons for the low level of the income of the county's urban residents. In the past 20 years, the faster the non-public owned economy developed, the faster the income of employees grew. The income of residents tends to grow more slowly, if the local non-public enterprise economy develops slowly.

Different income sources system of urban and rural residents. As can be seen from the comparison with China as a whole, the disparity between the incomes of urban and rural residents in Qinglong county is not due to the high income of urban residents, but mainly to the excessively low income of rural residents. The relatively steady income growth rate of urban residents in the county is due to the rapid growth of China's economy, which is mainly driven by development of secondary and tertiary industries. Increasing transfer payments are another reason. Therefore, although the growth rate fluctuates, the incomes of urban residents have kept to the general upward trend. Rural residents face different conditions, where income depends heavily on farming. The fall in agricultural product market prices and the adverse agricultural environment directly affect the growth of rural residents' income. As the incomes of the urban and rural residents of the county follow different growth paths, income disparities have widened. For example, in 2000, when Qinglong county endured a serious drought, the growth rate of county GDP declined by 6.8%, the net income of rural residents declined by 13%, while the disposable income of urban residents remained at a growth rate of 6.5%.

Conclusions and propositions

The economy is the foundation of income, and income growth in poverty-stricken areas relies primarily on economic development. The key to alleviating the disparity between urban and rural income is to improve the incomes of rural residents on the basis of the development of the rural economy. In order to develop the economy and enhance income growth, impoverished counties should rely not only on aid from the state, but also on their own efforts, and various measures should be taken, as follows:

Strengthen development-oriented poverty reduction work in impoverished counties. All levels of government, especially central and provincial governments, should give more support to strengthen infrastructure construction such as water, electricity, roads and communication facilities, in order to improve the conditions of production and the life of the people. Inputs should be increased to the training of farmers, so as to improve their skills. Importance should be also attached to science and technology, to make agriculture flourish, and improve the quality of farming and side-line production.

Adjust the structure of agricultural production. Township and village enterprises in non-agricultural industries and services should be encouraged; the production structure of rural areas should be optimised. Based on local resource conditions, an intensive process of agricultural product operation should be developed to improve the efficiency of the rural economy. Private enterprise should be encouraged, and the ownership structure should be reformed.

Protect farmers' rights and interests, especially land use rights. A reasonable lowest protective purchasing price of agricultural products should be set and implemented.

Push forward the urbanisation process. Farmers should be encouraged to work in cities and towns, relevant employment information should be provided, and various measures should be taken to increase the incomes of rural residents.

Chapter 6

INCOME DISPARITIES IN POST-REFORM CHINA: A REVIEW OF THE INTERNATIONAL LITERATURE

by
Marie-Ange Maurice,

Consultant

and

Peter Whiteford,

Principal Administrator,
Directorate for Employment, Labour and Social Affairs, OECD

Introduction[1]

China has experienced spectacular economic growth since 1978, averaging 8 to 9% per year. As a result, in general, the standard of living is far higher than ever before in China's history. However, economic disparities have also widened significantly at different times during this period, raising questions about the appropriateness and sustainability of some existing policies. The recent entry of China into the World Trade Organization (WTO) is likely to increase some social and economic pressures. Commitments taken will require sacrifices both in the short and medium term, with some groups in the population likely to be adversely affected, at least in the short run.

The purpose of this paper is to review the international literature on the evolution of economic disparities in China since 1978, and to identify the main factors causing these disparities. The first section reviews the main issues in the assessment of income inequalities with respect to data and measurement. The second describes trends in the distribution of income, and considers various levels of inequality: overall, regional and provincial, and urban and rural disparities. This is followed by a brief discussion of how China appears to compare with other countries. The third discusses trends in and levels of poverty, and assesses influences on poverty. In the fourth section, the main driving factors behind these inequality trends are discussed, while the final section discusses policy approaches to deal with these disparities.

---

1. We are particularly grateful to Michael Förster, Administrator, Directorate for Employment, Labour and Social Affairs (DELSA), OECD, for his help in reviewing the literature on which this paper is based, and for helpful comments from Anders Reutersward and Georges Lemaître, Principal Administrators, DELSA, OECD.

Before turning to detailed results, some caveats should be emphasised. Studies of inequality in China must deal with a nation with the world's largest population, spread over a very large area. China's huge population is spread across 31 provinces and prefectural level cities, with populations ranging in size from less than 3 million (Tibet) to roughly 113 million (Sichuan, including Chongqing). Studies of China also distinguish between three official territorial divisions – the eastern coastal provinces, the centre and the west. The urban/rural dimensions of inequality and poverty are particularly important, cutting across regional disparities and in some cases reinforcing them. It is also important to note that in China some municipalities are classified as rural which in other countries would be counted as large cities. In addition, China has a very significant "floating" population of migrant workers, variously estimated at between 50 and 200 million people, who may not be classified as resident in the area in which they are currently working and living, who send significant remittances to their "home" areas, and are generally difficult to capture in surveys and official statistics. A further factor is that the majority of the Chinese population live in rural areas, where a significant proportion of their resources is provided through home and self-production, rather than through market transactions. This complicates comparisons with the urban population, and also with other countries.

Statistical and measurement issues

There are many limitations to the data available, which should be borne in mind when assessing results. For example, the most comprehensive sources reviewed cover nearly all dimensions of income inequality and poverty in China, but look at only two years, and the period they review stops in 1995 (World Bank, 1997; Khan and Riskin, 2001). In more recent work, few studies are as comprehensive. A recurrent issue in the literature relates to the quality of data. Many researchers conduct their own surveys or undertake these jointly with Chinese authorities, because of inaccessibility of raw data or an over-high level of aggregation. These surveys often show different results from published official data, including higher levels of inequality.

Available research uses a number of different measures of income, further complicating analysis and comparison of results. These measures include the personal distribution of income by households, the distribution of gross domestic product across various regions, as well as disparities in average household incomes across regions or between urban and rural areas. Most of these studies have used household per capita income (PCI) or per capita GDP (PCGDP) to measure the level of inequality, based either on census data or on the annual separate households surveys (HHS) of rural and urban incomes. Some research is based on independent surveys, usually carried out with Chinese partner institutions. Studies also differ in their geographic focus. In addition, studies assessing inequality and poverty do not normally use equivalence scales to adjust household income to reflect variations in household size, as is common practice in OECD studies. However, it is common in studies of China to measure income on a per capita basis (*i.e.* dividing by the number of people in the household). This may reduce measured levels of inequality and poverty compared to an equivalent basis, but there appear to be no generally accepted equivalence scales for China, and in any case this approach may be less relevant in rural households where children contribute to production and well-being. Expenditure data are less often used because of data inconsistencies, and the impact of savings has been little studied. The literature on the impact of government tax and transfer, and redistribution policies, is even more limited.

China's official household income distribution is measured by the National Bureau of Statistics (NBS). The China Statistical Yearbook publishes data on income based on the separate annual rural and urban household surveys and are distinct from the census data (1982, 1990, 1995, 2000), conducted every five years. The HHS are panel surveys, which also collect information on expenditures. A number of problems have been identified in relation to official data on income distribution. Changes in statistical methodology pose some difficulties in interpreting trends over time.

Another issue is the number of regions included in the panel and the weight they are given in the survey over time. In addition, as households are required to record their expenses on a daily basis, it is clear that illiterate people – as well as ethnic minority populations in remote areas – are excluded from the survey. As poverty and illiteracy are strongly correlated, the panel may not completely reflect the income of poor households. The surveys are conducted in ways which may complicate international comparisons; for example, income data are collected for all 12 months, whereas in OECD countries they are usually based on either a week or a month, or by recall of annual income in the previous year. Analysis suggests that inequality would be higher if the OECD approach were used (although the Chinese approach may actually provide more accurate results) (Gibson *et al.,* 2002; Park and Wang, 2002).

The urban household survey covers more than 40 000 households in six administrative regions and is divided into 226 cities and towns of different sizes. Household sources of income are identified as either wages, bonuses, allowances or housing subsidies (in-kind). The survey presents data on household disposable income per capita, which includes: cash income, taxes, household production expenditures, other individual production activities, transfers (including pensions) and property income. The scope of the survey has changed many times since 1978. Apart from collecting demographic information, the survey questions households on 25 types of income. There are 150 categories of food items and 150 individual items of spending. It has been suggested that the scope of the survey is so wide that presumably some items are put in the wrong category or are not well identified (Park and Wang, 2001). The rural household survey covers 68 000 households in 7 100 villages across China. Incomes are decomposed into wages, household business income (including farming and other sources), property income (interest on savings and deposits, rents) and transfers. The household registration system (*hukou*), which limits rural and urban population mobility (and also distinguishes households engaged either in agricultural or non-agricultural activities) complicates inequality assessments. A rural move to an urban area, or *vice versa,* is considered as internal migration and if not registered, as illegal. Thus, the large-scale rural migration to cities since the mid-1980s is not well covered by official data, resulting in an under-estimation of urban inequality and poverty, and an under-valuation of rural income (Khan and Riskin, 2001).

It is also hard to assess the proportion of income coming from the growing informal activities (for instance, unreported work by laid-off workers and second jobs). Available data on urban incomes only partially reflect the role formerly played by fringe benefits and in-kind benefits for those working in state-owned enterprises (SOEs). It has been argued that the understatement of subsidies leads to an overstatement of inequality in urban areas (Bramall, 2001). Coupled with the fact that enterprise and wage reform has resulted in the inclusion of some fringe benefits into basic wages, there is obviously an impact on inequality assessment that is difficult to measure. There appears to be no available study which has reconciled old and new benefits, or assesses their impact on the measurement of inequality. Some authors have criticised official statistics as not reflecting spatial variations in prices and the cost of living. There are three consumer price indices in China, at the regional, rural and urban levels. Because the food basket can vary widely between each of the 54 national minorities in China, there are doubts that these differences are integrated into the overall food basket and in prices (Park and Wang, 2001; World Bank, 1997; Khan and Riskin, 2001; Hermann-Pillath *et al.,* 2002, and Kanbur and Zhang, 2001). The assessment of living standards at different points in time is further complicated by historical control of prices. The minimum expenditure for food has been calculated using a combination of planned and market prices, leading to problems of assessment of rural living standards, which includes a significant component of production for self-consumption.

Trends in inequality

Because of the different income definitions used by different studies, as well as the limitations of National Bureau of Statistics (NBS) data, a range of differing estimates of inequality emerge from the literature. The longest time series are given by Bramall (2001) and Chang (2002). Both give separate time series for urban and rural inequality and for China as a whole, and while both state that their source for these series is the National Bureau of Statistics, the series are different. Despite these differences, these (and other) studies agree that there has been a significant increase in income inequality since 1978 (Table 6.1). Depending on the individual study, the Gini coefficient for China as a whole moved from around 0.28 to 0.33 in the 1978-1980 period, to between 0.386 and 0.457 in 1999. The upward trend has not been consistent however and there appears to have been a fall in overall inequality between 1994 and 1997, according to Bramall (2001). Inequality appears to have risen since 1997 (Chen and Wang, 2001). The differences between estimates shown in Table 6.1 reflect differences in approaches, with some measures showing higher and others showing lower inequality. The lower estimates are produced when account is taken of differences in the cost of living between urban and rural areas (Chen and Wang, 2001), while the higher are produced when account is taken of a wider range of subsidies and imputed income from housing, and rural home production is valued at market prices (Bramall, 2001).[2]

Rural-urban disparities and the rural-urban gap

Inequality can be decomposed into disparities within and between urban and rural areas. The urban Gini coefficient has generally always been lower than the rural Gini, ranging from 0.16 to 0.32 for the former, and 0.21 to 0.35 for the latter, in the period between 1978 and 1999. Thus, both intra-rural and intra-urban disparities appear to have widened over the period. According to the statistics from the NBS (Table 6.2), the rural Gini coefficient started to increase after 1978, apparently at different rates in different periods, with an initial rapid increase, some stability in the mid-1980s, and again in the early 1990s, followed by slight falls between 1995 and 1998, and an increase in 1999 (Bramall, 2001).

Overall, the widening of the rural income distribution is mainly explained by the diversification of income sources (Khan and Riskin, 2001), which are more unequally distributed than farm income, combined with the slow growth of farming income. While farming remained the main and most equalising source of rural household income (46% of total income in 1995), its share in total income fell with the increase in new components: individual wages (22% of 1995 total income), property income and private activities. The last turn out to be the main factors tending to increase inequality, along with taxes. Wage disparities accounted for 40% of overall rural inequality in 1995, as wages were concentrated in the top decile group of incomes. Moreover, the burden of income taxes is borne by the poorest, and subsidies are concentrated in the two richest deciles (Khan and Riskin, 2001). State and collective transfers are also directed more to the richest than the lowest income groups.

For urban incomes (Table 6.3), the NBS estimates of the Gini coefficient (0.16 in 1978) varied little until the early 1980s, when it started to increase, and then more rapidly after the mid-1980s, reaching a peak of 0.30 in 1994, before falling somewhat (Bramall, 2001). The series given by Chang (2002) shows a very similar pattern, but without the decline in inequality after 1994. Wages remained as the main source of urban income in 1995 (61%) and still appear to be the most equally distributed component of overall urban incomes (Khan and Riskin, 1998; Gustafsson and Li, 2001). Bonuses used

2. Since both adjustments are desirable in theory, this means that the "true" level of inequality cannot definitely be said to be either higher or lower than the official estimate.

to be an important component of wages, but their share fell sharply between 1988 and 1995 (Khan and Riskin, 2001; Li and Zhao, 2001). Other components of incomes are in-kind income and subsidies. The former used to be a very important source of income in the centrally planned era, but the mid-eighties reforms transformed this situation. The rental value of owner-occupied housing (11% of income) and in-kind housing subsidies (10%) were major components of urban income in 1995. It is in subsidies that the picture of wage inequality saw the main shifts. Higher income groups benefited most from imputed income from housing and from subsidies. Even though housing subsidies were cut by half between 1988 and 1995, the privatisation of housing favoured mainly the higher income groups. In addition, there has been the suppression of ration coupons, which used to equalise urban incomes. All these changes have tended to make the urban income distribution less homogeneous.

However, the overall level of inequality in China has always been higher than either the rural or the urban Gini coefficients, reflecting the influence of the rural-urban income gap as a major contributor to overall inequality (World Bank, 1997; Kanbur and Zhang, 2001). These specific disparities are largely a result of low agricultural incomes – around 20% of average earnings per worker in non-agricultural jobs – combined with a much greater economic dependence on agriculture in some provinces than in others. Urban incomes on average have almost always been at least twice as high as rural incomes (Chart 6.1). A reduction in the rural-urban income ratio to 1.9 apparently occurred in 1985, owing to reforms that benefited rural incomes. The ratio then continuously increased, slowly during the second half of the 1980s, to reach a peak of 2.9 in 1994. A modest decrease in 1995-97 has been followed by a continuous increase back to a ratio of 2.9 by 2001. It should also be noted that it is likely that the incomes of the floating population of rural migrant workers would tend to decrease the urban-rural gap, as their incomes would be lower than the urban average, but higher than the rural average.

Regional disparities and inequalities

As shown in Table 6.4, inequality is neither homogeneous across regions, nor over the period discussed (Yao and Liu, 1998; Hermann-Pillath *et al.*, 2002). While economic growth has benefited all provinces and regions, the consensus among studies is that disparities between the three regions – the eastern, central and western regions – widened. While the early 1980s were characterised by a decline in regional disparities in terms of PCGDP growth, overall regional inequality started to widen at the end of the 1980s, mainly between the eastern and western regions, while the centre held a steady position. The decline in regional inequality in the 1980s appears mainly related to the catching-up effect for some coastal provinces. Regional income growth started to diverge after 1992, somewhat after Deng Xiaoping's southern tour, the usual benchmark for the foundation of the "socialist market economy", which reinforced the advantages of coastal cities. Since then, coastal areas have enjoyed a rate of growth at least twice that of the interior. However, the central-western disparity narrowed until 1994, and remains narrow.

The within-regions trends in inequality were different. Still in terms of PCGDP, the divergence within the eastern and within the central regions declined, whereas the opposite trend occurs within the western regions. There has been growing rural disparity within regions, most strongly in the east, and least in the west (Gustafsson and Zhong, 2000). In fact, the main shifts took place at the provincial level. However, trends were not uniform. The Gini coefficient in some provinces remained steady (Guangdong, Guangxi, Hunan and Qinghai) while others had declining inequality (Xinjiang), and others an extremely rapid increase in inequality (Tianjin, Sichuan, Heilongjiang and Henan) (Qian and Wong, 2000).

International comparisons

China's level of inequality in the late 1990s appears to be lower than in a number of other countries such as Brazil, Mexico, Russia, South Africa and Turkey, although well above the average for OECD countries (Table 6.5). What seems to be distinctive in the Chinese case is the speed at which inequality has apparently increased. From World Bank estimates, the Gini coefficient rose by 10 percentage points between 1981 and 1995. This increase is very rapid, with only some of the Central Asian Republics, Russia and the United Kingdom experiencing such an increase in the level of inequality in so short a period of time.

The rise in inequality should be seen in the context of a pre-reform situation where open disparities were artificially repressed (as in the case of the transition economies of Central and Eastern Europe and the former Soviet Union). Privileges existed, but were not necessarily available through the medium of income. Nevertheless, pre-reform China can be described as being a relatively equitable country in terms of living standards for the majority of the population, but with low living standards for all. In addition, the implementation of public measures in health, sanitation, access to improved water and primary education, and their provision to the majority of the population – although very basic and debatable in many respects – contributed to enhance living conditions (expressed *inter alia* in rising life expectancy and a reduction in child mortality). One of the main egalitarian aspects of Chinese society during the Maoist era was its land redistribution policy, which enabled the eradication of the problem of the landless poor. This is of particular importance in an agrarian country where the great majority live in rural areas.

Poverty trends and levels

The links between inequality and poverty are complex. A majority of studies emphasise the nature of poverty as a rural phenomenon (although existing in urban areas at a much lower level, albeit increasing), reflecting the agrarian characteristics of Chinese society. Inequality measures often concentrate on relative incomes, while in China, poverty measures usually focus on absolute income levels. China's official poverty estimates are based on income rather than expenditure, more precisely on annual net per capita income from the rural HHS. The poverty line was defined in the mid-1980s, after the government committed itself to eradicate poverty. For this purpose, the Leading Group for Poverty Reduction was created to set the goals of the regionally targeted programme on rural areas, called the "8-7" National Poverty Reduction Plan (1993). The plan promised to raise 80 million people out of poverty in seven years. Assistance is provided to national poor counties under the central programme, and provincial poor counties receive provincial assistance.

The official rural poverty headcount is based on a "very severe" poverty line (World Bank, 1997), even as compared to the international standard of USD1 per day. It has been set at CNY100 to CNY625 between 1978 and 2000 (around USD0.66 per day). The poverty line is based on a food consumption standard of either 2 100 or 2 400 Kcal, corresponding to a basic food basket, with non-food expenditure calculated using an Engel coefficient of 0.60. The official urban poverty line, in use since 1991, is about 2.9 times higher than the rural one, falling between USD1 and USD2 a day. On this basis, the Chinese authorities have an impressive record in poverty reduction since 1978, as shown in Table 6.6. Depending on the source, around 200 to 270 million persons are said to have been lifted out of poverty since that time. In aggregate, the rural poverty headcount decreased from 30.7% to 3.4% between 1978 and 2000. Overall, the poor population is estimated to have been 65 million in 1995 and 30 million in 2000. All studies agree that the official poverty rate reduced rapidly between 1978 and the mid-1980s, halving during this period. Thereafter, results differ in regard to the speed and the magnitude of the poverty reduction, which continued to fall over the 1980s and the 1990s, but at a slower absolute pace.[3]

The regional poverty map is similar to the inequality map, that is, poverty increases in moving from the east to the centre and to the western provinces (Li, 2001). However, poverty is not limited to remote areas, but occurs in all provinces (Khan, 1998; Khan and Riskin, 2001). From 1988 to 1995, the poverty headcount fell from 9.37, 19.97 and 26.96% to 5.24, 8.29 and 13.29%, respectively, in the eastern, central and western regions (Li, 2001). Urban poverty is significantly lower than rural poverty, and according to Khan and Riskin (2001), fell from about 20% to 6% between 1981 and 1993. Studies have suggested that urban poverty may have risen slightly after 1998, reflecting the impact of the Asian financial crisis (Chen and Wang, 2001). However, urban poverty varies significantly across provinces. For instance, Henan's urban poverty headcount was 11.24% in 1995, when Guangdong, one of the richest provinces of China, only had 0.16% of its urban population identified as poor (Li, 2001).

Behind the apparent impressive reduction in poverty since 1978, the literature describes a complex situation, which suggests some reservations about these trends. For example, Charts 6.2 and 6.3 illustrate trends in rural and urban poverty, respectively. While official rural poverty has continued to fall, the level at higher poverty lines (both USD1 and USD2 a day) has been stable since the mid-1990s. Moreover the proportion of the rural population with incomes between USD0.66 and USD1 a day has increased somewhat since 1996. This means that around 20% of the rural population have incomes just over the official poverty line, suggesting potential vulnerability to external shocks, a situation reminiscent of a number of South East Asian economies before the 1997 crisis (OECD, 2001).

The finding that rural poverty stopped falling after the mid-1990s seems linked to a pattern of growth which did not benefit rural incomes. There is also some indication that the problem of extreme urban poverty (albeit affecting a very small proportion of the population) has recently worsened, for example, with the poorest being hurt more severely by the Asian crisis (as measured with poverty gap measures). In addition, poverty eradication programmes have had some unequal features in relation to geographic location and ethnic composition (Gustafsson and Zhong, 2000; Khan and Riskin, 2001). As a means of targeting, these programmes designate only some regions or villages as poor. Most of these regions or villages are located in the south, the north-west and west, but one-third of the Chinese rural poor live outside these designated areas, and cannot benefit from these programmes or funds (World Bank, 1997). The concentration of poverty in the western region has long been interpreted as a consequence of the region’s natural disadvantages. The divergence of both output and living standards which drove the coast-interior disparity is partly due to the preferential policies implemented in favour of the coastal provinces. Low public investment in the western regions (especially remote areas) is another factor. But this is expected to reduce in the medium to long run, with the implementation of the western development project.

It also appears that there is a further link between ethnic minorities living in autonomous regions and poverty. Poverty rates in ethnic minority provinces have been found to be above average and to have increased markedly between 1988 and 1995 (Khan and Riskin, 2001). The poverty headcount is estimated to have decreased for households in the plains to 6%, and to roughly 14% for people living in the hills, but the rate increased to 34% for people living in mountains and also from 30% to 35% for ethnic minorities, mainly living in geographically austere areas. Overall, a person is more likely to be

3. In relative terms, the reduction is not slowing – having halved between 1978 and 1985, the rate halved again by 1995, and halved again by 2000.

poor when living in a rural hilly or mountainous area, in a large family or when belonging to the dependant age group. In urban areas, the typical groups of the poor include the retired, female laid-off workers from an SOE or collective-owned enterprise (COE), the unemployed, and the unskilled, or low-skilled or migrants working in the informal sector.

Understanding the driving factors behind the increase in inequality

The reforms of the first half of the 1980s boosted the rural economy, particularly with the implementation of the household responsibility system, the re-opening of rural markets and the spread of non-agricultural activities. In addition, the development of rural industry through township and village enterprises (TVE) brought a new source of income: wages. The growth of wage income has contributed to the widening of intra-rural and inter-provincial disparities. Moreover, TVEs are unequally distributed among regions. Among other reasons, due to their low integration in domestic markets, well-off TVEs are located in the eastern coastal region, contributing to the widening of inter-regional inequalities. Their natural advantages and the dynamism of the region have enabled the development of activities that are more export-oriented, and thus more profitable than TVEs in the interior of the country. East-west disparities have been exacerbated by preferential policies granted to special economic zones (SEZ), including export subsidies, access to foreign exchange, tax exemptions, and access to investment, among others, during the 1980s and whose privileges increased thereafter. These policies are at the heart of the dynamism of coastal areas, and also of inter-regional disparities. In fact, in the first phase of their implementation, these policies re-balanced the country-wide distribution of industry.

Economic reforms have also changed the Chinese labour market. In the pre-reform era, the labour market was entirely segmented, first by the *hukou* and second, by the organisation of work through the work unit (*danwei*) in urban areas and communes in rural areas. The agricultural sector used to be the main provider of employment, but its share in overall employment fell from 70.5% to 50% between 1978 and 2000. In urban areas, the de-*danweisation* process aimed to allow firms to concentrate on their productive role, by reducing their social protection activities and related financial burdens. As a result, more than 20 million people have been laid off over the period 1998-2001. Changes in the Chinese labour market have been affected by the introduction of new types of enterprises and new activities, which have transformed the employment structure. Although currently SOEs are still the main provider of urban employment, they are now accompanied by foreign enterprises, joint ventures and private firms (Coady and Wang, 2000; Qian and Wong, 2000). In these new types of enterprise, more driven by efficiency and productivity, social obligations are less restrictive, and wages are higher and more dispersed. The secondary and especially the tertiary sector are much more dynamic, and bring more returns to human capital and productivity, for instance in sectors like insurance or banking.

There is a diversity of opinion and analysis of the relation between trends in economic growth and trends in income inequality. Some research has emphasised that economic growth increased the country's wealth but not sufficiently to overcome rising inequality, nor to eradicate poverty, in part because personal incomes grew at a slower rate than national income (World Bank, 1997; Khan and Riskin, 2001). Inequality also appears to have grown more when output growth did not lead to personal income growth. The early 1980s reduction in inequality is related to reforms of the rural economy, enabling rural dwellers to increase and diversify their incomes, as well as a better distribution of land, which became much more equally distributed among households in the post-reform era. These rural reforms seem to have had a positive impact on the very bottom income group until 1984-1985. When growth slowed down between 1984 and 1989, personal incomes stagnated, except for the top income group. In fact, each time agricultural product purchasing prices increased, rural inequality was reduced, partly reflecting the little incentive to production. Others have interpreted the periods of falling inequality as corresponding to periods of tightening of monetary policy, which had a negative impact on labour intensive industries and non-farming activities, thus impacting more on urban incomes (Wan, 2001). It has also been argued that the unevenness of growth across regions is in part related to the pattern of China's opening and integration into the world economy, which has entailed growth in the coastal area and in central level municipalities, which are the main recipients of foreign direct investment (FDI) and technological exchanges (Khan and Riskin, 2001).

It is generally agreed that China's fiscal system is ineffective at redistribution between households and regions (Zhang and Zhou, 1998; Tian, 1999; Fang *et al.*, 2002). The 1994 fiscal reform has not changed the situation. Research and the official press report that taxes and fees are far higher in rural areas compared to urban areas. In contrast, farmers paid a range of different taxes, some specific to localities or villages. These taxes included a combination of national taxes and a multiplicity of local taxes and fees, such as for education, village road maintenance or construction, health, family planning, military training, but also illegal fees levied by officials. Moreover, rural workers do not receive as much in transfers as urban workers, whether in housing or social security, while paying higher taxes and spending directly for public services.

Government fiscal transfers appear also to have been misused, with specific purpose grants actually used to subsidise state-owned enterprises to cover pension debts, unpaid wages and other social security obligations (Ethisham *et al.*, 2002). Furthermore, the transfers designed to equalise inter-provincial resources have always been under-funded and shrank in size over the period. The fiscal decentralisation process since 1978 has given more autonomy to localities in tax collection and spending, but the central government budget decreased, and hence its capacity to invest and redistribute. The size of the state budget fell from 30.8% to 18.3% of GDP between 1978 and 1992. Overall, the impact of fiscal decentralisation has been to reduce redistribution from rich provinces to poorer provinces. Both media reports and researchers have highlighted the issue of rural taxes. The government made it a priority for 2002 to reduce the tax burden on peasants. It has been decided to unify rural taxes, and a two-years pilot reform is currently being experimented in Anhui and Jiangsu, as well as in nine provinces and autonomous regions. In the new taxation system, there will be only one agricultural tax, limited to some agricultural products. It is reported that this reform has already enabled savings of 10% average annual income for those affected, and a 31% fall in rural tax collections. However, this taxation reform, if extended to all China, would certainly put pressure on local finances.

To summarise, China's growing inequalities have been influenced by the conjunction of a range of factors as part of the reform and the globalisation processes. The coastal-oriented reforms, with their preferential policies for some regions, entailed an uneven distribution of growth. This has been reinforced by the policy focus on urban areas, which appears to have limited rural income growth. Policies such as "some get rich first" have also been conducive of a new social stratification, with more obvious high differences in living standards and wealth between the richest and the other income groups. Other disparities reflect the legacy of unreformed institutions and practices.

Other issues

Economic development in China has been accompanied by improvements in social conditions, such as life expectancy, infant mortality and literacy. This process improved somewhat after 1978, but the pace of improvements has slowed over time and in some aspects social development regressed. For example, the distribution of education appears to have worsened. Recent reforms in education have mostly been concerned with higher education, and the goal of the current five-year plan to raise participation in higher education to 15% has been quite successful. Comparatively speaking, primary and secondary education have been neglected during the last 20 years, especially in rural areas.

Education inequalities are observed mainly in relation to coverage and access to basic education. In both rural and urban areas, educational costs are said to have markedly increased in the 1990s.

The national illiteracy rate fell from 23% to 6.7% between 1982 and 2000. But the situation is extremely unequal: first, the urban illiteracy rate is 4%, compared to 8% among the rural population and, second, some regions have very high illiteracy rates, for instance, 23.5% in Qinghai and 17% in Gansu. In Tibet, more than 47% of the population aged 15 years and over have an instruction level at or under the primary level, most of whom are women (60%). Overall, the great majority of illiterate or semi-illiterate persons remain rural females.

Conclusions and policy questions

This review has emphasised that the task of assessing income disparities in China is very much complicated by significant problems of measurement, limited availability of data, the use of different income concepts, the divergent coverage of surveys, and differences in the geographic scale and focus of different studies. These problems point to the need for significant improvements in the area of statistics. Data on household incomes and expenditures need to be more accessible and transparent, and further development needs to go into improvement of concepts and coverage. Such improvements should help in increasing the understanding of income inequalities and poverty in China, and thus provide a better framework for possible policy responses. Nevertheless, in summary, it can be concluded that while there appears to be no agreement about the level of inequality in China (and therefore nor precisely how it compares with other countries), there is a consensus of research that income inequalities have increased significantly since 1978. This conclusion is reinforced by the evidence of public and government concern about the trend in income disparities. It can also be concluded that disparities between urban and rural areas, and between provinces and regions, are significant and are viewed as requiring policy attention.

What would be a wider agenda for public action? Broadly speaking, one approach is that China should address the issues of inequality and poverty through growth rather than redistribution (World Bank, 1997). While continued economic growth is a fundamental pre-requisite for sustained improvements in living standards for all of the Chinese population, it can also be argued that appropriate economic and social policies can improve growth prospects, and also improve the distribution of incomes. Earlier OECD work concluded that the initial steps to reduce inequalities are first, to create more employment opportunities, with the initial stage being to address the institutional barriers inherent in the household registration system, which constrains labour market development and mobility. Improvements in labour standards and their application are the second short to medium-term step. Another urgent task with long-term effects is the enhancement of educational levels.

One of the conclusions of earlier OECD work is that China must find ways to create employment for the rural under-employed. Rural under-employment is extremely large – 18.6% of the rural population (*People's Daily*, January 2003) – but China's internal migration is still constrained by the *hukou* system, creating inequitable access to the labour market, among other problems. The *hukou* is however in the process of change, and this is likely to continue as the country develops and urbanisation proceeds. However, China's arable land potential is limited, suggesting the continuing need to create employment opportunities for rural dwellers. For rural areas, the development of non-farming activities has resulted in higher rural incomes through self-employment and the development of TVEs, although at the cost of increasing inequalities within rural areas. Despite predictions of further increases in inequality with the development of non-farming activities, it seems desirable to promote their development simultaneously with the higher urbanisation of rural areas.

In addition, China needs to find jobs for a mounting number of urban workers who do not fit into the contemporary labour market. This is the case for laid-off workers and those belonging to the age groups not far from retirement, and who are identified as among the poorest of urban residents. Long-term unemployment also threatens those who are out of the current labour market and those who have limited skills. Active policies are thus required to promote the re-employment of these groups. Public policies, including social protection programmes, are an important theme to be considered, especially as current redistributive policies appear to be weak. As discussed in previous OECD work, social security is mainly provided to SOE workers, civil servants and more recently to the well-off in other types of enterprises in the best performing provinces and cities, even some TVEs. The extension to all urban formal workers is desirable on an equity basis, but also to raise coverage and to improve funding. Privatisation of health and the dismantling of the co-operative medical system has become an important issue for the population, who used to benefit from almost free access to health. The escalation of health costs raises the risk that people will not be able to access healthcare, especially in rural areas. Poor health is an important factor affecting the probability of falling into poverty. OECD analysis has also suggested that in order to reduce inequality between rural and urban dwellers, and to enhance China's human capital and to improve the quality of the labour force, the 12 years of compulsory school should be the target for the whole population.

BIBLIOGRAPHY

Adikhari, R. and Y. Yang (2002), "What Will WTO Membership Mean for China and Its Partners?", *Finance and Development*, International Monetary Fund (IMF), Washington DC, September.

Alvin, Y. So (2001), "The State, Economic Development and the Changing Pattern of Classes and Class Conflict in China", Paper presented at the International Conference on Money, Growth and Distribution, Chinese Taipei.

Arneberg, M. (2001), "Geographic Mobility: Urban Migrants", in D. Drury and M. Arneberg (eds.), *No More Forevers: The Chinese Labour Force in a Time of Reform*, FAFO Report, No. 356.

Atkinson, A.B. *et al.* (2001), *Inégalités économiques,* Conseil d'analyse économique, La Documentation française, Paris.

Benjamin, D., L. Brandt, *et al.* (1999), "Markets and Inequality in Rural China: Parallels with the Past", *American Economic Review,* Vol. 89, No. 2, pp. 292-295.

Berkowitz, D.M. and Li Wei (1997), *Decentralisation in Transition Economies: A Tragedy of the Commons?,* Working Paper, No. 45, The William Davidson Institute, University of Michigan, May.

Bramall, C. (2001), "The Quality of China's Household Income Surveys", *The China Quarterly*, Vol. 167, pp. 689-705.

Brown, P. and A. Park (2002), "Education and Poverty in Rural China", *Economics of Education Review,* Vol. 21, pp. 523-541.

Cai Fang (2001), "Regional Disparity and Regional Development Policy", in K.T. Lee, J.YF. Lin and S.J. Kim (eds.), *China's Integration with the World Economy: Repercussions of China's WTO Accession,* Institute for International Economic Policy, Seoul, Korea.

Chan, J. (2001), "Rural Revolts in China Reveal Widespread Disaffection over Tax Burdens", *Washington Post*, 8 May, *http://www.wsws.org/articles/2001/may2001/chin-m25.shtml*

Chan, J. (2003), *Social Discontent Escalates in China*, 12/02 on www.wsws.org.

Chan, K.W., T. Liu and Y. Yang (1999), "Hukou and Non Hukou Migration in China: Comparisons and Contrasts", *International Journal of Population Geography*, Vol. 5, No. 6.

Chang, G.H. (2002), "The Cause and the Cure of China's Widening Income Disparity", *China Economic Review*, Vol. 13, pp. 335-340.

Chen Shaohua and Wang Yang (2001), *China's Growth and Poverty Reduction: Recent Trends between 1990 and 1999*, Working Paper, No. 2651, World Bank, Washington DC.

Chua Hwee Yong and J.G. Bauer (1996), "The Income Distribution of China: Regional Disparities", *Regional Issues in Economics*, Vol. II, Part III, pp. 159-174.

Coady, D.P. and Wang Lm (2000), "Equity, Efficiency and Labour Market Reforms in Urban China: the Impact of Bonus Wages on the Distribution of Earnings", *China Economic Review*, Vol. 11.

De Brauw, A., E.J. Taylor and S. Rozelle (2000), "Migration and Incomes in Source Communities: A New Economics of Migration Perspective from China", *American Economic Review*, Papers and Proceedings, Vol. 89, No. 2, pp. 267-271, May 1999.

Démurger, S. (2001), "Infrastructure Development and Economic Growth: An Explanation for Regional Disparities in China?", *Journal of Comparative Economics*, Vol. 29, pp. 95-117.

Démurger S. *et al.* (2001, 2002), *Geography, Economic Policy and Regional Development in China*, CID, Working Paper No. 77, Harvard College, *www.nber.org/papers/w8897*.

Ethisham, A., *et al.* (2002), *Recentralisation in China*, WP/02/168, IMF, Washington DC.

Fabre, G. *et al.* (2000), "Chine : le piège des inégalités", *Problèmes politiques et sociaux*, No. 834, La Documentation française, Paris.

Fang Cheng, Zhang Xiaobo and Fan Shenggen (2002), "Emergence of Urban Poverty and Inequality in China: Evidence from Household Survey", *China Economic Review*, Vol. 13, pp. 430-443.

Förster, M. and M. Pearson (2002), "Income Distribution and Poverty in the OECD Area: Trends and Driving Forces", *OECD Economic Studies*, No. 34, OECD, Paris.

Fujita, M. and D.P. Hu (2001), "Regional Disparity in China 1985-1994: The Effects of Globalization and Economic Liberalization", *The Annals of Regional Science,* No. 35.

Fur, A., P. Gentelle and T. Pairault (1999), *Économies et régions de la Chine*, HER/Armand Colin, Paris.

Gentelle, P. (1994), *Économie de la Chine*, HER/Armand Colin, Paris.

Gibson, J., J.K. Huang and S. Rozelle (2002), *Improving Estimates of Inequality and Poverty from Urban Household Income and Expenditure Survey*, University of Waikato, Working Paper in Economics, No. 1/02.

Giraud, P.N. (1996), *L'inégalité du monde : économie du monde contemporain,* Collection Folio/Actuel, Éditions Gallimard, Paris.

Giraud, P.N. (1999), "La politique économique à l'époque de la globalisation", *Notas Economicas*, No. 12, CERNA, France.

Giraud, P.N. (2002), "Inégalités : faits et débats", *Sociétal*, No. 35, CERNA, France.

Gustafsson, B. and Li Shi (2001), "The Anatomy of Rising Earnings Inequality in Urban China", *Journal of Comparative Economics,* No. 29, pp. 118-135.

Gustafsson, B. and Wei Zhong (2000), "How and Why has Poverty in China Changed? A Study Based on Microdata for 1988 and 1995", *The China Quarterly,* No. XX, Research Note, pp. 983-1024.

Hansen. P. (2001), "Long March, Bitter Fruit: The Public Health Impact of Rural-to-Urban Migration in the People's Republic of China", *Stanford Journal of East Asian Affairs*, Vol. 1.

Haski, P. (2002), "L'instabilité sociale derrière la prospérité chinoise", *Libération,* 6 mars.

Herrmann-Pillath, C., D. Kirchert and Pan Jiancheng (2002), "Disparities in Chinese Economic Development Approaches on Different Levels of Aggregation", *Economic Systems,* No. 26, pp. 31-54.

Hu Angang (2001), "China's Urban Unemployment and Social Safety", in K.T. Lee, J.YF. Lin and S.J. Kim (eds.), *China's Integration with the World Economy: Repercussions of China's WTO Accession*, Korea Institute for International Economic Policy, Seoul, Korea.

Hussain, A., P. Lanjouw and N. Stern (1994), "Income Inequalities in China: Evidence from Household Survey Data", *World Development,* Vol. 22, No. 12, pp. 1947-1957.

Iredale, R. and Guo Fei (2000), "Contemporary Minority Mobility in China and its Implications", Paper prepared for the Conference on Social Transformation in the Asia-Pacific Region, University of Wollongong.

Kanbur, R. and Zhang Xb (2001), *Fifty Years of Regional Inequality in China: A Journey Through Revolution, Reform and Openness,* Working Paper, Cornell University, United States.

Khan, A.R. (1998), *Poverty in China in the Period of Globalisation: New Evidence on Trends and Patterns: Issues in Development*, Discussion Paper No. 22, International Labour Office (ILO), Geneva.

Khan, A. and C. Riskin (1998), "Income and Inequality in China: Composition, Distribution and Growth of Household Income, 1988 to 1995", *The China Quarterly*, No. 154.

Khan, A. and C. Riskin (2001), *Inequality and Poverty in China in the Age of Globalisation,* Oxford University Press, New York.

Lee Jongchul (2000), "Changes in the Source of China's Regional Inequality", *China Economic Review*, Vol. 11.

Li Shi (2001), *Changes in Poverty Profile on China,* Discussion Paper No.°2001/21, UNU/Wider.

Li Shi and Zhao Yaohui (2001), *The Decline of In-kind Wage Payments in Urban China*, CCER, July, *http://old.cenet.ccer.edu.cn/en/Articles/Papers/Paper2001-10-22-171346.doc*

The Luxembourg Income Study (2001), "Final Report and Recommendations", Expert Group on Household Income Statistics, The Canberra Group, Ottawa.

Ma Jun (1995), *Macroeconomic Management and Intergovernmental Relations in China,* Policy Research Paper, No. 1408, World Bank, Washington DC.

Moinuddin, K.H. (1992), *Poverty in the People's Republic of China: Recent Developments and Scope for Bank Assistance*, ADB Occasional Papers, No. 1.

OECD (2001), *Territorial Outlook*, OECD, Paris.

OECD (2002a), *Financing Education Investments and Returns: Analysis of the World Education Indicators,* OECD, Paris

OECD (2002b), *China in the World Economy: the Domestic Policy Challenges*, OECD, Paris.

OECD (2002c), *Agricultural Policies in China after the WTO Accession*, OECD, Paris.

Pairault, T. (1999), "Développements et dynamiques provinciales", *Économies et régions de la Chine*, HER/Armand Colin, Paris, pp. 32-35; also presented at an OECD Development Center Workshop, June 1999.

Park, A. and Wang Sangui (2001), "China's Poverty Statistics", *China Economic Review*, Vol. 12.

Qian Zhihong and Wong Taichee (2000), "The Rising Urban Poverty: A Dilemma of Market Reforms in China", *Journal of Contemporary China*. Vol. 9, No.°23, pp. 113-125.

Raa, Thijsten and Pan Haoran (2001), *Competitive Pressures on China: Income Inequality*, Center Discussion Paper, No. 2001-2053.

Ravallion, M. and Chen Sh (1998), *When Economic Reform is Faster than Statistical Reform: Measuring and Explaining Inequality in Rural China,* Policy Research Working Paper, No. 1902, World Bank, Washington DC.

Rawski, T.G. and Xiao Wei (2001), "Roundtable on Chinese Economic Statistics Introduction", *China Economic Review*, Vol. 12, pp. 298-302.

Rozelle, S., *et al.* (1999*)*, "Leaving China's Farm: Survey Results of New Paths and Remaining Hurdles to Rural Migration", *The China Quarterly*, No. 158.

Scharping, T. (2001), "Hide and Seek China's Elusive Population Data", *China Economic Review*, Vol. 12, pp. 323-332.

Sen, A. (1999), *Un nouveau modèle économique : développement, justice, liberté* (Development as Freedom), Odile Jacob, Paris.

Shan, J. (2002), "A Macro-econometric Model of Income Disparity in China", *International Economic Journal,* Vol. 16, No. 2, Summer.

Tian Xiaowen (1999), "Market Orientation and Regional Economic Disparities in China", *Post-Communist Studies*, Vol. 11, No. 2.

Tsui Kai-yuen (1996), "Economic Reform and Inter-provincial Inequalities in China", *Journal of Development Economics*, Vol. 50, No. 2, pp. 353-368.

Wade, R.H. (2001), "The Rising Inequality of World Income Distribution", *Finance and Development*, Vol. 34, No. 4, IMF, Washington DC.

Wan Guanghua (2001), "Changes in Regional Inequality in Rural China: Decomposing the Gini Index by Income Sources", *Australian Journal of Agriculture and Resource Economics*, Vol. 45, No. 3.

Wei Dennis Yehua (2002), "Multiscale and Multimechanisms of Regional Inequality in China: Implications for Regional Policies", *Journal of Contemporary China,* Vol. 11, No. 30.

Wei Shangjin (2002), "Is Globalisation Good for the Poor in China", *Finance and Development*, IMF, Washington DC, September.

World Bank (1997), *Sharing Rising Incomes: Disparities in China*, China 2020, World Bank, Washington DC.

World Bank/BIRD (2001), *China: Overcoming Rural Poverty*, Country Study, World Bank, Washington DC.

Xu Lixin, C. and Zou Hengfu (2000), "Explaining the Changes of Income Distribution in China", *China Economic Review*, Vol. 11, Amsterdam.

Yao Shujie and Liu Jirui (1998), "Economic Reforms and Regional Segmentation in Rural China", *Regional Studies*, Vol. 32, No. 8.

Yu Zhou (2002), *Urban and Rural Income Inequality in China – Review of Theories Relevant to China Economic Reforms*, Association of Pacific Rim Universities.

Zhang Tao and Zhou Hengfu (1998), "Fiscal Decentralisation, Public Spending and Economic Growth", *Journal of Public Economics,* Vol. 67, pp. 222-240.

Zhang, Liu and Yao (2002), *Convergence of China's Regional Incomes*, Discussion Paper, *http://mubs.mdx.ac.uk/research/Discussion_Papers/Economics/econ_dpap95.pdf*

Zhao Yaohui (2001a), *Causes and Consequences of Return Migration: Recent Evidence from China*, Working Paper, China Center for Economic Research, Beijing University, Beijing.

Zhao Yaohui (2001b), *The Role of Migrant Network in Labor Migration: the Case of China,* Working Paper No. 2001012, China Center for Economic Research, Beijing University, Beijing.

Zheng Fei, Xu Lida, Tang Bingyong (2000), "Forecasting Regional Income Inequality in China", *European Journal of Operational Research*, Vol. 124, pp. 243-254.

Zheng Jingping (2001), "China's Official Statistics Growing with Full Vitality", *China Economic Review,* Vol. 2, pp. 333-337.

Table 6.1. **Alternative estimates of overall inequality in China, 1978-1999**

Gini coefficient

Source	Measurement	1978	1980	1982	1984	1985	1986	1988	1990	1992	1994	1995	1996	1997	1998	1999
Bramall (2001)	NBS	-	0.28	-	-	-	-	-	0.36	-	-	0.41	0.39	-	-	-
	Improved measure	0.32	-	-	-	-	-	0.38	0.41	-	-	0.45	-	-	-	-
Chen & Wang (2001)	HH income	-	-	-	-	-	-	-								
	CLD=0	-	-	-	-	-	-	-	0.348	0.390	0.433	0.415	0.398	0.398	0.403	0.416
	CLD=20%	-	-	-	-	-	-	-	0.321	0.358	0.399	0.385	0.368	0.369	0.374	0.386
Chang (2002)	HH income	0.330	-	-	-	-	-	-	-	-	0.400	-	0.424	-	0.456	0.457
Chen & Wang (2001)	Consumption															
	CLD=0	-	-	-	-	-	-	-	-	-	-	-	-	-	0.429	0.445
	CLD=20%	-	-	-	-	-	-	-	-	-	-	-	-	-	0.399	0.415

-: Data not available; CLD: Cost of living difference; HH: Household; NBS: National Bureau of Statistics, China.
Source: OECD.

Table 6.2. **Alternative estimates of rural inequality in China, 1978-1999**
Gini coefficient

Source	Measurement	1978	1980	1982	1984	1985	1986	1988	1990	1992	1994	1995	1996	1997	1998	1999
Ravallion & Chen (1998)	HH PCI 4 provinces									-	-	-	-	-	-	-
	Original					0.291	0.301	0.330	0.339							
	Measure 2	-	-	-	-	0.275	0.288	0.306	0.309							
	Measure 3					0.271	0.283	0.281	0.287							
Yao & Liu (1998)	Disposable PCI	-	-	-	-	-	0.288	0.301	0.294	0.314	-	-	-	-	-	-
Benjamin & Brandt (1999)	PCI. 22 villages	-	-	-	-	-	-	-	-	-	-	0.380	-	-	-	-
Benjamin & Brandt (1999)	PC land. 22 villages	-	-	-	-	-	-	-	-	-	-	0.450	-	-	-	-
Bramall (2001)	NBS	0.21	0.24	0.23	0.26	0.26	0.29	0.30	0.31	0.31	0.33	0.34	-	0.33	0.33	0.35
	Improved measure	0.22	-	-	-	-	-	0.34	-	-	-	0.42	-	-	-	-
Chen & Wang (2001)	HH income	-	-	-	-	-	-	-	0.299	0.320	0.340	0.340	0.330	0.331	0.331	0.339
Khan & Riskin (2001)	HH PCI. CASS micro data.	-	-	-	-	-	-	0.338	-	-	-	0.416	-	-	-	-

Table 6.2. **Alternative estimates of rural inequality in China, 1978-1999** (contd.)
Gini coefficient

Wan (2001)	HH disposable PCI	-	-	-	0.106	0.910	0.107	0.113	0.108	0.125	0.148	0.162	0.160	-	-	-
Chang (2002)	HH income	0.212	0.241	0.246	0.227	0.304	0.305	0.310	0.307	0.329	0.342	0.323	0.329	0.337	0.336	-
Chen & Wang (2001)	Consumption	-	-	-	-	-	-	-	0.31	0.32	-	-	0.34	-	0.35	0.35

-: Data not available. CASS: Chinese Academy of Social Sciences; HH: Household; NBS: National Bureau of Statistics, China; PCI: Per capita income.
Source: OECD.

Table 6.3. **Alternative estimates of urban inequality in China, 1978-1999**

Gini coefficient

Source	Measurement	1978	1980	1982	1984	1985	1986	1988	1990	1992	1994	1995	1996	1997	1998	1999
Coady & Wang (2000)	Total wage, Liaoning	-	-	-	-	-	0.18	0.20	0.20	-	-	-	-	-	-	-
Coady & Wang (2000)	Standard wage, Liaoning	-	-	-	-	-	-	0.17	0.17	-	-	-	-	-	-	-
Qian and Wong (2000)	Average income		0.16			0.19			-		0.30	0.28		-	-	-
Xu & Zou (2000)	HH income	-	-	-	-	0.171	0.164	-	0.202	0.208	0.246	0.234	-	-	-	-
Bramall (2001)	NBS	0.16	0.16	0.15	0.16	0.19	0.19	0.23	0.23	0.25	0.30	0.28	0.28	-	-	-
	Improved measure	0.17	-	-	-	-	-	0.23	-	-	-	0.33	-	-	-	-
Gustafsson & Li (2001)	Total earnings	-	-	-	-	-	-	0.240	-	-	-	0.304	-	-	-	-
	East	-	-	-	-	-	-	0.236	-	-	-	0.315	-	-	-	-
	Centre	-	-	-	-	-	-	0.219	-	-	-	0.269	-	-	-	-
	West	-	-	-	-	-	-	0.243	-	-	-	0.255	-	-	-	-
Khan & Riskin (2001)	HH PCI. CASS micro data.	-	-	-	-	-	-	0.233	-	-	-	0.332	-	-	-	-

Table 6.3. **Alternative estimates of urban inequality in China, 1978-1999** (contd.)
Gini coefficient

Chang (2002)	HH income	0.160	0.150	0.150	0.190	0.190	0.200	0.230	0.240	0.270	0.280	0.280	0.290	0.300	0.295	-
Chen & Wang (2001)	HH income	-	-	-	-	-	-	-	0.234	0.241	0.292	0.283	0.285	0.294	0.299	0.297
Chen & Wang (2001)	Consumption	-	-	-	-	-	-	-	-	-	-	-	0.29	0.3	0.32	0.32

-: Data not available. CASS: Chinese Academy of Social Sciences; HH: Household; NBS: National Bureau of Statistics, China; PCI: Per capita income.
Source: OECD.

Table 6.4. **Estimates of regional inequality in China, 1978-1999**

Gini coefficients

Source	Coverage	Measur- -ement	1978	1980	1982	1984	1986	1988	1990	1991	1992	1993	1995	1998	1999
Kanbur & Zhang (2001)	Overall	Real CPC	0.259	0.249	0.244	0.216	0.255	0.234	0.236	0.243	0.257	0.262	0.271	0.283	0.303
Zhang, Liu &Yao (2002)	All except Tibet Hainan	Provincial PCGDP	0.201	0.198	0.195	0.195	0.200	0.212	0.209	0.218	0.227	0.236	0.249	-	-
Tsui (1996)	Overall	PCGDP	0.226	0.222	0.215	0.216	0.221	0.218	-	-	-		-	-	-
Zheng, Xu & Tang (2000)	Overall	Regional PCI	0.365	0.353	0.321	0.309	0.303	0.293	0.269	0.278	0.288		-	-	-
World Bank (1997)	Urban & rural	PCI and PCGDP	-	-	-	0.297	-	-	0.339	-	-		0.388	-	-
Yao & Liu (1999)	Rural	PC PDI	-	-	-	-	0.288	0.301	0.294	0.314	-		-	-	-
Herrmann-Pillath *et al.* (2002)	China; Provinces Prefectures	PCGDP	-	-	-	-	-	-	-	-	-	0.211 0.366	-	0.244 0.378	-
Herrmann-Pillath *et al.* (2002)	China Provinces Prefectures	TPCI	-	-	-	-	-	-	-	-	-	0.143 0.244	-	0.138 0.230	
Herrmann-Pillath et al. (2002)	Rural Provinces Prefectures	RPCI	-	-	-	-	-	-	-	-	-	0.148 0.238	-	0.141 0.233	
Herrmann-Pillath *et al.* (2002)	Urban; Provinces Prefectures	UPCI	-	-	-	-	-	-	-	-	-	0.086 0.157	-	0.092 0.170	

-: Data not available. CPC: Consumption per capita. PCI: Per capita income.
Source: OECD

Table 6.5. **Inequality in China in comparative perspective**

Country	Gini	Date	Source
China	0.458	2001	*China Daily*
OECD average	*0.288*	*Mid-90s*	*OECD*
Armenia	0.444	1996	WDI
Australia	0.305	Mid-90s	OECD
Austria	0.266	1997	WDI
Belgium	0.272	Mid-90s	OECD
Brazil	0.607	1998	WDI
Canada	0.305	1998	LIS
Chile	0.567	1998	WDI
Estonia	0.361	2000	LIS
France	0.278	1994	LIS
Germany	0.252	2000	LIS
Greece	0.336	Mid 90s	OECD
Hungary	0.244	1998	WDI
India	0.378	1997	WDI
Indonesia	0.317	1999	WDI
Italy	0.342	1995	LIS
Japan	0.260	Mid-90s	OECD
Kazakhstan	0.354	1996	WDI
Kyrgyz Republic	0.346	1999	WDI
Korea	0.316	1993	WDI
Mexico	0.531	1998	WDI
Norway	0.256	Mid-90s	OECD
Paraguay	0.577	1998	WDI
Poland	0.316	1998	WDI
Spain	0.325	1990	WDI
Russia	0.487	1998	WDI
South Africa	0.593	1993-94	WDI
Slovak Republic	0.195	1990	WDI
Slovenia	0.249	1999	LIS
Sweden	0.252	2000	LIS
Turkey	0.491	Mid-90s	OECD
Ukraine	0.290	1999	WDI
United Kingdom	0.345	1999	LIS
United States	0.368	2000	LIS
Uzbekistan	0.447	1998	WDI
Venezuela	0.495	1998	WDI

Note: This table presents different Gini's measured by income or by expenditure and made as comparable as possible by providers to international standards.

Source: Förster and Pearson (2002); World Development Indicators (WDI) (2002); Luxembourg Income Study (LIS) (2003).

Table 6.6. **Estimates of poverty in China, 1978-1999**

% of population below respective poverty line

Source	Coverage	Poverty threshold	1978	1985	1986	1988	1990	1991	1992	1994	1995	1996	1998	1999	2000
SSB Park & Wang (2001)	Rural	Official	30.7	14.8	15.5	11.1	9.5	10.4	8.8	7.6	7.1	6.3	4.6	3.7	3.4
SSB Park & Wang (2001)	Urban	Official	-	-	-	-	-	5.8	4.5	5.1	5.7	4.4	-	-	-
Chen & Wang (2001)	Overall	USD1/day	-	-	-	-	31.5	-	29.6	25.0	22.0	17.2	17.1	17.4	-
		USD2/day	-	-	-	-	69.9	-	65.7	61.2	56.6	51.3	50.3	50.7	
World Bank (2001)	Rural	USD1/day, PCI					31.3	31.7	30.1	25.9	21.8	15	11.5	-	-
Wei & Xu (1999)	Rural	USD1/day					35				27				
Gustafsson & Zhong (2000)	Overall	CNY439 in 1988, 908 for 1995, FGT=0 50% 1998 median	-	-	-	13.5	-	-	-	-	10.6	-	-	-	-
	Rural		-	-	-	17.6	-	-	-	-	14.9	-	-	-	-
	Urban		-	-	-	0.4	-	-	-	-	0.2	-	-	-	-
Chen & Wang (2001)	Rural	USD1/day	-	-	-	-	42.5	-	40.6	34.6	30.8	24.1	24.1	24.9	-
		USD2/day	-	-	-	-	87.6	-	85.7	80.3	75.8	68.7	69.0	68.7	
Khan & Riskin (2001	Rural	CNY810	40.8 (1980)	14.04	-	16.09	13.87	-	13.63	13.62	-	-	-	-	-
Khan & Riskin (2001)	Urban	CNY1 604	-	12.7	-	-	7.39	4.73	-	5.9	-	-	-	-	-

FGT: Foster-Greer-Thorbecke poverty index; PCI: Per capita income; SSB: State Statistical Bureau.
Source: OECD.

Chart 6.1. **Rural and urban household incomes per capita and income and consumption since 1978**

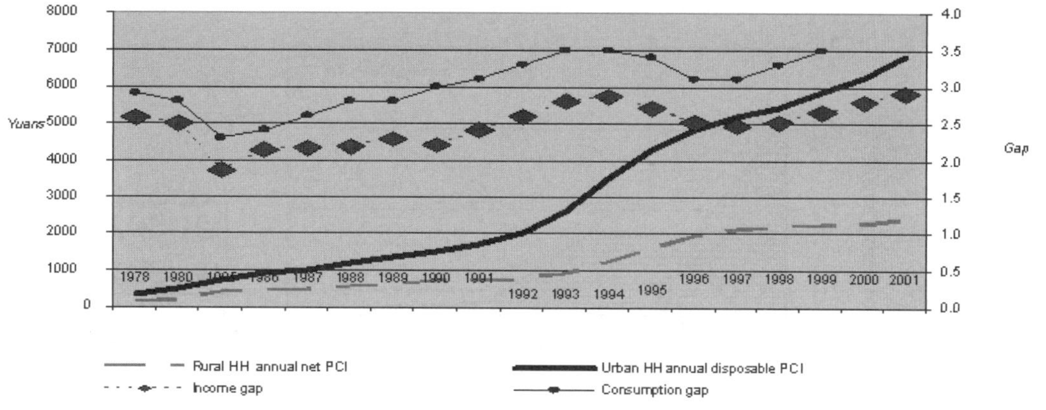

HH: Household; PCI: Per capital income.

Source: OECD.

Chart 6.2. **Trends in rural poverty, 1990-1999**

% below differing poverty lines

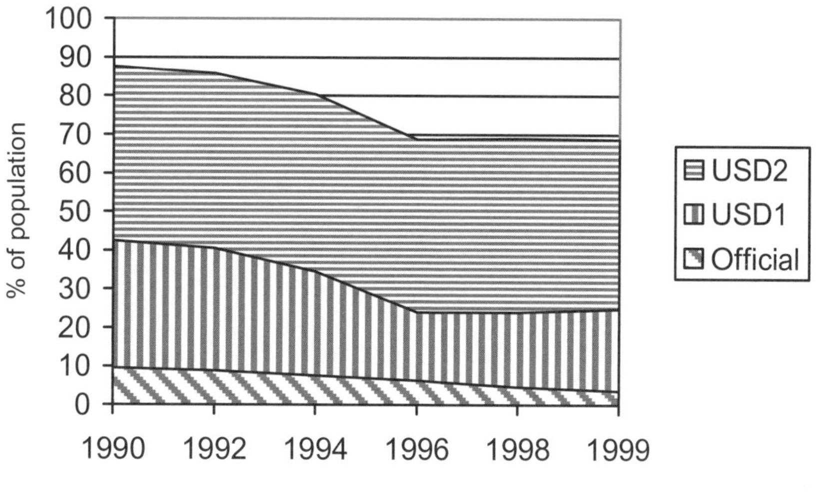

Source: OECD.

Chart 6.3. **Trends in urban poverty, 1990-1999**

% below differing poverty lines

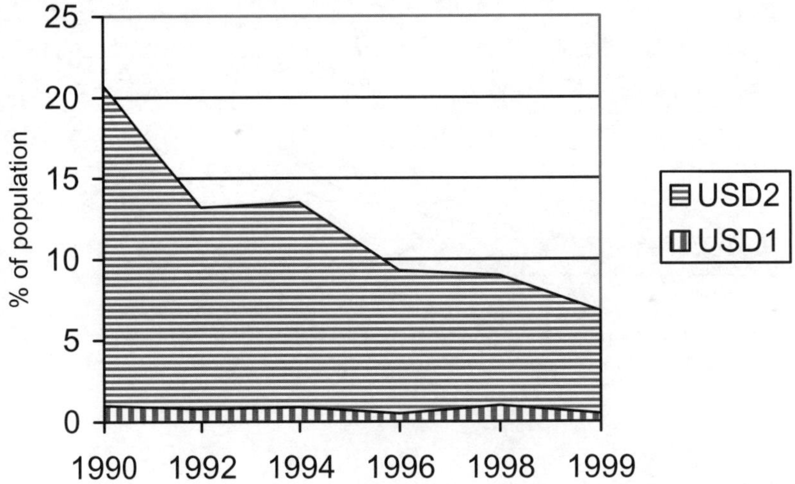

Source: OECD.

Chapter 7

APPARENT SOURCES OF INCOME INEQUALITY IN CHINA *OR* PLAUSIBLE AND LESS PLAUSIBLE INTERPRETATIONS OF IMPERFECT DATA

by
Anders Reutersward,

Principal Administrator,
Directorate for Employment, Labour and Social Affairs, OECD

What are the main causes of income inequality in China? A variety of possible causes have been suggested in the literature. But a closer look suggests that caution is necessary because the underlying data sources in China – notably household budget surveys – can be quite misleading if due account is not taken of statistical caveats. Many of the papers in this volume focus on standardised indicators such as Gini coefficients. These are statistical artefacts, estimated from a single type of data derived from surveys that supposedly are so uniform that they permit comparison across countries, regions and, in China, across the urban-rural divide. Authors generally assume (with or without discussion) that the data are comparable, which probably is true for some comparisons, but not for all of them.

When we know – as in China – that household budget survey data suffer from considerable limitations, it is prudent to consider different indicators before drawing conclusions, so as to avoid relying too much on only one type of data. Chapter 16 of *China in the World Economy: The Domestic Policy Challenges* (OECD, 2002) looks at a variety of indicators of potential relevance to the income distribution, also using statistics about employment, productivity, wages and households' actual *vs.* registered places of residence. I will first mention what appears as the most crucial shortcomings of China's household budget data, and how they might affect results. (We can't measure statistical bias, but we often know its direction.) The second part of this paper will briefly consider what we can say about possible causes of income inequality using such a broader range of data.

Chinese household budget surveys have serious limitations

To be sure, China's National Bureau of Statistics (NBS) does not publish Gini coefficients or similar measures, at least not in internationally available publications like the *China Statistical Yearbook*. For good reasons, NBS staff are undoubtedly aware of the caveats and they are careful when they use the results. Nevertheless, to us – outside researchers and policy makers – the potential interest of calculating comparable indicators is so great that we are at risk of unduly playing down the statistical problems. The most fundamentally confusing problem is that urban and rural household budget surveys are not only separate and use partly different definitions, but also fail to cover many migrants. The 2002 population census indicated that 12% of the population, or 150 million, did not live where they were registered. Most of them were probably rural citizens living in urban areas. As a result, perhaps one-third of the actual urban population – including many of the poorest – are either counted in the rural surveys, or not counted at all. (In theory, they belong to the "rural" population, but a majority of them probably escape the attention of any household budget survey.)

If we understand "urban" and "rural" as indication of where people actually live, the oft-mentioned "result" that China's "urban" income distribution is more equal than the "rural" one has no scientific support. (It holds only if we underline that residence is recorded primarily by register status, a terminology that is well-known in China, but misleading to non-Chinese readers.) Migrants' average incomes probably fall between the urban and rural averages, so the urban Gini coefficient could have been much higher if it were counted for all urban inhabitants. We don't know how this would affect the rural and overall Gini coefficients, except that they might also be quite different from the figures we now have.

Principal causes of income inequality in China

The principal causes of income inequality in China are:

- Low productivity in agriculture.
- Uneven distribution of non-farm job opportunities.
- Education.

Other important factors include:

- Wage discrimination against non-urban workers.
- Migration controls.
- For urban workers: those in the biggest cities are especially privileged.
- Public income transfers mainly to urban workers.

The following is a summary of information from the population census, national accounts, labour force surveys and wage statistics, as well as household budget surveys, all quoted from the *China Statistical Yearbook* (2002). Table 7.1 shows a ranking of China's 31 provinces by average household income per capita according to household budget surveys in 2001. The table then shows selected variables of potential explanatory interest. All the data sources – and not only household budget surveys – must be assumed to suffer from various degrees of under-reporting of the migrant population.

The principal explanatory factor is the low productivity of agriculture. Value added per employed person in farming is less than one-fifth of that in all other sectors together. By comparison, the per capita income ratio is about 3 between urban to rural households and about 1.7 between the average wages in urban enterprises compared with township and village enterprises (TVE) (not counting the smallest firms). The income ratio between the nine richest provinces (in the east) and the other 22 provinces is also a little less than 2 (Chart 7.1). With such low productivity in agriculture, the key factor behind inequality is the unequal access to non-farm job opportunities. Contrary to the impression one can get from superficial analysis, this is much more than the simple urban-rural divide. The richest provinces have high proportions of urban population, but that's not all: they also stand out with a high incidence of non-farm employment in rural households.

However, non-farm incomes are important in all provinces, including the poorest. In most provinces, the non-farm share in rural incomes is higher than the non-farm share in rural employment – but not as much higher as one might expect from the likely productivity difference. This is partly due to short working time. The First Agricultural Census in 1997 showed that farmers' participation in the labour market was often quite irregular.

Township and village enterprise wages are about 40% lower than urban wages on average. This probably has several reasons:

- Labour market segmentation due to migration controls, the household registration system *(hukou)*.
- Lower investments in TVEs, due to policies that favour state-owned enterprises (SOEs).
- The rural population has less education.

In other words, the fact that TVEs pay lower wages than urban enterprises may result both from low productivity – due to low education levels and low investment – and from labour market segmentation, related to the migration controls. *Hukou*-related migration controls distort competition between urban and rural labour markets. As noted also in Feng Jianlin's paper (Chapter 2), wages would become more equal if a national labour market could be established, with more circulation of labour. But perhaps education is most important. In conjunction with the information offered in Yin Yanlin's paper (Chapter 3), it is notable that youth with rural *hukou* in general are at a big disadvantage in terms of access to education. Furthermore, if one considers only the urban population, education facilities tend to be much better in big cities compared with smaller ones. Both the impact of migration controls, education and other government policies have probably favoured the big cities over small and medium-sized cities.

The final factor I should mention is social protection. Public income transfers in China are highly concentrated in urban areas. Because the poor provinces tend to be the least urbanised, they receive the least income transfers (Charts 7.2. and 7.3). In OECD countries – as Michael Förster's paper shows (Chapter 8, Table 8.6.) – taxes and public income transfer have a considerable equalising effect on disposable incomes. But the opposite may well be true in China, as in many developing countries. The Chinese papers in this volume suggest that it should be possible to reduce taxes in rural areas. But it is probably not possible to finance more social insurance when incomes are as low as they are in China's agriculture. The most important policy recommendation is perhaps to enhance competition in the markets (Feng Jianlin, Chapter 2). It is not possible to address more than, at best, a small part of China's huge rural poverty problem with social transfers. But the situation could certainly be much improved by policies to enhance competition, both in labour markets, capital markets and product markets. The aim should be to "establish a level playing field" – thus, to give everybody equal chances.

Table 7.1. **Urban and rural average wages, 2001**

China, total in 2001 = 100

	Urban	Township and village enterprise (TVE) (excl. the smallest)	Small rural business
China	**100**	**58**	**50**
Beijing	176	74	67
Tianjin	132	93	81
Zhejiang	151	86	125
Guangdong	144	66	111
Fujian	111	67	28
Jiangsu	109	65	55
Shandong	92	53	39
Liaoning	93	54	42
Heilongjiang	82	45	32
Hubei	79	53	37
Jilin	81	44	44
Hainan	77	47	51
Hunan	89	54	34
Chongqin	88	60	35
Inner Mongolia	76	59	52
Hebei	80	49	60
Xinjiang	95	52	41
Guangxi	83	48	49
Shanxi	75	38	44
Sichuan	91	41	22
Jiangxi	74	46	38
Qinghai	119	34	43
Anhui	73	54	51
Ningxia	96	41	46
Henan	73	45	67
Shaanxi	84	77	32
Yunnan	97	42	46
Gansu	92	38	38
Guizhou	83	48	45

Source: *China Statistical Yearbook*, 2002.

Chart 7.1. **Income ratios for key indicators**

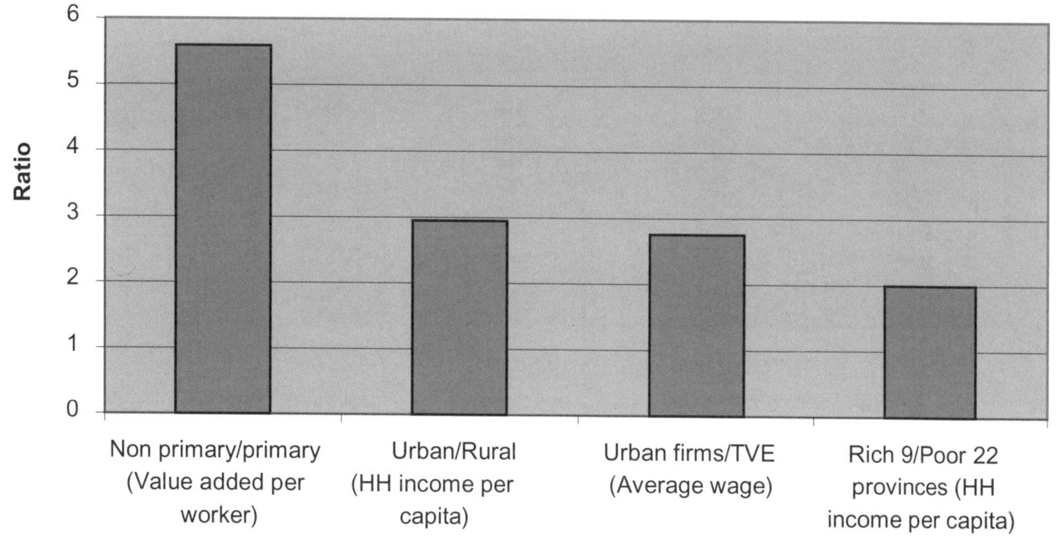

HH: Household; TVE: Township and village enterprises.

Source: *China Statistical Yearbook*, 2002.

Chart 7.2. **Indicators of urbanisation**

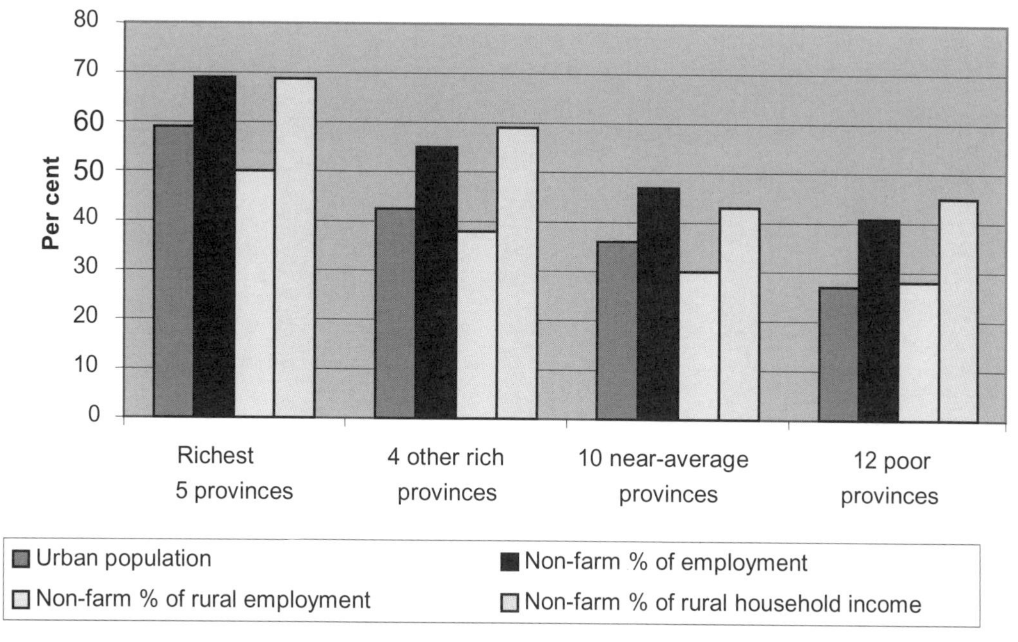

Source: *China Statistical Yearbook*, 2002.

Chart 7.3. **Transfers as a percentage of household income**

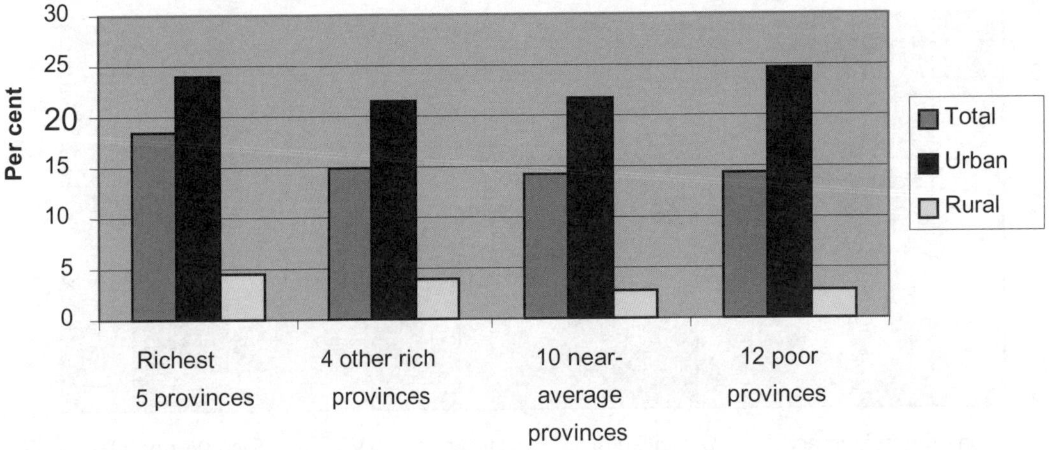

Source: *China Statistical Yearbook*, 2002.

PART II.

INCOME DISPARITIES IN OECD MEMBER COUNTRIES

Chapter 8

TRENDS IN THE DISTRIBUTION OF HOUSEHOLD INCOMES IN THE OECD AREA

by
Michael Förster,

Administrator,
Directorate for Employment, Labour and Social Affairs, OECD

Introduction[1]

There is an increasing literature of national empirical analyses of trends in the distribution of household income in OECD member countries. The main impression gained from these studies is that of broad stability during the decade of the 1970s and increasing polarisation since the 1980s, starting in the Anglo-Saxon countries and followed by many continental European countries in the 1990s. Those studies, however, make use of different definitions and concepts of income and inequality, and often focus particularly on earnings rather than other components of household income. The final distribution of household income (disposable incomes) is the result of a complex set of relationships, including family formation and dissolution, longevity and fertility, as well as the more obvious trends in earnings, transfers, taxes and the returns on capital.

This chapter uses comparable data and definitions to look at 26 OECD countries, a coverage sufficient to determine whether one can truly speak of OECD-wide trends, rather than a few country-specific tendencies. Due to data limitations, the main part of the analyses looks at the period from the mid-1980s to the mid-1990s, for which comparable estimates for all countries are available. The chapter considers the working-age population separately from the retirement-age population. Influences of income components *(e.g.* earnings, transfers) to total inequality differ substantially between those two populations, and considering only the entire population – as is usually the case in inequality analyses – blurs the picture. The same holds for analyses of the effects of taxes and transfers on inequality. When the entire population, including the retirement-age population, is considered, the inequality-decreasing effects of the tax/transfer system will be higher in countries with public pension scheme arrangements. The results therefore reflect partly the extent to which national retirement

1. This chapter draws on the OECD project on income distribution and poverty trends, undertaken between 1997 and 2002, and updated results for additional countries. It summarises and updates two recent OECD publications: "Trends and Driving Factors in Income Distribution and Poverty in the OECD Area" (*OECD Labour Market and Social Policy Occasional Paper,* No. 42, 2000, by Michael Förster and Michele Pellizzari); "Income Distribution and Poverty in the OECD Area: Trends and Driving Forces" (*OECD Economic Studies,* No. 34, 2002/1, pp. 7-39, by Michael Förster and Mark Pearson).

income systems rely on earnings-related social security transfers. It is important to isolate this effect, to understand the way in which transfer systems work.

The second part of this chapter documents levels and recent trends in the overall distribution of disposable household income[2] in OECD countries. It identifies population groups who were among the "winners" and "losers" of relative income changes. The third part analyses the driving forces underlying these trends for the working-age population, including the frequently off-setting trends in the distribution of market-based incomes and the redistributive impact of taxes and transfers. The concluding fourth part assembles 10 stylised facts emerging from this analysis and provides an important context for making policy choices in this difficult area. The conclusion also briefly discusses the relevance of these findings for the Chinese situation.

Main trends in the distribution of disposable incomes

Levels of income inequality in OECD countries

A first question refers to the differing levels of income inequality across OECD countries. The first two columns in Table 8.1 display two commonly used indicators of income inequality in 26 OECD countries in the mid-1990s, the Gini coefficient and the P90/P10 percentile ratio (see Box 8.1 on the definition of income for an explanation of the methodology followed). The values of the Gini coefficient *per se* do not allow assertions as to whether a society is "equal" or "unequal", the extreme cases being 0 ("perfect equality") and 1 ("perfect inequality"). Nevertheless, it is generally perceived that Gini coefficients of around 0.20 to 0.25 describe "equal distributions", while values of 0.30 to 0.35 are perceived as rather unequal distributions, and values in excess as stronger inequalities. The values in Table 8.1 allow to distinguish four groups of countries in terms of increasing levels of inequality:

i. "Lower-inequality" countries with Gini coefficients below 0.26: the Nordic countries (Denmark, Sweden, Finland and Norway), together with Austria, the Czech Republic and the Netherlands. P90/P10 values are below 3, except for the Netherlands

ii. "Rather equal" countries with Gini coefficients between 0.26 and 0.30: most of the remaining continental European countries, together with Japan and Canada. Their P90/P10 values are between 3 and 4, except for Japan (4.4).

iii. "Rather unequal" countries with Gini coefficients between 0.30 and 0.36: the remaining Anglo-Saxon countries (Australia, Ireland, New Zealand, the United Kingdom and the United States), southern European countries (Greece, Italy, Portugal and Spain) and Poland. These countries display P90/P10 values of between 4 and 5, except for the United States (5.5).

iv. "Highly unequal" countries: Mexico and Turkey are clearly outliers in this league table: their Gini coefficients are around 0.50. The distance to the next highest unequal income

2. "Household income" is often used synonymously with "household resources". This is not accurate: households have access to goods and services provided to them at no cost by the state; indirect taxes affect the purchasing power of a given amount of resources; barter, charity and mutual exchange between and within families play a greater or lesser role in different countries. Therefore, the absolute level of measured income inequality or poverty, however interesting, cannot be used to make reliable cross-country comparisons. But trends in income distribution and poverty, if measured on a comparable basis, do permit a number of key findings to be drawn from the analysis.

distribution, that of Portugal, is greater than the distance between Portugal's and Denmark's income distributions.

The (unweighted) OECD average is 0.31 for the Gini coefficient and 4.1 for the P90/P10 ratio. The respective values are 0.29 and 3.7, when Mexico and Turkey are excluded from the average. Differences in levels of inequality across OECD countries are therefore rather pronounced, even when disregarding the two outliers. The most common summary inequality measures, the Gini coefficient and the P90/P10 percentile ratio, are just two possible measures of income concentration and are sensitive to particular points of the income distribution. However, sensitivity analyses using three alternative income inequality indicators – the squared coefficient of variation (SCV), the mean-log deviation (MLD), and the S80/S20 quintile share ratio – suggest that the above-described broad country rankings are robust. For all five summary indicators and two different equivalence scale assumptions, Denmark and Sweden display the lowest levels of inequality, and Turkey and Mexico the highest. In general, the Nordic countries have the lowest inequality levels among OECD countries. This lower-inequality group is joined, according to the indicator, by one or other western European country: Austria, the Netherlands – but also the Czech Republic (especially in the case of percentile ratios and shares). The second central eastern European country, Hungary, clusters together with the remaining western European countries, Canada and Japan around the average, while Poland forms part of the country group with rather unequal distributions, according to all indicators used. Higher inequality levels are also consistently recorded for the Anglo-Saxon countries (especially the United States) and southern Europe (especially Portugal).

Box 8.1. **The definition of income**

The income concept used in this paper is that of equivalent disposable household income per individual. The income unit is the household, defined as a group of persons sharing a set of common resources. Incomes are recorded on an annual basis and all possible types of cash income have been grouped into four categories:

i) Gross earnings: the salary income of the household from dependent employment (excluding employers' contributions to social security, but including sick pay paid by social security).

ii) Gross capital and self-employment incomes: financial gains, real estate rents, occupational pensions and all kinds of private transfers, as well as self-employment incomes (but not including imputed income from owner occupation).

iii) Social security transfers: all kinds of cash transfers from public sources.

iv) Taxes: direct income taxes and employee social security contributions paid by households.

Household disposable income is defined as total market income (I + ii) plus transfers from general government (iii), less income taxes and social security contributions (iv).

The analysis has been conducted for individuals rather than households, and their personal income has been defined as equivalent disposable income and calculated as follows: First, the sum of the disposable incomes of all household members equals household disposable income. Household disposable income then is adjusted for differences in household size to obtain equivalent household disposable income. This adjustment recognises some "economies of scale" of consumption within the household. In particular, household disposable income is divided by the square-root of the number of persons in the household: for example, the equivalent income of a four-person household is household income divided by two. (This is usually referred to as "equivalence-scale elasticity" of 0.5. A higher elasticity value assumes less economies of scale in consumption, until the elasticity value of 1.0 which assumes no economies of scale.) Third, equivalent household income is attributed equally to all individuals in the household, even though the incomes they receive as individuals may be different. Children and spouses are assumed to benefit equally from household income. Finally, individuals are ranked by the (ascending) levels of their equivalent disposable income (Atkinson *et al.,* 1995).

Overall trends in income distribution

Over a longer time-span from the mid-1970s, there has been no clear general trend in final income inequality. Table 8.2 summarises the evidence on trends in the distribution of income, based on the movements in the value of the Gini coefficient. In the eight countries for which a relatively long time span of over two decades can be considered, starting from the mid-1970s, there are four countries where the income distribution widened, three where it narrowed, and it remained stable in the remaining one. In three of the eight countries, movements in the first decade (decline in Finland and Sweden; increase in Australia) tended to be offset by opposite movements in the second. However, there are signs of a more general trend across OECD countries in more recent times. According to the Gini coefficient, from the mid-1980s to the mid-1990s, inequalities decreased only in three of the 23 countries for which trend data are available, remained stable in another six, but increased in the other 14 countries, in a majority of them by considerable amounts. This latter observation does not support, however, the hypothesis of an international "convergence" to common inequality levels. Looking at all available sub-periods, it can be seen that trends in inequality were not systematically related to original levels of inequality across countries, and international divergence persists.

Different measures of inequality can give different results, and a careful reading of Table 8.1 shows that during the earlier sub-period – from the mid-1970s to the mid-1980s – inequality trends among the entire population were diverse but significant: inequality increased unambiguously – *i.e.* all four indicators pointed to a rise – in four of the eight countries for which longer trend data are available. These are shown in bold in Table 8.1. And it decreased unambiguously in another three (values shown in italics). As for the sub-period from the mid-1980s to the mid-1990s, there are more uncertainties. Inequality among the entire population increased unambiguously in 12 of the 26 countries considered and decreased in just two. In all other countries, inequality indicators moved in different directions.[3] This implies at the same time that in no country except Denmark and Spain was an unambiguous trend towards greater income equality recorded during that period. The OECD overall average indicates a slight but unambiguous increase in disposable income inequality for the entire population between the mid-1980s and the mid-1990s.

Of course, real incomes have grown in most countries. In 16 of the 24 countries for which trend data for the second sub-period are available, the mean income of each decile in the mid-1990s lies above that for earlier years. In other words, the bottom 10% in the mid-1990s are better off on average than the bottom 10% in the mid-1980s; the second 10% in the mid-1990s have higher average incomes than their counterparts in the mid-1980s, and so on up the income distribution. This general increase in real mean incomes does not mean, however, that all parts of the income distribution gained in overall prosperity to the same extent. In particular, the general pattern has been that the three lower deciles did not share in overall growth to the same extent as higher decile groups. A more significant and above-average increase of real mean incomes for the lower three income deciles took place only in Belgium, Denmark, France, Ireland and Spain.

Changes in aggregate inequality can hide other trends. If, for instance, groups in the middle deciles lose ground whilst both bottom and top incomes increase their shares, one can speak of a "hollowing out" of the distribution. Table 8.3 shows that this was generally not the case during the period between the mid-1980s and the mid-1990s. A widening of the income distribution could happen if the poor become relatively poorer, the rich have relatively more, or a combination of the two. Table 8.3 suggests that the second of these possibilities has predominated in countries where inequality increased: there has been a trend for those at the top of the income distribution to receive a

3. For two countries, New Zealand and Turkey, only two inequality indicators were available and for Switzerland, no trend data were available.

greater proportion of household income. In 17 of the 24 countries, the top income quintile now has a greater proportion of household income than in the mid-1980s, substantially so in Belgium, the Czech Republic, Finland, Hungary, Italy, Mexico, New Zealand, Portugal and Turkey. Persons at the bottom of the income ladder lost ground slightly, relative to the average in 12 countries, these losses being larger only in Italy.

Both levels and developments in inequality were not the same for the working-age and for the retirement-age population.[4] While in the 1980s, only in a minority of countries was the level of inequality among the retirement-age population lower than that of the working-age population, this was the case of a large majority in the 1990s. Going back even further, in the 1970s, all countries for which this information is available displayed a higher level of inequality among the retirement-age population, with one single exception (Sweden). On OECD average, the Gini coefficient of the retirement-age population exceeded that of the working-age population by almost 1 percentage point in the mid-1980s, while it was 1 percentage point lower in the mid-1990s. Inequality trends therefore seem to have been more favourable for those in their retirement age.

"Winners" and "losers" of relative income changes

The classic life-cycle pattern would predict that income increases when individuals enter working life; continues to rise as individuals gain experience in the labour market and accumulate capital assets and declines when moving into retirement. Broadly speaking, this is indeed the pattern found in most countries. Table 8.4 shows that children are, on average, a little under 10% poorer than the population average.[5] The richest age group are individuals aged 41 to 50 (and indeed this is true in every country, other than Japan, Sweden, Switzerland and the United States). Beyond 65, average incomes are 13% below the population average, falling to 23% below average for those aged over 75.

However, the changes in this distribution have been significant. In nearly all countries people aged 41-50 have seen an increase in incomes relative to the average of all age groups between the mid-1980s and mid-1990s. Even more strikingly, in most countries, elderly age groups also benefited from changes in the income distribution, in particular those just before or just after retirement: relative incomes of those aged 51 to 65 increased by 3 percentage points on average, and relative incomes of those aged 66 to 74 increased by 1 percentage point (a fall in income beyond the age of 65 being found only in Australia, Greece, Ireland, Japan, the Netherlands and, in particular, Mexico and Turkey). However, relative incomes of those aged 75 and over increased by less, if at all. In stark contrast, younger age groups lost ground during the 1990s: relative incomes of children remained at a low level, and those of persons aged 18 to 25 decreased by 4 percentage points.[6] This latter development is linked to delayed labour market entry of younger people, due to longer education periods and/or unemployment.

---

4. In the following, the working-age population refers to individuals aged 18-64, and the retirement-age population to individuals aged 65 and over. This clearly underestimates the retired population in many countries. It has, however, been preferred to choose a standardised upper limit of the age cut-off.

5. It should be noted that "incomes of children" refer to equivalent income of the households of which children are members. These equivalent incomes are then assigned to the respective household members, including children.

6. Care should be taken when interpreting results for this age group. Students' income, for instance, might be counted separately if they live independently, or lumped together with parents' income if they live in a shared household, or not counted in the survey if they live in students' homes.

Within the working-age population, there are large differences in standards of living across different family types. Persons living in households with only one adult generally have lower relative incomes than those living in households with two or more adults (Table 8.5). The gap between the incomes of the two types of households has not become smaller over time. Lone parents have – by far – the lowest relative incomes, usually between half to two-thirds the level of the average income of the entire working-age population. Only in the four Nordic countries, Austria, Belgium, Greece, Hungary, Mexico and Poland, did they have relative incomes above two-thirds of the average. Their income position relative to the rest of the population has declined between the mid-1980s and mid-1990s in half of the countries, in particular in New Zealand and the United Kingdom. Relative incomes of persons living in two-adult households with children did not move very much (less than 2 percentage points up or down) except in Austria, where they increased, and in the Czech Republic, Hungary and Mexico, where they decreased. Those living in two or more adult households without children (the richest family type in all countries) improved their income position in a number of countries, particularly in the Czech Republic, Hungary and Mexico, but lost ground in a few other countries, particularly in Austria and Spain.

These patterns in the distribution of income are replicated to some extent when looking at poverty rates.[7] Taking the average of all countries, people aged under 25 and over 65 have higher than average poverty rates. The only two countries in which poverty rates of all ages increased between the mid-1980s and mid-1990s were the Netherlands and the United Kingdom, and relative poverty declined across all age groups in Australia. Elsewhere, the age profile of poverty has shifted. Overall, whereas the probability of the younger age groups being poor has been rising relative to the average since the mid-1980s for the older age groups, it has been declining generally (particularly in Canada, Denmark, France, Hungary and Poland). At the same time, the number of people in the younger age groups has been declining, and the number of older persons has been rising. As a result, despite a higher proportion of young people having low incomes, the proportion of poor people who are young has not changed much.

Child poverty has risen in about half of all countries, and declined in half. The issue of child poverty has moved sharply up the political agenda in many countries, reflecting much greater concern about the effects of poverty in childhood on future life-chances. It is becoming relatively common for countries to set targets for reducing child poverty. Children are, in general, represented in the poor population as much as in the entire population. The exceptions are the four Nordic countries, with child poverty rates well below the average for the population, and Canada, Hungary, the Netherlands, New Zealand, the United Kingdom and the United States, where child poverty exceeds the average by more than a third. There are some remarkable differences between countries. In Hungary, Italy, Mexico, Turkey, the United Kingdom and the United States, persons in families with children have a considerably higher poverty risk than families without children. The other extreme is Belgium and the four Nordic countries, where childless families are more likely to experience poverty than families with children (Oxley *et al.*, 2001).

On average, single parents are represented three times as often in the poor population than in the working-age population as a whole. This over-representation has however been decreasing over time in about half the countries and this decline was especially notable in Australia, Canada and the four Nordic countries. Poverty rates of single parents, however, remain high in almost all countries studied. In some countries (Germany, Japan, Netherlands, Portugal, Spain, United Kingdom) their poverty rates are as much as four times higher than for the total working-age population. A remarkable

7. Defined in terms of relative low-income: *i.e.* the percentage of persons with incomes below 50% of the median disposable income in each country.

exception is Sweden. In this country, poverty rates for persons living in single-parent households fell significantly during the past 10 to 20 years, and are today at the same low level as for the entire population, and slightly lower than for the working-age population.

Whilst the risk of being poor varies sharply across groups, this information is not enough to give a full picture of poverty. Persons in families with children made up around one-third or less of the poor population in the four Nordic countries and Belgium, but a majority in the other countries, and more than 70% in the Czech Republic, Hungary, Italy, Mexico, Turkey, the United Kingdom and the United States. Single parents are particularly likely to be poor, but they remain a relatively small part of the poor population. Single parents account for 20 to 25% of the poor population in Australia, Austria, Canada, the Czech Republic, the Netherlands, New Zealand, Norway and the United States, and over one-third of those with low incomes in the United Kingdom. On the other hand, their share is below 6% in Greece, Italy, Mexico, Poland, Portugal and Spain, and negligible in Turkey.

Driving factors of changing income distribution

The distribution of income in OECD countries can best be understood as being determined by two factors: differences in market income and the redistributive impact of fiscal and social policy. In policy discussions, most attention is given to the effects of taxes and transfers, *i.e.* how much governments take from one group and give to another. This is indeed of great importance, and there are large differences in the extent of this redistribution of income across countries. However, before looking at how government redistributes income, it is important to understand why it is that some groups have little income other than income transfers, and why others have sufficient incomes for governments to tax them for redistribution.

The analysis in the following two sub-sections is confined to the working-age population, in order to abstract from changes that took place in shares of public and private pensions.[8] These sections explore the extent to which shifts in components of disposable income (market income, transfers and taxes), and trends in employment concentration within and across households, contributed to changes in income inequality. What is particularly interesting is that whereas governments have taken different approaches to redistribution over the past 10 or 20 years (in some countries redistribution has increased, in others it has not), there is a common, underlying trend in the distribution of income before taxes and transfers towards increasing inequality.

Market incomes

- *Market income distribution*

In OECD countries, market incomes are distributed far more unequally than disposable incomes and, moreover, their distribution evolved differently from that of final income. First, the average Gini coefficient of market incomes among the working-age population in the mid-1990s was as high as 0.40, and the range of values between countries was much lower than that for disposable incomes (Table 8.6). Second, there was a clear trend for the distribution of market incomes to become more unequal, until the mid-1990s. With the exception of Finland in the earlier period and Ireland in the latter, this holds for all countries and for both periods of time. On OECD average, the Gini coefficient for market incomes increased by almost 4 percentage points between the mid-1980s and mid-1990s, which is a sizeable increase. For those countries for which longer-term estimates were available, the

8. As public transfers are the main component of income for retired persons in most OECD countries, an increasing transfer share in the incomes of the entire population, and effects on inequality, might simply reflect the increased share of pensioners in the population.

increase in inequality has mainly taken place in the earlier period, the mid-1970s to mid-1980s, exceptions being the Canada, Finland and Sweden, where the main increase took place in the later period.

In many national studies, the distribution of market income in OECD countries has been described as widening, and gross earnings have been identified as the main contributor to increased overall income inequality. Table 8.7 confirms this picture. It shows the allocation market income and its two components – gross earnings and capital/self-employment income – across three income groups among the working-age population: the bottom two deciles ("low incomes"), the six middle deciles ("middle incomes"), and the top two deciles ("high incomes"). The shares of earnings and other market incomes going to the lower incomes are small: the poorest 20% of the population receive between 3 and 8% of total market income in most countries. These shares are lower in Anglo-Saxon countries than in the Nordic countries, Japan and western Europe (Belgium and the Netherlands excepted). While it should not be surprising that very few people in the bottom deciles have much income from capital, it is striking that one-fifth of the working-age population has so little income from labour. This suggests that barriers to working play a critical role in explaining low incomes, a linkage that is examined in greater detail below. In contrast, the richest 20% of the working-age population have something between 40 and 50% of all market income, the exceptions being Mexico and Turkey, where the richer part of the population commands an even greater share of market income, close to 60%. On average, 53% of market income is going to the middle 60%, hence somewhat less than their share in the population.

The distribution patterns differ between the two components of market income: earnings and capital/self-employment income. The latter income source is more concentrated to both extremes of the income distribution, *i.e.* the proportion of capital/self-employment income going to both the poorest and the richest parts of the population is higher than the respective proportions of earnings. As a consequence, the share of capital/self-employment income going to the middle incomes is as low as 43% on OECD average (57% in the case of earnings). This means that these sources of income play a more important role for both richer and poorer people than income from wages and salaries. Furthermore, the trend between the mid-1980s and the mid-1990s has been for the top 20% of the population to receive an ever larger proportion of capital and labour income, the only exceptions being Canada and Ireland. At the same time, those with incomes at the bottom of the distribution have seen a relative decline in market income in all countries (with the same two exceptions); and those in the middle of the distribution in most countries, as well. Among market incomes, the dispersion of capital and self-employment incomes increased particularly rapidly, although country patterns are much more diversified than for earnings.

This pattern of a widening distribution of market income predates the mid-1980s, going back to the 1970s in many, albeit not all, countries. The underlying trend in the distribution of market income has been towards widening, at least until the mid-1990s. Whatever governments have been doing to taxes and transfers in order to make economies and societies more or less equal according to political preferences[9] has been happening against this background of the richer groups getting relatively richer, and the poorer groups receiving relatively less income from their efforts in working or saving.

There have been trends in the economy which have widened the distribution of market incomes. Unemployment was higher in most countries in the mid-1990s than in the mid-1980s and the 1970s. Those with particularly valuable skills in the new economy have been able to command very high rates of remuneration. The rate of return on capital has been high in the 1990s. But these

9. It should be noted that government redistribution is not confined only to taxes and transfers, but also influences market distribution directly, *e.g.* via minimum wage policies.

"explanations" are only part of the story. After all, unemployment may have been high, but because female employment had continued to rise, employment rates were nearly as high as they had ever been. The main contributor to increased overall income inequality has been the distribution of gross earnings across households. The share of earnings going to the lower income groups has fallen in practically all countries. In addition, capital and self-employment income has also become more unequally distributed, although because such income is small in comparison with earnings, the overall effects are less important.

- *The importance of the earnings distribution and employment polarisation*

What, then, has been causing the widening in earnings distribution? An important part of the answer lies in the allocation of employment across and within households. "Work" is becoming more concentrated in some households. In other words, there are more households where all adults are working, more households where no adults are working, and fewer households where there is at least one adult working and one adult not working. This process – the simultaneous increase in both workless and fully employed households – has been described as a process of "employment polarisation" (see, for instance, Gregg and Wadsworth, 1996). OECD (1998) found this process at work in nine out of 11 European OECD member countries. Table 8.8 divides the population where the head of the household is still of working-age into three groups: those where every adult who is present in the household is working; those where no adult in the household is working, and "mixed" households where one adult is working and the other adult(s) is (are) not. The share of those living in households where there is full employment increased in all but seven of the 21 countries for which trend data are available. The share of people in workless households also increased in most countries, and the share of persons in "mixed" households (those with two or more adult households with only one earner) declined in all countries during the period between the mid-1980s and mid-1990s, with the only exceptions being the Czech Republic and Denmark. Overall, the evidence suggests that employment polarisation took place in 10 countries.

Of course, the quantity of work across households is only part of the story. The wage rates that people receive when they work must be added to the equation, in order to explain changes in earnings distribution. Here the story varies across countries. As described in OECD (1996), there has been little common trend across countries in wage rates of those in full-time work. Large increases in earnings dispersion certainly have taken place in some countries (the United Kingdom, the United States), but not in others (Canada, Finland, Germany). But of course trends in earnings are inextricably related to trends in employment. Low-skilled (low-wage) workers are much more likely to be without work than higher-skilled (high-wage) workers.

Consequently, poverty rates for those living in households with two or more earners are very low (under 1% of two-earner households in Austria, Belgium, Denmark, Germany, Norway and Sweden and under 6% in all countries other than Mexico and Turkey, where the poverty rate exceeds 13%), and these rates have been on a downward trend since the 1980s. On the other hand, poverty rates for those in workless households are very high – over 18% in all countries other than Belgium and Denmark, and over 40% in Canada, Germany, Ireland and the United States. The poverty rate of workless households has generally been increasing (but did actually decrease considerably in Australia, Denmark, Norway and Sweden). In most countries, people in workless households are represented three to five times as often in the poor population as in the total working-age population.

The importance of work in explaining income distribution and poverty changes can be seen as the primary cause of many changes in the relative income of particular groups. Why has the position of youth declined? At least in part because employment rates have declined. What explains the very low income of lone parents? The very low employment rates are often the key factor. Hence the striking result referred to above that lone parents in Sweden are not at greater risk of poverty than others in the population is explained mainly by the fact that a large majority of Swedish single parents are working – almost nine out of ten – whereas in most other countries the share of single parents who are working is between 50% and 70%. Poverty rates for single parents who do not work are very high in all countries and, with the exception of Japan, Mexico and Portugal, are at least twice as high as those for working single parents. In Canada, the Czech Republic, Spain, the United Kingdom and the United States, more than 65% of non-working single parents are poor.

Transfers and taxes

Across the income distribution, most household income is market income – income which comes from work, or from the returns to investment. However, governments tax that income, and distribute cash transfers, so altering disposable income. When juxtaposing trends in the distribution of market incomes with trends in the distribution of disposable incomes, it can be seen that in almost all countries, the gains in the shares of the highest income quintile were substantially higher for market income than for disposable income. By contrast, market income shares for the lowest quintile (and most often for both lowest quintiles) declined substantially (exceptions being Ireland and, to a lesser extent, the United States). In a great majority of countries, the workings of tax/transfer systems thus resulted in disposable household incomes falling by less than the fall in market incomes for the shares of the lower quintiles, and in a number of countries the falling trend of market income shares actually was reversed (Australia, Canada, Denmark and France).

- *(Re)distributive patterns of social cash transfers*

Benefit systems in OECD countries redistribute income. But they do not primarily redistribute from rich to poor. Rather, they redistribute from young to old, from those who work to those who do not, and from childless families to families with children. In most countries (Australia and New Zealand being exceptions), most benefits are based not on the income of the individual or family, but on the circumstances of the family and the individuals who make up the family more generally. Even so, the distribution of non-pension transfers altogether was slightly progressive in all OECD countries studied in the mid-1990s – progressive in the sense that higher transfer shares are going to poorer than to richer income groups. In most countries, between one-third and 40% of those transfers went to the lower three decile income groups in the working-age population, and between 20% and 25% to the higher income groups (top three deciles). The progressive pattern was stronger in Australia, Ireland, New Zealand and the United Kingdom, where 50% to 60% went to the lower income groups, and less than 10% to 20% to the higher incomes. These latter countries rely on means-tested benefits to a greater extent than most other countries, so this pattern is not surprising – it simply confirms the effect of these policies in restricting the benefit entitlements of higher-income groups.

Non-pension transfers have become more progressively distributed over the mid-1980s to mid-1990s in a large majority of OECD countries. In most of those countries, the lower three deciles of the income distribution were the sole beneficiaries of this trend, but in a number of countries – Finland, Ireland, Spain and Sweden – middle-income groups also benefited from this trend in distribution. In two southern European countries – Greece and Portugal – and in Japan, the middle-income classes benefited considerably from these changes at the expense of both lower and higher-income groups. Canada and, in particular, Italy and the United States, stand apart. In these countries, a change towards a less progressive distribution of non-pension transfers among the working-age population took place.

Förster and Pellizzari (2000) compared the distribution patterns of two of the most important benefits among non-pension transfers in 14 OECD countries: family cash benefits and unemployment benefits.[10] For family cash benefits, two groups of countries emerge:

- Australia, Canada, Denmark, France, Ireland, the Netherlands, the United Kingdom and the United States all show a progressive distribution of family cash benefits; moreover, most of these countries (the exceptions being Denmark, the Netherlands and the United States) also clearly moved towards a more progressive distribution during the last decade.

- In Austria, Belgium (data for 1995 only), Finland, Hungary, Norway and Sweden in the mid-1980s, family cash benefits seemed to be distributed more equally across the income distribution with an emphasis on the middle class; a distributional pattern sometimes described as "targeted to the middle classes". However, Hungary moved towards a progressive pattern in the 1990s.

By 1995, in all countries considered except Belgium, the proportion of family benefits going to the bottom three deciles was higher than the proportion going to the top three income deciles. Family benefits, therefore, played a role in the redistribution of incomes to lower segments among the working-age population.

As to unemployment benefits, the country patterns are different:

- Unemployment benefits show a clear progressive pattern in seven countries: Australia, Austria, Belgium, Finland, Hungary, Ireland and the United Kingdom. In Hungary, they became considerably more progressively distributed over the years, while their distribution became somewhat less progressive in the United Kingdom. In Ireland, changes favoured lower-middle and middle-income groups, and in Australia and Finland, no significant change occurred.

- In the remaining seven countries, unemployment benefits are almost equally distributed across income groups of the working-age population. This is particularly the case in the Netherlands. In Canada, Norway and Sweden, and, to a lesser degree, Denmark, the distribution of unemployment benefits showed some signs of a "targeting to the middle class": and in France and the United States, the distribution of these benefits moved from such a pattern to a slightly regressive one.

Taken together, family cash benefits seemed to be a more important tool for redistributing incomes from higher to lower segments than unemployment benefits in Canada, Denmark, France, the Netherlands and the United States, whereas the inverse was the case in Austria, Belgium, Finland and Hungary. In Australia, Ireland and the United Kingdom, both benefits played an important redistributive role. Only in Norway and Sweden were both benefits more middle-income class oriented. This has to be seen against the background that, in a majority of the countries considered here, the prime aim of these benefits is not a redistribution of incomes towards lower income groups, but the maintenance of the income status in case of child-rearing and compensation for loss of employment, regardless of income status.

---

10. Other cash transfers going to the working-age population, such as housing benefits or social assistance payments, have not been included in the detailed analysis, because information often was not available separately; lumped together, these "other" transfers constitute approximately 10% to 20% of all non-pension transfers in most countries (30% in Sweden and the United Kingdom).

- *Overall effects of tax/transfers among the working-age population*

Just because a benefit system is not progressive does not mean that it plays no role in redistributing income. Poor households (by definition) have less other income than richer ones, so the higher the level of a benefit, the greater will be the reduction in inequality, even if everyone receives exactly the same amount of benefit. It follows that just because a benefit system is not particularly targeted on the poor, it cannot be concluded that the effects on inequality (and poverty) are necessarily small.

Table 8.9 summarises the distribution of all benefit payments taken together, with tax payments and social security contributions of employees across the income distribution of the working-age population. On average, the bottom 20% of the population do get more than 20% of total benefit payments, but not by much. The top 20% of the population get, on average, 15% of all benefits. In other words, the benefit system does not have a very different effect on final income inequality from paying everyone in the population a fixed amount of benefit, regardless of income level. Of course, averages hide a lot of cross-country variation. The Anglo-Saxon and some of the Nordic countries, as well as the Netherlands, target payments towards the poorer end of the distribution to a much greater extent than Austria, Greece, Hungary, Italy, Japan, Poland, Portugal, Spain and Switzerland, where the poorest 20% of the population receive less than 20% of all benefit payments. In Turkey and Mexico, benefits are even more likely to be targeted towards richer groups, reflecting "dual" labour markets – individuals have to be in the "modern" sectors of the economy to qualify for social insurance.

Taxes, on the other hand, are very strongly related to income. Of course, this is not the full story as regards taxes – the figures in the table exclude consumption taxes and social security contributions paid by employers, both of which bear much more heavily on lower income groups than the personal income taxes and employee social security contributions which are included. But nevertheless, it is readily apparent that direct income taxes have a great effect in equalising incomes across households. The trend has been towards a greater share of taxation being paid by higher income groups. This is not the same as saying that there is greater progressivity in the tax system than previously. In fact, only in a few countries has the share of taxes paid by the top 30% gone up significantly more rapidly than market income. In the Nordic countries, the increases in taxes paid by the upper income groups were less than the increase in their market incomes – in other words, their average tax rate fell relative to lower income groups.

The analysis above referred to the distribution of a given overall level of non-pension transfers among the working-age population. However, although a specific transfer might be distributed more progressively in one country than in another, its weight for the lower income groups might be higher in another country because of a higher overall level of this transfer. An equally important question therefore concerns the relative importance of those transfer payments in the disposable incomes of lower, middle and higher income groups. Förster and Pellizzari (2000) analysed non-pension transfer shares in the disposable income of income groups. These shares rose for the working-age population as a whole in the last ten years, from below 10% on average, to 11.4%. The increase for the lower income groups, however, was much stronger: it varied on average across the countries from around one-quarter of their disposable income to around one-third. Those increases were recorded in all countries, but were strongest in the four Nordic countries (where more than 10 percentage point increases were recorded). This underlines the growing importance of non-pension transfers for the lower income groups of the working-age population.

Underlying demographic changes

Putting the two pieces of the equation together – trends in market income and trends in government tax and transfer policy – gives most of the information necessary to understand the overall picture of income distribution. One last piece of the jigsaw puzzle remains to be inserted: changes in the demographic structure of the population. There are considerable differences between countries and country groups as to the levels of these shares: in the Nordic and the continental European countries, children make up 20% of the population; in the Anglo-Saxon countries, they account for around 25%, and in Mexico and Turkey, the share of children in the population is much higher, around 40%. At the same time, there have been very large changes in the structure of populations in OECD countries. In nearly all countries, the proportion of children in the total population decreased from the mid-1980s to the mid-1990s, on average by some 2 percentage points. Similarly, the share of young people – those aged 18 to 25 – fell in most countries, on average by 1 percentage point. On the other hand, the proportion of persons aged 65 and over increased in all countries except Sweden, on average by over 1 percentage point (Förster and Pearson, 2002).

The changes do not stop there. The fewer children are much more likely to be in households where there is only one adult – the proportion of lone-parent families has been increasing. In the Anglo-Saxon countries and the Nordic countries, between 10 and 20% of those in households with children live in lone-parent households. In the continental European countries, their share is just below 10%, and in the southern European countries, Turkey and Mexico, below 5%. The proportion of children who are in lone-parent households rather than households with two or more adults has also been rising, and is around 25% of the total in Sweden. Within the working-age population, fewer people live in households without children than in households with children, but their share increased from one-third to almost 40% in the ten years from the mid-1980s to the mid-1990s.

Furthermore, mainly as a consequence of population ageing (but also reflecting an increased preference for living alone among younger age groups), the average household size has also been falling for the last 10 to 20 years throughout the OECD area, and is close to being just two people in some of the Nordic and continental European countries. The average household size is closer to three in the southern European countries, and still above four in Mexico and Turkey.

Such changes may not sound very significant. In fact, taken together they amount to a huge change in the structure of the population, in many countries to an extent unprecedented in recent times outside of war, famine or epidemic. Here, it is worth noting simply that these demographic trends directly affect trends in inequality. If older people have less income than younger people, then as there are more of them in the population, so income distribution will apparently widen. Similarly, if small households are poorer than large ones, so will the trends described above lead to a stretching out of the income distribution, regardless of whether the average income of small households is changing relative to larger ones. Finally, differences in living arrangements across countries, *e.g.* a lower or higher share of multi-generational households, can also affect the results of how redistributive social security systems appear.

Conclusions

Ten stylised facts on trends in income inequality in the OECD area

Overall distributional trends:

1) There has been no generalised long-term trend in the distribution of disposable household incomes since the mid-1970s; neither has there been a convergence across OECD countries

towards similar levels of income inequality. However, during the period from the mid-1980s to the mid-1990s, income inequality has increased in a greater number of countries, while only two of the OECD countries recorded an unambiguous decrease in inequality.

2) There was no trend towards a "hollowing out" of the income distribution at the expense of the middle-income class. Rather, there has been a trend for those at the top of the income distribution to receive a greater proportion of household income in a majority of OECD countries.

Changes in the relative positions of specific social groups:

3) In those countries where inequalities increased, this happened mostly among the working-age population, whilst there were fewer changes among the retirement-age population.

4) Changes in income distribution between the mid-1980s and mid-1990s generally favoured the prime-age and elderly age groups, particularly those around retirement age. Younger age groups lost ground, in particular those aged 18 to 25, reflecting delayed labour market entry. Similarly, poverty rates for the elderly fell in a large majority of countries, youth poverty rates increased, and child poverty rates increased slightly in a number of countries.

5) Relative income levels of single parents and persons in workless households are very low and have worsened in a number of countries.

Driving factors:

6) Market income inequality has widened in almost every country until the mid-1990s. The increased dispersion from gross earnings has been the main cause. A variety of factors have explained this, in turn, increased inequality in earnings and a trend towards "employment polarisation" in many countries, leading to a simultaneous increase in "work-rich" and "work-poor" shares of households.

7) Capital and self-employment incomes are distributed more unequally than earnings. However, as their share in total disposable income is lower, their contribution to levels and, in most cases, changes in overall inequality, is less important than that of earnings.

Distributional effects of public transfers and taxes:

8) The effectiveness of taxes and transfers in reducing inequality and poverty has increased. As a result, the increase in market income inequality was not, or not entirely, translated into higher inequality of disposable incomes for the working-age population.

9) Targeting of benefits has increased. The shares of family cash benefits and/or unemployment benefits going to lower income groups among the working-age population increased in a majority of countries.

10) Non-pension social transfers form an increasingly large part of the income of low-income households among the working-age population in all countries.

Relevance of the OECD experience for China

To what extent are the experiences of OECD countries with regard to income inequality trends relevant for the current situation and development in China? First, the continuing diversity in levels of household income inequality across OECD countries suggests that, apart from (international and national) economic forces and demographic changes, political preferences also play an important role in outcomes in terms of income disparities. There are no "natural" levels of income inequality corresponding to specific stages in the development of a market economy. Second, and in line with recent experiences in China, disparities in the distribution of gross market incomes have increased in all OECD countries during the past 10 to 20 years, but specifically during the 1990s – the main component having been increased earnings inequality. Third, and perhaps most in contrast to the current situation in China, the contribution of fiscal and social policies through income taxes and social cash transfers was to equalise substantially the income distribution in all OECD countries, and increasingly so in most OECD countries.

BIBLIOGRAPHY

Atkinson, A.B., L. Rainwater and T.M. Smeeding (1995), "Income Distribution in OECD Countries, Evidence from the Luxembourg Income Study", *Income Distribution in OECD Countries*, OECD Social Policy Studies, No. 18, OECD, Paris.

Förster, M. and M. Pearson (2002), "Income Distribution and Poverty in the OECD Area: Trends and Driving Forces", *OECD Economic Studies,* No. 34, OECD, Paris.

Förster, M., assisted by M. Pellizzari (2000), "Trends and Driving Factors in Income Inequality and Poverty in the OECD Area", *OECD Labour Market and Social Policy Occasional Papers*, No. 42, OECD, Paris.

Gregg, P. and J. Wadsworth (1996), "It Takes Two: Employment Polarisation in the OECD", *Centre for Economic Performance Discussion Papers*, No. 304, London.

OECD (1996), *Employment Outlook*, OECD, Paris.

OECD (1998), *Employment Outlook*, OECD, Paris.

OECD (1999), *A Caring World – The New Social Policy Agenda*, Chapter 3: "The Distribution of Income", OECD, Paris.

OECD (2001), *Employment Outlook*, OECD, Paris.

Oxley, H., T.-T. Dang, M. Förster and M. Pellizzari (2001), "Income Inequality and Poverty Among Children and Households with Children in Selected OECD Countries: Trends and Determinants", in Smeeding and Vleminckx (eds.), *Child Well-being, Child Poverty and Child Policy in Modern Nations: What Do We Know?*, The Policy Press, Bristol, pp. 371-405.

Table 8.1. **Levels and trends in four income inequality indicators for the entire population**

	Levels, mid-1990s		Absolute change							
	Gini coefficient	P90/ P10 ratio	Gini		P90/P10 Decile ratio		Squarred coefficient variation (SCV)		Mean log deviation (MLD)	
			A	B	A	B	A	B	A	B
Australia	30.5	3.9	**2.1**	-0.7	**0.2**	-0.4	**3.2**	1.2	**1.8**	0.5
Austria	23.8	3.0	..	0.2	..	0.1	..	1.4	..	-0.2
Belgium	27.2	3.2	..	1.2	..	-0.0	..	9.1	..	0.4
Canada	28.3	3.6	-0.8	-0.4	-0.6	-0.2	4.0	0.7	-2.5	-1.0
Czech Republic	25.7	2.9	..	**2.6**	..	**0.4**	..	**17.1**	..	**2.8**
Denmark	21.3	2.6	..	*-1.6*	..	*-0.2*	..	*-6.2*	..	*-1.7*
Finland	22.8	2.8	*-2.8*	**2.1**	*-0.5*	**0.1**	*-3.7*	**7.8**	*-3.0*	**1.2**
France	27.8	3.4	..	0.3	..	0.1	..	6.9	..	-0.8
Germany	28.2	3.7	..	..	..	..	..	..	..	..
Germany, old *Länder*	28.0	3.5	..	1.7	..	0.4	..	-2.2	..	1.6
Greece	33.6	4.7	*-7.7*	0.0	*-2.1*	-0.2	*-47.9*	1.1	*-11.5*	-0.3
Hungary	29.4	3.5	..	**2.1**	..	**0.3**	..	**12.1**	..	**1.7**
Ireland	32.4	4.2	..	-0.6	..	-0.1	..	32.0	..	-3.0
Italy	34.8	4.8	..	**4.2**	..	**0.9**	..	**29.6**	..	**7.6**
Japan	29.5	4.4	..	**1.2**	..	**0.2**	..	**5.3**	..	**1.5**
Mexico	52.0	10.9	..	**6.3**	..	**2.2**	..	**154.0**	..	**11.8**
Netherlands	25.5	3.2	**0.7**	**2.1**	**0.1**	**0.4**	**2.7**	**2.5**	**0.6**	**2.3**
New Zealand	33.1	4.0	..	**6.1**	..	**0.6**	..	..	..	..
Norway	25.6	3.0	..	**2.2**	..	**0.1**	..	**2.3**	..	**3.1**
Poland	34.8	4.4	..	..	..	..	..	..	..	..
Portugal	35.9	5.1	..	**3.0**	..	**0.4**	..	**14.5**	..	**3.6**
Spain	30.3	4.1	..	*-2.5*	..	*-0.8*	..	*-41.7*	..	*-5.6*
Sweden	21.1	2.5	*-1.6*	1.4	*-0.2*	-0.2	*-2.1*	8.0	*-1.8*	2.0
Switzerland	29.1	3.5	..	..	..	..	..	..	..	..
Turkey	49.1	6.8	..	5.6	..	0.3	..	..	..	..
United Kingdom	31.2	4.1	**3.8**	**2.5**	**0.5**	**0.5**	**10.3**	**8.6**	**3.1**	**3.0**
United States	34.4	5.5	**2.7**	0.4	**0.8**	-0.2	**7.7**	1.2	**3.2**	0.5

Note: Absolute change is the difference in the value of the index. A = Mid-1970s to mid-1980s. B = Mid-1980s to mid-1990s (except for Czech Republic, Hungary and Portugal: early to mid-1990s). Values for Gini coefficients multiplied with 100.

Source: Calculations from OECD questionnaire on distribution of household incomes.

Table 8.2. **Overall trends in income inequality: summary results for the entire population**

	Down a lot	**Down**	**Down a bit**	**No change**	**Up a bit**	**Up**	**Up a lot**
Mid-1970s to mid-1990s	Greece		Canada Finland	Sweden	Australia	Netherlands United States	United Kingdom
Mid-1970s to mid-1980s	Greece	Finland Sweden	Canada		Netherlands	Australia United States	United Kingdom
Mid-1980s to mid-1990s		Spain	Australia Denmark	Austria Canada France Greece Ireland United States	Belgium Germany Japan Sweden	Czech Republic Finland Hungary Netherlands Norway Portugal United Kingdom	Italy Mexico New Zealand Turkey

Note:

Up a lot: significant rise in income inequality (more than 12% increase).
Up: rise in income inequality (7 to 12% increase).
Up a bit: modest rise in income inequality (2 to 7% increase).
No change: -2% to +2% change.
Down a bit: modest decrease in income inequality (2 to 7% decrease).
Down: decrease in income inequality (7 to 12% decrease).
Down a lot: significant decrease in income inequality (more than 12% decrease).

No comparable data is available for countries not included.

The results are based on the values of the Gini coefficient for all countries in three reference years which may vary among countries. For the Czech Republic, Hungary and Portugal, the period mid-1980s to mid-1990s refers to early to mid-1990s. Results for Germany refer to western *Länder*.

Source: Calculations from OECD questionnaire on distribution of household incomes.

Table 8.3. **Gains and losses of income share by income quintile: entire population, mid-1980s to mid-1990s**

	Bottom quintile	Middle quintiles	Top quintile
Australia	=	=	=
Austria	=	=	=
Belgium	=	---	+++
Canada	=	=	=
Czech Republic	-	-	+++
Denmark	+	+	-
Finland	=	---	+++
France	=	-	+
Germany	-	=	+
Greece	=	=	=
Hungary	-	-	+++
Ireland	+	=	=
Italy	---	-	+++
Japan	-	=	+
Mexico	-	---	+++
Netherlands	-	=	+
New Zealand	-	---	+++
Norway	-	-	+
Portugal	-	---	+++
Spain	+	+	---
Sweden	-	=	+
Turkey	-	---	+++
United Kingdom	-	-	+
United States	=	-	+

Note:
+ increase of between half and 1.5 percentage point.
+++ increase of more than 1.5 percentage points in the share of final disposable income received by the decile group.
= -0.5 to +0.5 percentage point change.
- decrease of between half and 1.5 percentage point.
--- decrease of more than 1.5 percentage points.
The results are based on percentage point changes of quintile shares in disposable income. For the Czech Republic, Hungary and Portugal, the period mid-1980s to mid-1990s refers to early to mid-1990s. Results for Germany refer to western *Länder*.

Source: Calculations from OECD questionnaire on distribution of household incomes.

Table 8.4. **Relative disposable incomes, by age groups (average income of entire population = 100)**

	Age 0-17	Age 18-25	Age 26-40	Age 41-50	Age 51-65	Age 65-75	Age 75+
Australia, 1984	87	130	..	107	..	72	..
Australia, 1994	86	122	..	112	..	68	..
Austria, 1983	90	110	104	117	109	82	79
Austria, 1993	90	109	101	116	108	91	80
Belgium, 1995	105	83	102	118	108	83	71
Canada, 1985	88	102	103	116	110	91	84
Canada, 1995	88	100	100	114	114	99	95
Czech Republic, 1992	99	110	103	117	95	72	71
Czech Republic, 1996	94	114	102	118	103	73	71
Denmark, 1983	99	102	110	116	103	75	66
Denmark, 1994	100	95	104	120	108	78	69
Finland, 1986	98	97	103	116	103	80	74
Finland, 1995	101	88	102	114	108	82	75
France, 1984	95	102	106	112	103	86	82
France, 1994	95	97	100	115	109	94	82
Germany, 1984	93	98	102	113	109	85	81
Germany, 1994	91	96	99	118	110	93	77
Greece, 1988	94	104	108	111	102	84	79
Greece, 1994	98	104	110	113	100	80	72
Hungary, 1991	100	109	104	116	98	79	77
Hungary, 1995	93	111	102	119	101	85	78
Ireland, 1987	87	130	105	103	112	85	83
Ireland, 1994	89	117	109	112	111	77	71
Italy, 1984	90	107	106	106	108	82	78
Italy, 1993	87	105	105	107	111	88	83
Japan, 1985	92	108	96	108	111	91	92
Japan, 1994	91	106	98	109	113	90	87
Mexico, 1984	88	114	113	108	114	110	84
Mexico, 1994	84	110	117	131	124	94	77
Netherlands, 1984	89	104	102	109	112	93	84
Netherlands, 1995	89	97	105	114	112	90	79
New Zealand, 1986	84	121	102	116	112	84	72
New Zealand, 1996	83	112	103	129	113	75	76
Norway, 1986	97	105	104	118	109	78	60
Norway, 1995	98	94	101	120	117	84	61
Poland, 1995	87	97	113	101	94	86	103
Portugal, 1990	95	110	110	112	101	76	73
Portugal, 1995	94	107	110	115	104	77	68
Spain, 1985	92	102	112	101	104	88	93
Spain, 1995	93	101	108	111	103	86	95
Sweden, 1983	101	71	105	119	119	91	70
Sweden, 1995	99	60	100	120	127	96	78
Switzerland, 1998	84	105	101	108	120	94	80

Table 8.4. **Relative disposable incomes, by age groups (average income of entire population = 100)** (contd.)

	Age 0-17	Age 18-25	Age 26-40	Age 41-50	Age 51-65	Age 65-75	Age 75+
Turkey, 1987	89	109	100	117	116	103	106
Turkey, 1994	85	111	103	127	119	89	102
United Kingdom, 1985	90	114	105	124	105	74	72
United Kingdom, 1995	86	112	106	123	108	80	74
United States, 1985	82	99	104	118	121	99	84
United States, 1995	84	94	102	118	124	99	82
Average 22, mid-1980s	92	106	105	113	108	86	79
Average 22, mid-1990s	92	102	104	117	111	87	79

Note: For Australia, the group "41-50" refers to age 26-65, and the group "65-75" to age above 65. For calculating relative income changes, population shares have been kept constant at the beginning of the period. Australia, Belgium, Poland and Switzerland excluded from averages. Data for Germany refer to western *Länder*.

Source: Calculations from OECD questionnaire on distribution of household incomes.

Table 8.5. **Relative disposable incomes, by family types (average income of working-age population = 100)**

	Single adult, with children	Single adult, no children	Two adults, with children	Two adults, no children
Australia, 1984	53	99	92	131
Australia, 1994	57	92	93	129
Austria, 1983	63	93	95	121
Austria, 1993	87	85	98	110
Belgium, 1995	70	80	107	113
Canada, 1985	50	90	94	121
Canada, 1995	55	84	93	122
Czech Republic, 1992	64	74	101	107
Czech Republic, 1996	63	80	97	115
Denmark, 1983	67	78	99	110
Denmark, 1994	67	73	99	112
Finland, 1986	75	75	100	113
Finland, 1995	76	75	100	112
France, 1984	73	95	96	113
France, 1994	66	94	97	113
Germany, 1984	55	87	95	113
Germany, 1994	57	90	95	112
Greece, 1988	68	104	95	112
Greece, 1994	82	98	97	107
Hungary, 1991	69	68	100	109
Hungary, 1995	74	83	96	115
Italy, 1984	57	97	91	118
Italy, 1993	57	94	90	120
Japan, 1985	57	81	94	117
Japan, 1994	53	87	93	118
Mexico, 1984	65	133	97	160
Mexico, 1994	72	143	94	191
Netherlands, 1984	60	90	92	121
Netherlands, 1995	55	80	93	123
New Zealand, 1986	60	93	91	135
New Zealand, 1996	50	97	93	133
Norway, 1986	65	81	99	115
Norway, 1995	67	73	99	117
Poland, 1995	72	75	100	103
Portugal, 1990	65	77	97	112
Portugal, 1995	60	108	96	114
Spain, 1985	57	119	94	122
Spain, 1995	51	115	96	115
Sweden, 1983	78	78	103	128
Sweden, 1995	74	83	101	129

Table 8.5. **Relative disposable incomes, by family types (average income of working-age population = 100)** (contd.)

	Single adult, with children	**Single adult, no children**	**Two adults, with children**	**Two adults, no children**
Switzerland, 1998	68	102	86	126
United Kingdom, 1985	59	87	94	124
United Kingdom, 1995	51	92	93	127
United States, 1985	46	100	92	130
United States, 1995	49	99	93	127
Average 21, mid-1980s	63	90	96	121
Average 21, mid 1990s	63	92	96	122

Note: Two adults refer to two and more adults. For calculating relative income changes, population shares have been kept constant at the beginning of the period. No data are available for Ireland and Turkey. Averages exclude Belgium, Poland and Switzerland. Data for Germany refer to western *Länder*

Source: Calculations from OECD questionnaire on distribution of household incomes.

Table 8.6. **Levels and trends in market income inequality**

Gini coefficients of market income concentration, working-age population

	Levels, mid-1990s	Changes mid-1970s to mid-1980s	Changes mid-1980s to mid-1990s
Australia	42.3	6.5	3.4
Belgium	46.9		
Canada	39.0	1.9	2.3
Czech Republic	37.1		
Denmark	34.8		5.2
Finland	38.2	-1.4	7.6
France	41.4		2.2
Germany	36.6		0.2
Ireland	44.6		-0.5
Italy	46.4		7.2
Japan	33.8		2.9
Netherlands	37.7	4.4	0.4
New Zealand	42.8		6.6
Norway	34.1		4.7
Portugal	43.1		3.5
Sweden	37.4	0.2	6.9
Switzerland	33.6		
United Kingdom	42.4	7.7	3.4
United States	41.3	3.3	1.6
Average 16	**39.7**		**3.7**

Note: Absolute change refers to the difference in the value of the Gini coefficient. Values for Gini coefficients multiplied with 100. Data for Germany refer to western *Länder*. Average exclude Belgium, Czech Republic and Switzerland.

Source: Calculations from OECD questionnaire on distribution of household incomes.

Table 8.7. **Distribution of market income: proportion of different sources of income received by different income groups of the working-age population**

	Share of earnings, mid-1990s			**Share of capital and self-employment income, mid-1990s**			**Share of total market income, mid-1990s**		
	Poorest 20%	Middle 60%	Richest 20%	Poorest 20%	Middle 60%	Richest 20%	Poorest 20%	Middle 60%	Richest 20%
Australia	1.8	72.6	25.6	6.7	50.1	43.3	2.5	54.1	43.4
Belgium	3.3	57.7	39.1	4.3	28.1	67.6	3.5	51.2	45.3
Canada	4.5	56.5	39.0	6.4	42.1	51.5	4.8	54.2	41.0
Czech Republic	6.1	57.4	36.5	4.9	30.2	64.9	5.9	52.8	41.3
Denmark	4.3	58.0	37.6	8.0	42.6	49.5	4.8	56.1	39.1
Finland	3.3	55.2	41.5	10.2	50.4	39.4	5.0	54.0	41.0
France	5.4	54.6	40.0	7.9	31.7	60.4	5.8	51.3	42.9
Germany	6.2	56.4	37.4	6.4	43.4	50.1	6.2	54.8	39.0
Greece	4.4	57.4	38.2	8.6	46.0	45.3	6.3	52.1	41.5
Hungary	4.5	52.8	42.8	5.2	40.3	54.5	4.7	49.3	46.0
Ireland	1.7	53.6	44.6	5.5	39.1	55.4	2.6	50.5	46.9
Italy	5.2	59.2	35.6	3.9	29.8	66.3	4.8	49.6	45.6
Japan	5.1	56.2	38.7	16.0	47.6	36.4	6.4	55.2	38.4
Mexico	2.8	40.7	56.5	5.1	35.5	59.4	3.5	39.1	57.4
Netherlands	4.2	57.8	38.0	5.0	47.3	47.7	4.3	56.2	39.5
New Zealand	3.2	55.5	41.3	5.2	36.9	57.8	3.6	51.5	44.8
Norway	5.4	61.1	33.6	4.5	33.8	61.7	5.2	55.9	38.9
Poland	5.9	59.7	34.4	3.5	29.5	67.0	4.9	47.9	47.2
Portugal	4.3	49.8	45.9	8.9	47.9	43.3	5.5	49.3	45.2
Spain	5.9	59.7	34.4	3.5	29.5	67.0	4.9	47.9	47.2
Sweden	5.2	56.6	38.2	9.4	43.5	47.0	5.6	55.4	39.0
Switzerland	6.8	56.8	36.4	14.0	42.3	43.7	7.8	54.7	37.5
Turkey	6.9	54.8	38.3	3.4	29.0	67.6	4.5	37.5	58.0
United Kingdom	2.9	54.3	42.7	5.5	44.9	49.6	3.4	52.5	44.0
United States	4.1	53.9	42.0	4.8	40.6	54.6	4.2	52.1	43.7
Average (16)	**4.2**	**56.8**	**39.0**	**7.7**	**43.4**	**49.0**	**4.8**	**53.3**	**41.9**
Change mid-1980s to mid-1990s	-1.0	0.1	1.0	-1.6	-0.8	2.5	-1.1	-1.2	2.2

Note: Data for Greece, Hungary, Mexico, Poland, Spain and Turkey refer to market incomes net of taxes and are therefore not entirely comparable with the results from the other countries. They are excluded from the average. For calculating the average of percentage point changes, Belgium, the Czech Republic and Switzerland have also been excluded, due to lack of mid-1980s data. Income groups were built on the basis of final disposable adjusted income.

Source: Calculations from OECD questionnaire on distribution of household incomes.

Table 8.8. **Changes in household employment concentration**

Percentage point change in the distribution of working-age households

	Population shares		
	Fully employed	**Workless**	**"Mixed"**
Australia, 1984-1994	5.2	1.7	-7.0
Austria, 1983-1993	13.7	0.6	-14.4
Canada, 1985-1995	1.9	1.9	-3.8
Czech Republic, 1992-1996	-1.5	-0.2	1.6
Denmark, 1983-1994	-3.1	2.3	0.7
Finland, 1986-1995	-0.8	4.1	-3.3
France, 1984-1994	4.1	1.1	-5.2
Germany, 1984-1994	0.1	1.4	-1.5
Greece, 1988-1994	8.4	-1.3	-7.1
Hungary, 1991-1995	-1.5	1.8	-0.3
Italy, 1984-1993	-0.2	5.5	-5.4
Japan, 1985-1994	0.9	1.6	-2.6
Mexico, 1989-1994	7.8	-0.1	-7.7
Netherlands, 1984-1995	14.4	1.6	-16.1
New Zealand	-4.1	5.8	-1.8
Norway, 1986-1995	2.0	4.8	-6.8
Portugal, 1990-1995	7.2	0.1	-7.3
Spain, 1985-1995	11.2	-0.4	-10.7
Sweden, 1983-1995	-1.2	3.4	-2.2
United Kingdom, 1985-1995	4.8	0.6	-5.4
United States, 1985-1995	3.1	-0.6	-2.5
Average change	3.5	1.7	-5.2
Average levels mid-1990s	63.7	9.6	26.7

Note: "Fully employed households" are households in which all adult persons have an employment; "workless households" households in which no person is employed; and "mixed households" two or more adult households with only one earner. Data refer to households with a head of working-age. Changes are percentage point changes.

Source: Calculations from OECD questionnaire on distribution of household incomes.

Table 8.9. **Redistribution by government: proportion of total transfers (taxes) received (paid) by different income deciles of the working-age population**

	General government transfers			Taxes		
	Poorest 20%	Middle 60%	Richest 20%	Poorest 20%	Middle 60%	Richest 20%
Distribution of benefits received and taxes paid, mid-1990s						
Australia	45.3	51.7	3.1	0.8	46.8	52.3
Austria	17.5	62.3	20.2	..	..	..
Belgium	21.9	63.4	14.7	1.3	49.4	49.3
Canada	26.2	56.9	16.9	3.7	51.4	44.9
Czech Republic	31.4	58.9	9.7	4.3	50.0	45.6
Denmark	30.5	60.2	9.3	7.0	55.1	37.9
Finland	29.8	60.7	9.5	5.0	51.1	43.9
France	24.2	58.7	17.1	5.9	37.2	56.8
Germany	20.7	57.9	21.4	4.7	54.8	40.6
Greece	13.4	57.0	29.6	..	..	..
Hungary	18.8	62.0	19.3	..	..	..
Ireland	31.5	59.7	8.8	1.3	47.3	51.4
Italy	10.0	60.1	29.9	3.6	48.1	48.3
Japan	18.7	61.1	20.2	6.4	51.5	42.1
Mexico	7.6	46.0	46.4	..	..	..
Netherlands	34.6	54.4	11.0	6.1	54.6	39.3
New Zealand	37.9	57.4	4.8	1.9	49.9	48.2
Norway	31.4	57.4	11.2	4.7	54.5	40.8
Poland	13.3	65.4	21.3	..	..	..
Portugal	14.0	50.0	36.0	3.8	39.5	56.6
Spain	17.8	61.4	20.8	..	..	..
Sweden	26.1	59.9	14.0	7.1	53.9	39.0
Switzerland	18.9	59.9	21.2	11.3	54.5	34.2
Turkey	8.0	60.1	31.9	..	..	..
United Kingdom	38.8	54.9	6.3	2.6	48.6	48.8
United States	29.7	54.1	16.2	2.8	45.6	51.6
Average, 16	**28.1**	**56.9**	**15.0**	**4.2**	**49.6**	**46.2**
Average change mid-1980s to mid-1990s	0.0	-0.1	0.1	-1.1	-2.0	3.2

Note: General government transfers include all public cash transfer benefits. Taxes include all direct income taxes, including employees' social security contributions. Averages exclude Greece, Hungary, Mexico, Poland, Spain and Turkey (no tax data available), as well as Belgium, Czech Republic and Switzerland (no trend data available). Income groups were built on the basis of final disposable adjusted income. Income groups were built on the basis of final disposable adjusted income.

Source: Calculations from OECD questionnaire on distribution of household incomes.

ANNEX 8.A.1. PER-CAPITA OR EQUIVALISED HOUSEHOLD INCOME: DOES IT MATTER FOR INCOME INEQUALITY ESTIMATES?

Estimates of income inequality in China are usually based on per capita household incomes. This contrasts with the common use of household-size adjusted (or "equivalised") income for micro-economic comparisons across and within most OECD countries. Therefore, this Annex considers the question to what extent the use of these different income concepts influences the results and distorts comparisons between the OECD and China.

It can be assumed that household resource needs grow with each additional member, but, due to economies of scale, not in a proportional way. Needs for housing, electricity, etc. will not be three times as much for a household with three members, as for a single person. With the help of equivalence scales, each household type in the population is assigned a value in proportion to its needs. The factors commonly taken into account to assign these values are the size of the household and its age-structure (whether adults or children). Ideally, sophisticated equivalence scales would also consider the different ages of adults and children themselves, as well as other factors, such as health status or region.

Using household size as the sole determinant, equivalence scales can be expressed by one single parameter, the equivalence elasticity, *i.e.* the power by which economic needs increase as the household size increases:

$$N = S^e \text{ , or}$$

$$e = \frac{\ln(N)}{\ln(S)}, \quad 0 \leq e \leq 1$$

where e: equivalence elasticity
N: economic need
S: household size

The equivalence elasticity, *e*, thus can range from 0 (when unadjusted household disposable income is taken as the income measure) to 1 (when per capita household income is used). The smaller the value for *e*, the higher are the assumed economies of scale. As pointed out above, this paper uses a value of $e = 0.5$, while most of the published estimates on income inequality in China use a value of $e = 1$.

Chart 8.A.1. **Levels of inequality in 19 OECD countries under two equivalence scale assumptions**

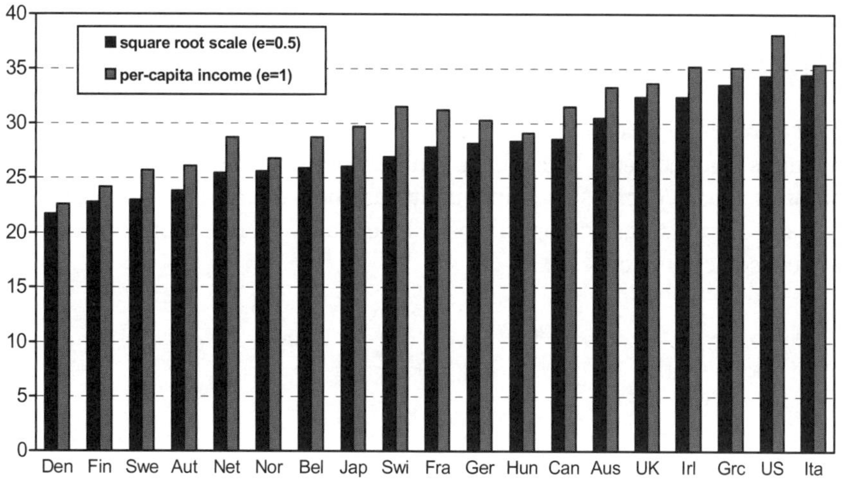

Note: Inequality levels refer to Gini coefficients of income concentration in the mid-1990s. Values for Gini coefficients multiplied with 100. Germany refers to western *Länder*.

Source: Calculations from OECD questionnaire on distribution of household incomes.

Chart 8.A.2. **Trends in inequality in 19 OECD countries under two equivalence scale assumptions**

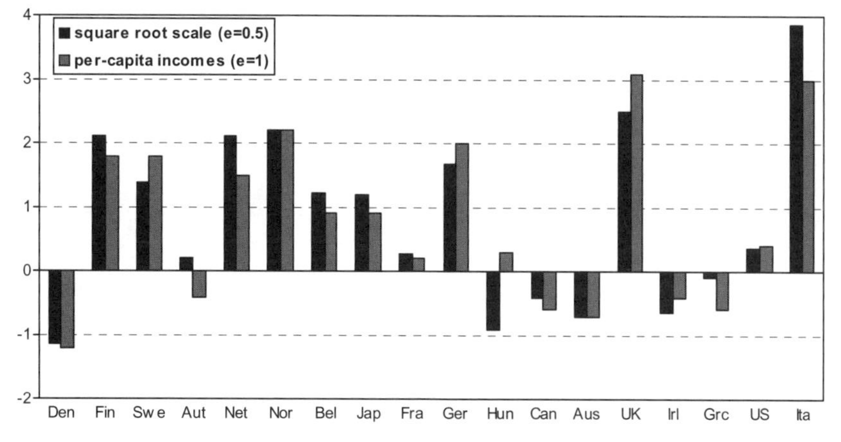

Note: Inequality trends refer to percentage point changes of Gini coefficients between the mid-1980s and the mid-1990s, except for Hungary (early to mid-1990s).

Source: Calculations from OECD questionnaire on distribution of household incomes.

Chart 8.A.1 therefore compares levels of Gini coefficients for OECD member countries under these two alternative adjustments: the flat square root scale and per capita adjustment. Clearly, in all countries, inequality levels are reported to be higher on a per-capita basis than when accounting for household size, namely between 1 and 4 percentage points (2 percentage points on average). At the same time, the ranking across countries does not seem significantly affected, with a few exceptions:

among the low-inequality countries, the Netherlands and Norway change places; among the middle-inequality countries, Germany and Hungary would score lower, and France and Switzerland higher; and among the high-inequality countries, the United States would have higher inequality than Italy. Similarly, alternative indicators of income inequality (decile ratios, percentile shares and other indexes) would be higher when calculated on a per-capita basis (results not shown).

Are reported trends in inequality affected by the use of different equivalence scales? Chart 8.A.2 suggests that this is not the case. Trends, in general, point in the same direction, and differences in percentage point increases/decreases of inequality are below half a point except in the Netherlands, Hungary and Italy. International comparisons of inequality trends therefore do not seem to be very sensitive to the chosen equivalence scale.

Chapter 9

COMMENTS ON CHAPTER 8, "TRENDS IN THE DISTRIBUTION OF HOUSEHOLD INCOMES IN THE OECD AREA" by MICHAEL FÖRSTER

by
Pascal Mazodier,

Institut National de la Statistique et des Études Économiques (INSEE), France

Introduction

First, I thank the OECD for having asked me to discuss Michael Förster's superb paper on "Trends in the Distribution of Household Incomes in the OECD Area" (Chapter 8), despite the fact that I am not a specialist in income statistics (which has some obvious drawbacks, but may also have a few advantages, I hope). Anyway, I am sure that anybody – be she/he a specialist or no – who reads this paper carefully is struck by *1)* the considerable amount of craftsmanship involved in it, and *2)* the fact that only an international agency such as OECD can undertake such a huge piece of research. Moreover, it is clear that it raises lots of very interesting questions as to its conclusions about the recent evolution of income inequality within the OECD area.

However, I will not raise my own questions on why one or other of the OECD countries has seen one or other specific evolution in its income distribution: first, because I think that, by and large, Mr. Förster's findings and conclusions are reasonably well substantiated and very clearly stated, so that my own contribution to such a debate could be, at best, marginal; and second, because I fear that such questions might be more interesting for OECD statisticians than for our Chinese colleagues, in so far as they assume a very good prior knowledge of the economic and social situation in a majority of OECD countries for the past thirty years or so. Rather, I will focus my comments on a few methodological points, in trying both to make clearer what, at first sight, seemed a bit difficult to grasp for a non-specialist like me, and also to relate such methodological points to what I know about the current Chinese statistical situation. In order to be brief, I have selected five points: the data collecting process, "meso" data, sample data, income data and grouped data, and inequality.

The data collecting process

It would have been much too expensive (and practically impossible) for OECD statisticians to have specific data on income distribution (and trends in these) gathered specifically for their study: remember that this OECD study deals with about 23 different countries, with a total population of about 800 millions. Therefore, OECD had to rely on statistical data already collected by national statistical offices, each with its own national specificities in terms of statistical organisation. And in asking national statistical offices for comparable data (both between countries and between different periods), OECD had to compromise upon the very definition of the main variables it was interested in – to the inevitable effect that each country could find some valuable reasons for questioning at least some of the results obtained by OECD concerning itself. But this is the usual price to pay for making comparative analysis, and it can safely be said that, if there are robust underlying patterns and trends in inequality of income distribution throughout the whole OECD area, they are bound to come out, whatever are the slight differences that remain in the definition of variables in each country. This is the whole point for making comparative analysis on a grand scale.

In this respect, China has a clear comparative advantage over OECD: even though Chinese provinces are somewhat homologous to average OECD countries in terms of size, they have an institutional, cultural and statistical framework, if not fully identical between themselves, at least roughly very similar, and in any case, much more similar than between OECD countries. So, such a study should be easier to do in China than in the OECD area. On the other hand, the study was made possible because each national statistical agency in OECD countries was willing to co-operate actively with the OECD team of statisticians in charge. For China, a prerequisite for such a study – with Chinese provinces playing the part of OECD countries – would be a fully co-operative attitude between provincial statistical offices and the National Bureau of Statistics of China (NBS). In such a sensitive area as income distribution (which is related closely to taxes and transfers), some guarantees of confidentiality and a good communication policy should be provided from the very beginning of the operation, in order to avoid any misplaced suspicion by the provincial offices.

"Meso" data

There is, however, an important consequence of the fact that OECD had to delegate data gathering to national statistical offices, and this consequence can be easily overlooked if Michael Förster's paper is not very carefully read, especially without access to the questionnaires sent by OECD to the national statistical offices themselves. If the data asked from national statistical offices by OECD were not the usual macroeconomic ones (GDP per capita, for instance), neither were they genuine micro-data, *i.e.* data about individual households themselves – these would have been much too cumbersome for OECD statisticians to deal with. Rather, they were what is sometimes called "meso-data", *i.e.* something in between macro – and micro-data: here, the data requested by OECD from national statistical offices concerned only sub-groups of households, for instance "deciles" in the income distribution as far as income is concerned (or a few age sub-groups, and so on). Of course, in order to provide these "meso"-data, national statistical offices had to start from their own national micro-data on household incomes, be they the result of specific past statistical operations, such as surveys of household budgets, or sub-products of regular administrative operations, such as tax collection.

Such a strategy – which was chosen out of simplicity and cost considerations, it can be imagined – has at least two kinds of consequences:

- It is quite possible, given the expected concavity of the Lorenz curve (the concentration curve which characterises the distribution of income in a given population), that inequality coefficients computed from these sub-groups underestimate the full income inequality between households which would stem from truly individual household data. To what extent? I, personally, cannot say, even though I am reasonably confident that the resulting bias should be of the second order of magnitude compared to the effects of the main factors considered in the study.
- Much more important, it makes it difficult (at best) to correlate income distribution inequality with other factors in a truly "all other things equal" way. Indeed, it makes it

practically impossible to consider covariation between more than two variables at once. To give an example: with these meso-data, it is possible to cross-tabulate relative disposable income with age groups (Table 8.4), on one side; then, separately, to cross-tabulate income with family types (with or without children, and the like, Table 8.5). This gives some idea of the correlation between income inequality and each of these two factors. But it is not possible to control the effect of age in estimating the effect of household structure, *i.e.* to say that, for a given age group, having children or not in the household has such and such consequences in terms of income, even though, obviously, we expect households with children to be, on the average, younger than households without children since, among the latter, there may be a majority who had children indeed, but whose children have grown up and no longer live in their parents' home. We will see below that truly individual data might allow for a more informative way of identifying "driving factors" at work behind the evolution of income distribution in different areas.

It may be the case that, due to the central part played by the National Bureau of Statistics of China with respect to the provincial offices, it could be easier to gather meso (or even micro) household income data for the whole of China. But one guesses that it would still be a complex and costly operation, especially since (to the best of our knowledge and at least up to now), there are many reasons why tax files can hardly be used in China as a source of quantitative reliable information on household incomes.

Sample data

It must be made clear also that, again for reasons of costs, most (if not all) of the income data collected originally by the national statistical offices, and then transmitted to OECD under a semi-aggregated form, are issued from a sample of households rather than from the whole population of national households (as could possibly be the case when complete sets of fiscal data can be used). However, given the large sizes of the household samples – in the several tens of thousands – this does not matter for the reliability of the main global results, *i.e.* those results which pertain to the whole population, or even to large subgroups of it. It may well happen, however, that for some subgroups, there are not enough households observed in the sample to get reliable results (*i.e.* the sampling error might be at least of the same order of magnitude than the effect one is looking for). In particular, given the skewness of the income distribution (and even more of the distribution of wealth among households), it is difficult to know to what extent some extreme values may affect the reliability of conclusions reached for these special cases (especially those derived from standard inequality coefficients).

For our Chinese colleagues, who, as far as I know, cannot rely too much on fiscal data, this implies that the sampling scheme for collecting income data would have to be worked out from the results of the most recent (2000) population census very carefully, *i.e.* according both to the precise questions they hope to answer and to practical considerations about cost and simplicity of implementation. Experience has taught that such a task is far from easy.

Income data

When thinking about economic inequality, one usually thinks first about inequality in money income. In fact, be it for political reasons or for policy purposes, what counts is rather inequality in standard of living or in well-being, and this raises lots of questions. Economists have devoted much effort to define what could be the most proper concept of income to explain microeconomic decisions by households (permanent income, relative income, life-cycle income, and the like), but we will not go into such debates here. On the other hand, statisticians have had many difficulties adopting an homogenous definition of income, given the very different structure of purchasing power in different countries, if only (for instance) because some important categories of goods and services (education, health) are provided to households at very different costs in different countries.

This is one of the main reasons why the OECD study on income inequality is focused on trends (or changes) rather than on levels. This amounts to assuming that such structural or institutional differences do not evolve too fast, which may be generally true. In any case, these points are well documented in Michael Förster's paper, and I will not insist upon them. Neither will I underline some well-known difficulties pertaining to the part played by non-earned income (such as capital gains and transfers). One should be aware, however, that in a country such as China, the differential evolution between urban and rural areas has been extremely fast, so that it might be even more difficult to summarise the well-being of households by their money income only, even if one takes into account all sorts of money income (as OECD does). And taking into account various sorts of in-kind benefits, for private as well as for public goods, always proves to be quite difficult.

There is one more classical difficulty in translating income into a relevant measure of well-being. The reason is that income has to be defined at the household level (rather than at individual level). Obviously, then, when one thinks in terms of well-being, one has to take into account the size and composition of households. This problem of equivalence scales to take into account economies of scale is clearly presented in Michael Förster's paper. However, the reader may not be made sufficiently aware that, in this OECD study, the equivalence scale takes into account only the size of the household (hence the letter S), not its composition.[1] Once this choice has been made, it is the square root of the household size which has been considered the most adequate correction factor by OECD. In plain words, it means that the standard of living of a household consisting of one single adult (whatever his/her age) with income Y is equivalent to that of a household consisting of S persons (be they adults or children, and whatever their age) with an income of square-root of S times Y. This is a very simple and convenient equivalence rule. Michael Förster says that this rule is robust with respect to other choices of the scale factor. Well, this robustness property is probably true when one looks at sufficiently aggregated results. Otherwise, some caution should be exercised: if one looks at Chart 8.A.2 at the end of Annex 8.A.1, for instance, one can see clearly that the relative evolution of income inequality between the mid-80s and the mid-90s in the United Kingdom and in Italy is inverted when one takes S or its square-root as a factor of equivalence scale.

This robustness to the scale factor should be of even more concern when looking at Chinese results, since we are told that the equivalence rule used by Chinese statisticians is such that a household of S persons needs an income of S times Y to be in the same equivalence class of standard of living as a household of one person with an income of Y (*i.e.* they use the scale factor S instead of the square root of S used in the OECD study; or, equally, they assume no economies of scale attached to the size of the household, which may be less and less realistic when households get richer). In China, given that the average size of households has evolved drastically since the 1980s, and possibly not to the same extent in urban and in rural areas, it might well be that choosing one or the other of these scale factors is not without influence on the conclusions about changes in income inequality.

---

1. So that it is different from the "Oxford" scale (1 for the first adult in the household, 0.7 for the other adults, 0.5 for the children (under 14 years of age), or even the so-called "modified OECD scale" (1, 0.5 and 0.3, respectively). The general view is that the choice of one or the other of these various ways of taking into account the size and composition of the household does not matter too much as far as global results are concerned, but might matter when looking at the well-being of specific categories of households.

Moreover, the choice of S as a scale factor for China is not without consequences, when one compares inequality coefficients such as the Gini index between China and OECD countries. If, among Chinese rural households, large-size households are, on the average, in the lowest part of the income distribution (as seems likely, if only because of the higher fertility rates of the ethnic minorities), then the average rural income should be smaller and the rural inequality coefficient higher when equivalent incomes are computed "the Chinese way" (*i.e.* without economies of scale) versus "the OECD way". In addition, if the opposite were true for urban households, *i.e.* if large-size urban households are rather in the highest part of the urban income distribution (which does not seem impossible in today's China), then the average urban income would be higher, as well as the urban inequality coefficient, when computed "the Chinese way" rather than "the OECD way". In any case, the total inequality coefficient for the whole of China would be higher. Off hand, I am unable to say whether this likely overestimation of Chinese income inequality due to the choice of a the equivalence factor S (rather than square root of S as in OECD countries) is significant or not, but this is a point which deserves to be studied by Chinese statisticians, in order to obtain meaningful comparisons between Chinese and OECD inequality coefficients.

Grouped data and inequality

There is a last statistical point I would like to stress. In statistical terms, dealing with inequality is akin to dealing with "dispersion". For any statistical distribution, the most common measure of dispersion is the variance, or second-order moment centred around the mean. As soon as one considers grouped data, there is an interesting (and intuitive) feature of dispersion measurement which can be stated this way, loosely speaking:

- Total dispersion = Dispersion between groups (*i.e.* between the group-means) + Dispersion within groups (*i.e.* the sum of dispersions in each group around the group-mean).

- (For variances, one often speaks of "inter" variance and "intra" variance components). Such an identity is valid in levels as well as in changes over time.

One must be aware, however, that such a decomposition holds true for most types of inequality coefficients (at least when they are properly defined) and for any type of grouping, not only geographical ones such as "countries" or "provinces", but demographic (age) or socio-economic groupings as well. With some care (which usually means introducing some co-variances when the grouping factors are not independent), it can even accommodate a whole embedding of groupings (for instance, first a geographical one, then a demographic one, and so on).

This has two different kinds of consequences. For analytical purposes, *i.e.* to assess the possible causes of an observed inequality in income distribution (or change of it), it is often much easier to look separately at the "between" and the "within" parts. From a statistical point of view, it is much easier to deal with "between" inequality than with "within" inequality, since one needs only group means, and this may be enough if one is looking at certain questions, for instance, the so-called "convergence" between different countries (or provinces) when there is a catching-up in economic terms. The problem is, if one is interested in total inequality, it may well be that, as seems to be the case in China, the levels of within inequality may be less pronounced than the level of between inequality; and, at the same time, within inequality is increasing much faster than between inequality. The result is that total inequality might be much more pronounced, both in levels and in changes, than one would surmise from looking only at within inequality (for levels) or at between inequality (for changes).

Conclusions

It is not easy to say whether it would be easier to make such a comparative study on income inequality in China. On the one side, it is very likely that many basic sources of statistics on household income are still missing, or are of a quality difficult to assess. Moreover, rapid demographic changes and even more rapid economic progress are introducing more heterogeneity in Chinese society, to the effect that estimating precise time trends in income inequality may be rather heroic.[2] On the other side, within the whole of China there is a single monetary unit, and prices are probably more homogenous than within the OECD area, as well as are traditional consumption patterns. All in all, it might well be that comparing the levels in income inequality is slightly easier between Chinese provinces than between OECD countries. Such information, anyway, is probably of the utmost importance for defining Chinese economic and social policy in years to come, and Chinese statisticians should be given the budgetary means to undertake the corresponding work.

As far as OECD statistical work is concerned (and probably for future Chinese statistical work as well), it seems to me that the time has come to put much more "descriptive modelisation" in the assessment of income inequalities within the OECD area: this would require *1)* Working with individual household data, possibly provided by fiscal data files, and *2)* At least using standard variance/covariance analysis on these individual data to estimate the proper descriptive contribution of each factor to the observed income inequality. In a more ambitious way, one could think of using panel-data models, which seem specially fit for dealing with cross-country or cross-regional analysis, and would allow to pick not only specific country or period effects, but really to test for various possible causes of income inequality – one can think of education or health, for instance.

The last conclusion is that we have to be thankful to OECD statisticians and to Michael Förster for providing such an interesting and stimulating paper.

2. In any case, it is always heroic to try summarising a whole statistical distribution by a single coefficient.

Chapter 10

EARNINGS DISPARITIES IN OECD MEMBER COUNTRIES: STRUCTURAL TRENDS AND INSTITUTIONAL INFLUENCES

by
Giuseppe Bertola,

Department of Economics, University of Turin

Introduction

Labour income is of course highly heterogeneous across working individuals, reflecting not only differences in working time but also (and for primary workers, especially) differences in wage rates. Since earnings are a very large fraction of total income for a very large proportion of the population, their dispersion plays a dominant role in determining the distribution of overall net income (Förster and Pearson, 2002) and has very important implications for welfare distribution. Wage differences depend importantly on individual characteristics, some of which can be changed through education and training. The impact of measurable "skill" attributes on earnings differs across countries, and has been increasing in most countries over the last few decades. But wages also differ across similar individuals, and for a given individual over time. A non-trivial portion of observed wage differentials results from good or bad luck in individuals' career histories, from shocks hitting each worker's job and geographical location, from differences in market organisation and bargaining strength. The welfare impact of both permanent and temporary earnings differentials motivates policy and institutional interventions. Wage differences are often smoothed out by collective contractual provisions which, on the basis of equal pay for equal work principles, specify wage rates that may only depend on simple observable characteristics of the worker (such as seniority) and of his/her duties (job description), and are otherwise identical.

This chapter outlines theoretical and empirical issues that arise when analysing the sources and welfare consequences of wage inequality, and the motivation and impact institutional interference with *laissez faire* configuration of earnings dispersion. An exhaustive literature review or full technical treatment lies outside its scope. Rather, it attempts to offer a structured framework linking theoretical, empirical, and institutional aspects, as well as a simple analysis of the main trends and cross-country differences observed in OECD member countries. The first section reviews concerns about and explanations of increasing wage inequality (especially in the United States since the 1980s), with special focus on demand and supply of skills, and on the relationship between labour income and consumption volatility. The second section discusses static and dynamic income inequality. The third discusses international evidence and outlines the role of labour market institutions in shaping observed earnings inequality. In the fourth section, a simple empirical analysis of available employment, unemployment and earnings inequality data suggests that compressed wage differentials tend to be associated with lower employment and higher unemployment rates. The last section concludes with brief remarks on the recent and prospective evolution of the relevant phenomena.

Sources and welfare effects of rising earnings inequality

Wage inequality indicators were observed to be increasing in US data during the 1980s, and this phenomenon motivated an extensive empirical literature (see Levy and Murnane, 1992; and Katz and Autor, 1999, for surveys). In particular, education appeared to command increasingly large wage premia. Widening earnings inequality across measured skill levels could in principle be explained by increasing effectiveness of each year (or level) of formal education in improving a given worker's productivity. In the absence of obvious technological progress or organisational change in the education sector, however, explanations of the phenomenon were more naturally explained by standard demand-and-supply mechanisms. If groups of workers with different education are viewed as imperfectly substitutable factors of production, higher relative wages for skilled workers can result from declining relative supply and/or from increasing relative demand for their services.

In the United States, the relative supply of college-educated and other skilled workers increased throughout the post-war period, reflecting the abundant post-baby-boom supply of school-age individuals and their higher school completion rates. Educational performance, of course, is in principle endogenous to the financing and organisational structure of the schooling system. Since those features were broadly stable in the United States, however, the literature has viewed increasing educational achievements as a by-product of exogenous population and income growth. In the 1970s, the stock of college-educated workers grew particularly sharply, while their wages remained roughly stable in relation to those of lower-skilled workers. Since the labour market did not require a fall in highly educated workers' wages in order to employ increasing numbers, this evidence indicates that demand for skilled-labour services was increasing already in the 1970s. The slowdown in the growth of skilled labour supply in the 1980s then unleashed relative demand influences on relative earnings, which began to become increasingly unequal across all steps of the skill distribution. This theoretical framework can rationalise empirical observations in terms of changing demand conditions, and opens the questions of:

- What might in turn determine demand trends?
- To what extent may earnings inequality bear on welfare, motivating policy concerns and reactions, and
- Whether the different possible sources of changing relative demand conditions might call for different concerns and different policy interventions.

Trade and technology

Research seeking sources of relative demand dynamics focused on two broad trends influencing the organisation of production over the post-war period: increasing openness of international economic relationships and technological progress. Throughout the post-war period, but particularly in the last three decades of the twentieth century, trade and capital flows displayed a strongly increasing trend. Standard trade theory indicates that the income of factors that are relatively abundant in autarchy (*i.e.* before integration) should increase, relative to that of scarce factors under autarchy, when economies integrate. As the United States (and other Western economies) increasingly traded with less-developed, unskilled labour-abundant economies, the US economy clearly was initially and remained endowed with a more abundant supply of skilled workers than its new trading partners. So, skilled labour was scarcer in the integrated trading area than it was in the US autarchic situation.

Hence, opportunities to import unskilled labour-intensive goods and export skill-intensive ones should indeed increase the relative demand, and earnings, of skilled labour within the United States.

Theory, of course, also indicates that trade opportunities improve the efficiency of production, and may therefore increase the real income of all workers. However, if the evidence indicated that the poor earnings experience of unskilled American workers (whose real wage actually declined during much of the period) was due to trade integration, political pressure to remedy this situation may be irresistible. Protectionist political tendencies remain strong, but empirical research has found little evidence that widening wage differentials across skill levels could be attributed to international trade. The intensity of US unskilled workers' exposure to competition from their counterparts in trading-partner countries can, to some extent, be measured and timed, using data on import penetration and/or on relative prices by industries across the skill-intensity distribution. These indicators empirically explain a very small portion of observed inequality trends, and the prediction (by at least the simplest two-country models) of narrowing skill differentials in less-developed trading patterns has also proved difficult to verify empirically.

Accordingly, "technological progress" is a more likely candidate for the demand effects needed to rationalise widening skill differentials. Technology has undoubtedly changed over the last 25 or so years of the past century but, of course, also throughout previous history. To explain skill-differentials evidence, skill-biased progress should have been faster than in previous decades. As in the case of trade, it is possible in principle to try and identify observable counterparts in the data (such as computer use). But while patterns of technology adoption appear consistent with patterns of skill wage differentials across sectors, it is even harder than in the case of international trade to find empirical support for a time-series relationship between technological indicators and wage differentiation. "Technological" features need not be well approximated by computer intensity and other observables, but might well take the form of less tangible organisational changes made possible and profitable by the so-called "knowledge economy". From this perspective, increasing wage premia for skilled workers would reflect realistic, but not directly observable increases in the relative productivity of workers able to take advantage of new information and co-ordination opportunities.

Static and dynamic earnings inequality

The theoretical perspective outlined above suggests that increasing wage differentials across skill levels may reflect higher relative demand for skilled labour. Observable worker characteristics, however, explain only a fraction of the overall earnings dispersion in microeconomic data sets. The data also give evidence of important job-specific effects on wages, of widening wage differentials across observationally equivalent workers, and of increasing instability over time of the wages earned by a given worker (Davis and Haltiwanger, 1991; Gottschalk and Moffitt, 1994; Bertola and Ichino, 1995). Many worker characteristics that are unobservable for researchers may of course play much the same role as formal education and other observable skill indicators, in determining individual suitability to fulfil the demands of a changing labour market. If the market value of unobservable skill components changes in parallel with that of readily measurable worker characteristics, then common factors such as skill-biased progress or trade may explain the similar trends of wage inequality "within" and "between" skills.[1]

A dynamic rather than static perspective on earnings differentials, however, offers important insights. Over time, individual workers should attempt to upgrade their observable and unobservable skills in response to increasing wage differentials. And to the extent that increasing wage

1. As argued by Juhn *et al.* (1993)

differentiation is observed across industries and regions for observationally equivalent workers (as well as for differently skilled workers within each region and industry), it is particularly important to take into account that mobility of workers towards higher-paying jobs is generally made difficult by costs of geographical and occupational mobility. From this perspective, increasing international trade and accelerating technological progress are relevant, not only through their point-in-time impact on relative labour demand across skill levels, but also through their influence on the instability of relative demand across jobs (industries, regions and occupations) (Bertola and Ichino, 1995; and Ljungqvist and Sargent, 1998). As labour demand becomes more volatile across the various jobs accessible to a given worker, if workers could supply their labour without cost to any such jobs, then observed earnings should remain equalised. But if reallocation towards higher-paying jobs is costly, then labour mobility will not completely arbitrate away job-specific wage differentials, which in dynamic equilibrium will need to be such as to compensate workers moving towards them for the costs incurred upon relocation. Higher volatility of labour demand will then imply wage differentials that are not only more volatile, but also more widely distributed at a point in time: to compensate a given mobility investment, wage premia need to be larger when they are expected to be temporary.

Wider and more volatile wage differentials have important welfare implications when individual workers cannot rely on private financial instruments or collective schemes in order to finance their mobility towards higher-paying jobs. When labour demand variability needs to be absorbed by individual resources, rather than aggregate ones, its trends and fluctuations will be primarily reflected in the level and volatility of workers' consumption. Not surprisingly, in fact, empirical earnings and consumption data track each other quite closely at the individual level, especially at the low end of their distributions (Attanasio and Davis, 1996; Cutler and Katz, 1991; Blundell and Preston, 1998; and Blundell *et al.,* 2002).

Cross-country evidence

In the previous section, conceptual issues were introduced and illustrated with references to the US concerns and empirical evidence. Turning now to consider evidence from other OECD member countries, it is appropriate to discuss briefly measurement issues before reviewing why and how institutional frameworks more heavily regulated than the American labour market may play a role in determining observed earnings inequality.

Measurement of earnings inequality

Many different dimensions of heterogeneity influence measured wage-inequality indicators, which are in general not easy to relate to the two concepts introduced above. The relationship between a worker's wages and his/her age, experience, or tenure on the job, for example, may well depend on job characteristics and job-specific investments, and need not coincide with individual productivity at a point in time. Ideally, if all relevant worker characteristics could be used as explanatory variables, a decomposition of earnings disparities between "explained" and "unexplained" components (and a time-series analysis of the latter component) would be most directly related to the static *vs.* dynamic distinction outlined in the above, and would in particular make it possible to determine the extent to which wage differentials are temporary, and to examine their impact on consumption dynamics. To the extent that the steepness of age-wage profiles may differ across countries, it would also be important to control for workers' age. The welfare effects of earnings differentials across stages of an individual's lifetime are conceptually different from those of permanent and random wage differentials: delayed receipt of wages need not matter if borrowing is possible (or unnecessary) (Bertola and Koeniger, 2003).[2]

Such a decomposition and analysis would need to be performed on internationally comparable micro data sets. These are relatively scarce, and rarely feature a long time dimension (see Blau and Kahn, 1996 and 1999, for a survey of the evidence). The results of such analyses, however, largely confirm the impression conveyed by the simple plots in Charts 10.1 and 10.2. The data are drawn from the OECD *Trends in Earnings Dispersion* electronic file, which collects comparably defined earnings inequality indicators. The charts report statistics for the whole employed population, with no adjustment for worker characteristics (only gender-disaggregated information is available for a subset of countries in the data source). Chart 10.1 plots the time path of ratio of the median observed wage to the 10th percentile of the wage distribution, and Chart 10.2 those of the 90th percentile to the 10th percentile. Thus, the graphs provide information as to the extent of inequality in the lower and higher portions of the earnings distribution. Other inequality indicators (available for some countries) may convey additional useful information, but broadly confirm the message of these charts.

Both charts organise the plots in four groups, primarily in order to reduce clutter, but also in preparation for the discussion of institutional features below. The top-left panel of the charts displays earnings inequality for a group of Anglo-Saxon countries: relatively long time series are available for Australia, Canada, New Zealand, the United Kingdom and the United States; a single observation is available for Ireland. The picture of high and broadly increasing inequality in this group of countries contrasts sharply with the low and decreasing earnings inequality displayed by the continental European countries (Austria, Belgium, France, Germany, Italy, the Netherlands and Switzerland) of the top-right panel of the charts, and with the even lower and also decreasing inequality observed in the Scandinavian countries (Denmark, Finland, Norway, Sweden) plotted in the bottom-left panel. The latter panel also displays Japanese data, which resemble continental European ones. For completeness, the bottom-right panel reports the remaining available statistics, for countries of more recent industrialisation or post-communist transition (the Czech Republic, Hungary, Korea, Poland, Portugal and Spain).

The impression conveyed by this organisation of the data is that the widening of earnings dispersion that motivated the research reviewed in the previous section is primarily a US phenomenon. The phenomenon is similar in some other Anglo-Saxon countries, which also feature persistently large earnings dispersion throughout the period. But it is far from evident in European data, which tend to feature instead declining earnings inequality.

Institutional influences

The clearest message of the overall picture conveyed by Charts 10.1 and 10.2 is that differences over time within the United States and within other countries, while far from being negligible in welfare terms, are dwarfed by cross-country differences. The degree of wage dispersion may of course reflect different degrees of labour force heterogeneity across countries. To the extent that wages are allowed to reflect individual productivity, they should tend to be more dispersed in countries where the labour force is more heterogeneous in terms of education, gender, age, experience and other productivity-relevant characteristics. The economic structure of industrialised countries, however, is sufficiently homogeneous to suggest that their very different degree of wage dispersion largely reflects institutional features, such as the structure of the educational system, wage-setting constraints from

2. Bertola and Koeniger (2003) analyse the welfare impact of borrowing constraints and their relationship to labour market structure. Lack of internationally comparable individual wage-growth data makes it impossible to assess interaction with lifecycle borrowing.

centralised bargaining and minimum wage arrangements, unemployment insurance schemes and employment protection legislation. Indeed, where comparable datasets are available, the evidence confirms that wage dispersion tends to be wider, both across and within observationally similar workers, in the same countries that display higher inequality on the unadjusted basis considered in the figures reported here (Blau and Kahn, 1996 and 1999; and Kahn, 2000).

By their "institutional" nature, policy and organisational features tend to be historically determined and remain constant over time, changing only slowly or, more rarely, as a result of drastic reforms. (Interestingly, the United Kingdom experienced a decline of earnings inequality even sharper that France's in the 1970s, when its labour market's institutional structure was much closer to the continental European one than it became after Mrs. Thatcher's reforms.) As regards earnings differentials across skills, the character of financing arrangements plays an important role from an equilibrium perspective with endogenous supply. The same Anglo-Saxon countries that display wider wage differentials also tend to rely more on privately financed education. Over all levels of education, the publicly financed portion of costs falls short of 80% in the United States, but approaches 100% in Italy and Sweden (OECD, 2000, *Education at a Glance,* Chart B2.1), and differences in such proportions are not surprisingly more marked as regards tertiary education. To the extent that privately financed investment needs to be rewarded by private returns in the form of higher earnings, a broad positive relationship between private incidence of costs and wage dispersion across education levels is not surprising.

Many other features of the educational system bear on its productivity and accessibility, however, and from this paper's labour market perspective, a different set of institutional differences is more directly relevant (Freeman and Katz, 1995, collect a group of country-specific studies of earnings dispersion). A vast literature studies unemployment and other aspects of labour market experience in light of labour market institutions, emphasising in particular the contrast between the United States (and other Anglo-Saxon countries) on the one hand, and European (especially continental European) countries on the other. The experiences of these two groups of OECD member countries have largely mirrored each other over the last few decades. If in the 1960s, and until most of the 1970s, the unemployment rate of typical European countries was much smaller than the American counterpart, by the late 1980s a virtually uninterrupted trend increase brought European unemployment rates to exceed North American ones by a large multiple (Bertola *et al.,* 2002a). The literature seeking explanations for this "reversal of fortune" phenomenon has focused primarily on labour market institutions, such as high levels of union coverage and generous social insurance benefits (Nickell and Layard, 1999; and Nickell *et al.,* 2003). Since cross-country differences in such respects were largely the same in the 1960s and 1970s as in the more recent period, the literature has also focused on restrictive monetary policy in Europe and other macroeconomic shocks are found to explain a large portion of diverging unemployment experiences, especially when interacted with institutional features (Blanchard and Wolfers, 2000; and Ball, 1999). Public employment patterns and demographic factors (such as the more rapidly falling size of the youth population) have also been shown to play a potentially important role (Algan *et al.,* 2002; and Bertola *et al.*, 2002a).

As regards institutional influences on earnings dispersion, centralisation of union wage setting plays a crucial role. Collective wage bargaining may or may not increase overall wages and unemployment, because the greater bargaining power associated with more extensive union coverage may be offset by wage restraint resulting from the union's awareness of macro-level wage effects (see Nickell and Layard, 1999, for discussion and references). Empirically, however, centralised wage setting is unambiguously associated with some compression of the distribution of wages (Blau and Kahn, 1996, 1999). Policies that induce wage equalisation across skill levels and other permanent worker characteristics can be sensible in the presence of distributional concerns, or of incomplete insurance against labour market risks (Agell and Lommerud, 1992; and Agell, 2002). As discussed in the second section, however, earnings differentials have important dynamic dimensions. Even identical workers could earn different wages when they hold different jobs, and mobility across jobs is costly; for example, residents in different regions within a potentially integrated labour market. At a point in time, geographic wage differentials may be observed if the labour mobility that would arbitrate them away is costly. Residents of southern Italy, for example, need not be enticed to move to the tighter northern Italian labour markets by earnings differentials when mobility entails substantial economic and non-economic costs. And the observed wage differentials across jobs held by similar workers can be very large, even when mobility costs are small, when they are temporary. Would-be migrants faced by volatile labour demand, in fact, need to weigh the advantages of higher wages in the near future against not only mobility costs, but also the value of waiting for local labour market conditions to improve.

The costs imposed on workers by job loss and by the subsequent mobility towards other jobs motivate both unemployment insurance schemes (UI) and employment protection legislation (EPL). UI offers income subsidies to unemployed workers financed by payroll contributions. EPL mandates costly procedures and/or redundancy payments upon individual and collective redundancies. Both institutions tend to reduce labour mobility across jobs: UI tends to increase reservation wages of unemployed workers, who are therefore less likely to obtain new employment; and EPL diminishes not only employers' incentives to fire redundant workers, but also their incentives to hire, since increasing employment in response to possibly temporary increases in labour demand increases the chance of encountering firing restrictions in the future. And both institutions also tend to reduce wage differentials, since the availability of unemployment subsidies limits competitive pressure on low wages, and EPL-induced redundancy payments can finance mobility towards new jobs, implying lower wage differentials in equilibrium between expanding and shrinking employment opportunities (see Bertola, 1999b, for a detailed treatment and references). The scope for wage differentiation is of course also influenced by the incidence and coverage of collective wage bargains, which unavoidably tend to constrain the extent to which wage rates can respond to both job and worker-specific circumstances.

In summary, institutional influences on wage dispersion and volatility are motivated by concerns with protecting workers' labour income from "unfair" differentiation and volatility. Such concerns and the policies they motivate are pervasive in all industrialised countries, but their intensity and the tightness of institutional constraints on wage formation and employment patterns is highly heterogeneous across countries. Referring to the OECD employment protection indicator as a summary index of employment relationship regulation, it is easy to see that in practice highly regulated labour market configurations do appear quite effective in sheltering workers from idiosyncratic labour-income fluctuations. The OECD index of EPL stringency is not surprisingly strongly associated with average tenure length data (Chart 10.3), and also with indicators of wage inequality (Chart 10.4) and of wage stability (Chart 10.6). In rigid labour markets, workers who are employed tend to remain employed, and their wages to remain stable over time.

Inequality tradeoffs

Stability of labour income has positive welfare implications for risk-averse workers' welfare, as financial markets offer limited opportunities for consumption smoothing in the face of labour market shocks. Empirically, inequality indicators within and across worker categories are related to each other, and to indicators of earnings volatility. And they are also related to measures of overall net income inequality at the household level which (controlling for capital income, government taxes and transfers, and less formal within-household transfers) are the most direct determinant of consumption and welfare inequality (Förster and Pearson, 2002). It is obviously desirable to enhancing equality and stability of income, and to shelter workers from uninsurable consumption fluctuations. This goal, however, is unlikely to be achieved without costs in an imperfect world. In the face of downward-sloping labour demand schedules, wage compression across heterogeneous workers and jobs implies employment divergence. The clearest instance of such phenomena is regional divergence of unemployment rates within Italy, Germany and Spain, where centralised bargaining of uniform wages (and other national institutions) tends to lower employment and increase unemployment in the regions where labour is less productive (see Bertola, 1999a, for evidence and references).

More generally, if employment of low-productivity workers is made unprofitable for firms by binding minimum wages, or undesirable for workers by generous unemployment and non-employment subsidies, compressed wage distributions for employed workers will be naturally associated with low employment rates, and with high unemployment rates if wage floors are binding.[3] The empirical importance of the relevant theoretical mechanism is also confirmed by disaggregate analysis of employment outcomes. By decoupling wages from productivity differentials, wage compression tends to reduce employment disproportionately for low-productivity labour force groups, or regions. Unemployment effects across disaggregated labour force groups are not easy to detect, since the same (youth, low-skilled) groups whose low-productivity employment may be prevented by wage floors in regulated markets also experience higher frictional unemployment in less regulated ones (Nickell and Bell, 1995). Employment rates in the labour markets of OECD member countries, however, do tend to be concentrated in female, youth and older labour force groups which are likely to have lower productivity.[4] This perspective has some explanatory power for time-series developments across countries and labour market performance indicators. As is well known, over the last three decades of the twentieth century, unemployment displayed a trend increase in continental European countries where earnings inequality tended to decline (Charts 10.1 and 10.2), while it remained broadly trendless in the United States and other Anglo-Saxon countries displaying trend increases in earnings inequality. Arguably, the same technological and trade forces that brought increasing earnings inequality to relatively less regulated labour market also brought increasing unemployment to more regulated ones.

Since many institutional and structural features jointly determine wage and employment outcomes, and not all of them are directly observable, it is empirically difficult to assess the practical relevance of this theoretical channel. Availability of earnings-differentiation data, however, makes it possible to detect a tendency for earnings compression to be associated with unfavourable employment outcomes. Charts 10.6 and 10.7 plot the same earnings inequality indicators displayed by Chart 10.1 against country-year unemployment and employment rates, respectively. The impression conveyed by these data is not one of a negative association between wage inequality and unemployment, or of a positive one between the former and employment. Quite the opposite: the raw time-series cross-section panel displays weak (and insignificant) overall associations in the opposite direction. The data plots, however, also indicate that observations tend to cluster along the country and time dimensions of the data (reported in each observation's label). For example, Canadian observations are grouped in the top-right region of Chart 10.7, while Italy's are grouped at the opposite corner. It is less easy to see, but confirmed by regression analysis, that for each country over time, observations tend on average to move towards increasing unemployment and decreasing employment for a given level of earnings inequality – or, as is the case in the United States and similar countries, to display increasing inequality for a given level of unemployment or employment. Neither

3. See Bertola, Blau and Kahn (2002a), and references therein, for a discussion of this "unified theory" (Blank, 1997) of wages and employment, and a discussion of five-year average evidence similar to that proposed here.

4. Bertola, Blau and Kahn (2002b) document this fact, and offer an explanation based on differently elastic supply across these and prime-age male groups of workers.

the relevance of country effects, nor that of time effects is surprising from the perspective of the previous sections. The former can be interpreted as country-specific institutional and structural features that change only slowly over time, if at all. The latter can offer a stylised summary measure of the common forces (whether technological or trade-related) that tended over the 1970-2000 period, to increase the differentiation and turbulence of labour demand in industrialised countries. After removing both country-specific and year-specific effects by regression on dummy variables, the relationship between residual wage inequality and unemployment or employment indicators in Charts 10.8 and 10.9 conforms nicely to the theoretical perspective outlined above. The data indeed give evidence of a trade-off between wage inequality and a labour market's ability to limit unemployment and generate employment, and sensibly indicate that the trade-off's position depends on both country-specific and time-dependent circumstances.[5]

As regards policy implications, the proposed theoretical and empirical perspective indicates that changing circumstances may well make a country's institutions unsuitable to pursue their own objectives.[6] As the turbulence of labour demand increases, or in the face of negative macroeconomic shocks, the employment-generation benefits of increased labour market flexibility generally tend to increase in relation to their costs in terms of income inequality and volatility. This has of course prompted reforms, albeit partial and hesitant, of the labour markets of OECD member countries. Time-varying institutional indicators would in principle make it possible to assess the role of policy in determining a country's deviation from its own long-run average position along the inequality/(un)employment trade-off depicted in Charts 10.8 and 10.9, and from the time variation of that trade-off.

In practice, data limitations make it difficult to do so. Nor are institutional features easy to define and measure at a point in time. Also, since many institutional features influence lifetime career choices and other forward-looking decisions, expected rather than actual settings and reforms should be taken into account. The bulk of the residual observations, however, lie in a rather narrow range: moving wage inequality by two standard deviations of the overall distribution changes the predicted employment rate by some 4 percentage points only, and the unemployment rate only by some 3 percentage points. The country effects are much larger, and country and time effects together explain over 80% of the variance of unemployment rates, and some 45% of the variance of employment rates.

Recent and possible future developments

Wage inequality ceased to be a headline concern in the United States in the late 1990s, when a booming economy and a tight labour market finally allowed the wages and employment prospects of even very low-skilled workers to improve after decades of stagnation and decline (Hines *et al.*, 2002). Indeed the raw inequality statistics plotted in Charts 10.1 and 10.2 above display a declining pattern over that period, if not one such as to compensate the previous trend increase. It is too early to tell whether the weaker labour market of the past two years has reversed this trend.

---

5. This evidence is similar to that reported by Bertola *et al.* (2002a) for time-averaged unemployment rates. Time-averaging usefully removes some of the data's cyclical variation. In principle, using structural unemployment measures would serve a similar purpose. In practice, empirical exercises using the OECD Employment Outlook Non-accelerating wage rate of unemployment (NAWRU) measure yield insignificant slopes for the relationships of interest.

6. For more detailed discussion, see Bertola *et al.* (2002a), Blanchard and Wolfers (2000), Bertola and Ichino (1995), and Ljungqvist and Sargent (1998).

Theory and historical data, however, indicate that:

- Relative demand for differently skilled and otherwise heterogeneous workers have tended to become more widely dispersed, and the same has been true of earnings in labour markets where these are more flexibly allowed to respond to market forces.
- Institutional features play an important role in shaping the distribution of earnings along all of its dimensions (skills, occupations, geographical location).
- Regulatory constraints on wage and employment formation processes can desirably stabilise and equalise earnings, but do so at a price in terms of higher unemployment and lower employment.

Just as the benefits of labour-income-stabilising institutions should not be forgotten when assessing their employment and fiscal costs, it should also be kept in mind that both the accelerated technological progress and the increasing trade integration associated with increasing earnings dispersion are also associated with increased efficiency. To the extent that this efficiency spurs economic growth, inequality will not necessarily continue to increase, and (as was the case in the latter portion of the 1990s in the United States) wages will be able to increase at the low end of the distribution as well as at the top. It remains to be seen whether the price in terms of employment and aggregate income of equality-enhancing institutions will be such as to spur incisive reforms in the countries that have so far not experienced increasing earnings inequality, and it is of course advisable to spur further improvements in both financial market and collective-intervention instruments meant to facilitate labour retraining and reallocation, and to shelter workers' consumption from labour income shocks.

BIBLIOGRAPHY

Agell, J. (2002), "On the Determinants of Labour Market Institutions: Rent Seeking vs. Social Insurance", *German Economic Review,* Vol. 3, No. 2, pp. 107-135.

Agell, J. and K.E. Lommerud (1992), "Union Egalitarianism as Income Insurance," *Economica,* Vol. 59, No. 235, pp. 295-310.

Algan, Y., P. Cahuc and A. Zylberberg (2002), "Public Employment and Labour Market Performance", *Economic Policy,* No. 34, pp. 9-65, April.

Attanasio, O. and S.J. Davis (1996), "Relative Wage Movements and the Distribution of Consumption", *Journal of Political Economy,* Vol. 104, No. 6, pp. 1227-1262

Ball, L. (1999), "Aggregate Demand and Long-Term Unemployment", *Brookings Papers on Economic Activity,* Vol. 2, pp. 189-236.

Bertola, G. (1999a), "Labor Markets in the European Union", Working Paper RSC, No. 99/24, European University Institute.

Bertola, G. (1999b), "Microeconomic Perspectives on Aggregate Labor Markets", in O. Ashenfelter and D. Card (eds.), *Handbook of Labor Economics*, Vol. 3C, Amsterdam, North-Holland, pp. 2985-3028.

Bertola, G., F.D. Blau and L.M. Kahn (2002a), "Comparative Analysis of Labor Market Outcomes: Lessons for the US from International Long-Run Evidence", in A.B. Krueger and R. Solow (eds.), *The Roaring Nineties: Can Full Employment Be Sustained?,* Russell Sage and Century Foundations, pp. 159-218.

Bertola, G., F.D. Blau, and L.M. Kahn (2002b), "Labor Market Institutions and Demographic Employment Patterns", Working Paper No. 9043, National Bureau of Economic Research (NBER).

Bertola, G. and A. Ichino (1995), "Wage Inequality and Unemployment: U.S. vs. Europe", *NBER Macroeconomics Annual*, MIT Press, Cambridge, Mass.

Bertola, G. and W. Koeniger (2003), "Consumption Smoothing and the Structure of Labor and Credit Markets", Discussion Paper, No. 1052.

Blanchard, O.J. and J. Wolfers (2000), "The Role of Shocks and Institutions in the Rise of European Unemployment, The Aggregate Evidence", *Economic Journal,* Vol. 110, No. 462, pp. C1-33.

Blank, M. (1997), "Is There a Trade-Off Between Unemployment and Inequality? No Easy Answers: Labor Market Problems in the United States Versus Europe", Public Policy Brief No. 33, Levy Economics Institute.

Blau, F.D. and L.M. Kahn (1996), "International Differences in Male Wage Inequality: Institutions Versus Market Forces", *Journal of Political Economy*, Vol. 104, No. 4, pp. 791-837.

Blau, F.D. and L.M. Kahn (1999), "Institutions and Laws in the Labor Market," *Handbook of Labor Economics*, Vol. 3A, in O. Ashenfelter and D. Card (eds.), Amsterdam, North-Holland, pp. 1399-1461.

Blundell, R., L. Pistaferri and I. Preston (2002), "Partial Insurance, Information and Consumption Dynamics", W.P. 02/16, IFS .

Blundell, R. and I. Preston (1998), "Consumption Inequality and Income Uncertainty", *Quarterly Journal of Economics,* Vol. 113, No. 2, pp. 603-640.

Cutler, D.M. and L.F. Katz (1991), "Macroeconomic Performance and the Disadvantaged", *Brookings Papers on Economic Activity*, Vol. 2, pp. 1-74.

Davis, S. and J. Haltiwanger (1991), "Wage Dispersion between and within US Manufacturing Plants, 1963-1986", *Brookings Papers on Economic Activity (Microeconomics)*, pp. 115-180.

Förster, M. and M. Pearson (2002), "Income Distribution and Poverty in the OECD Area: Trends and Driving Forces", *OECD Economic Studies,* Vol. 34, OECD, Paris, pp. 7-40.

Freeman, R.B. and L.F. Katz, (eds.) (1995), *Differences and Changes in Wages in Wage Structures*, University of Chicago Press, Chicago, Ill.

Gottschalk, P. and R. Moffitt (1994), "The Growth of Earnings Instability in the US Labor Market", *Brookings Papers on Economic Activity,* Vol. 2, pp. 217-254.

Juhn Chinhui, K.M. Murphy and B.Pierce (1993), "Wage Inequality and the Rise in Returns to Skill," *Journal of Political Economy,* Vol. 101, No. 3, pp. 410-442.

Hines, J.R., Jr., H.W. Hoynes and A.B. Krueger (2002), "Another Look at Whether a Rising Tide Lifts All Boats", in A.B. Krueger and R. Solow (eds.), *The Roaring Nineties: Can Full Employment Be Sustained?,* Russell Sage and Century Foundations, pp. 493-537.

Kahn, L.M. (2000), "Wage Inequality, Collective Bargaining and Relative Employment 1985-94: Evidence from 15 OECD Countries", *Review of Economics and Statistics,* Vol. 82, No. 4, pp. 564-579.

Katz, L.F. and D.H. Autor (1999), "Changes in the Wage Structure and Earnings Inequality", in O. Ashenfelter and D. Card (eds.), *Handbook of Labor Economics*, Vol. 3A, Amsterdam, North-Holland, pp. 1463-1555.

Levy, F, and R.J. Murnane (1992), "U.S. Earnings Levels and Earnings Inequality: A Review of Recent Trends and Proposed Explanations", *Journal of Economic Literature,* Vol. 30, pp. 1333-1381.

Ljungqvist, L. and T. J. Sargent (1998), "The European Unemployment Dilemma", *Journal of Political Economy*, Vol. 106, No. 3, pp. 514-550.

Nickell, S. and B. Bell (1995), "The Collapse in Demand for the Unskilled and Unemployment Across the OECD", *Oxford Review of Economic Policy,* Vol. 11, pp. 40-62.

Nickell, S. and R. Layard (1999), "Labor Market Institutions and Economic Performance", in O. Ashenfelter and D. Card (eds.), *Handbook of Labor Economics,* Vol. 3C, Amsterdam, North-Holland, pp. 3029-3084.

Nickell, S. *et al.* (2003), "The Beveridge Curve, Unemployment and Wages in the OECD," in P. Aghion *et al.* (eds.), *Knowledge, Information and Expectations in Modern Macroeconomics: in Honor of Edmund S. Phelps,* Princeton University Press, Princeton.

Chart 10.1. **Ratio of the 50th to the 10th percentile of countries' earnings distribution**

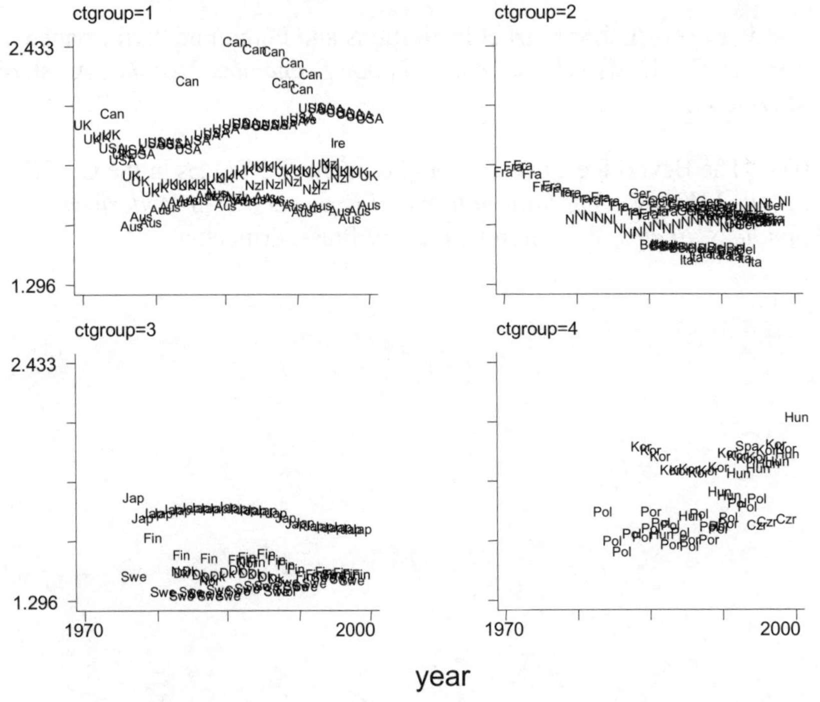

ctgroup: country group.

Source: OECD.

Chart 10.2. **Ratio of the 90th to the 10th percentile of countries' earnings distribution**

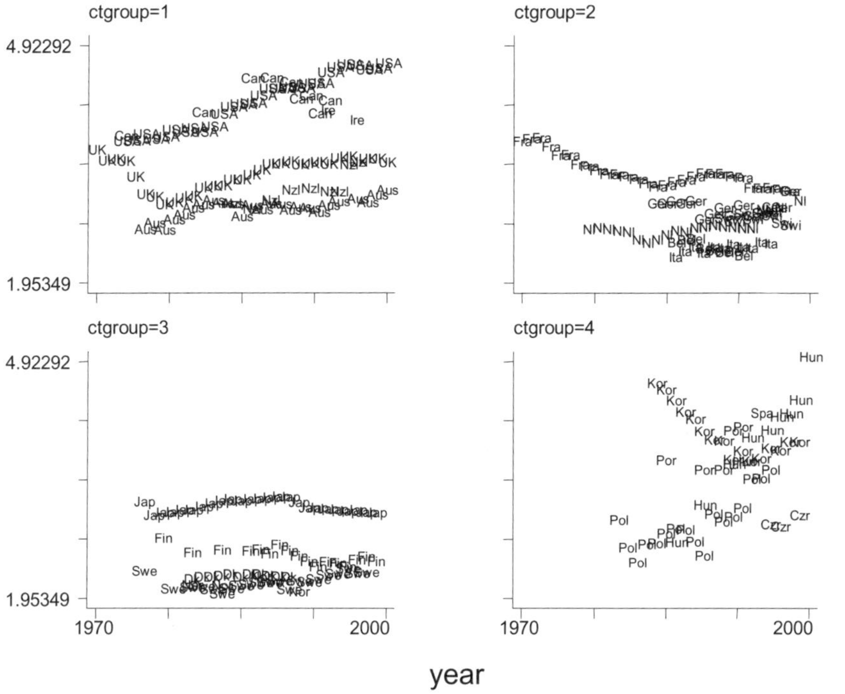

ctgroup: country group.

Source: OECD.

Chart 10.3. **Empirical relationship between tenure lengths and employment protection stringency indicator**

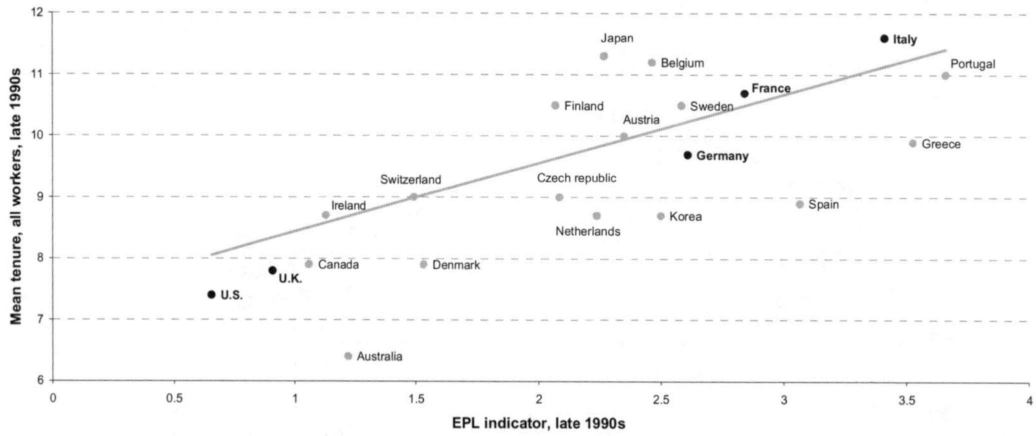

Chart 10.4. **Empirical relationship between wage inequality (ratio of the median to the 10th percentile of the male wage distribution) and employment protection legislation rank indicator**

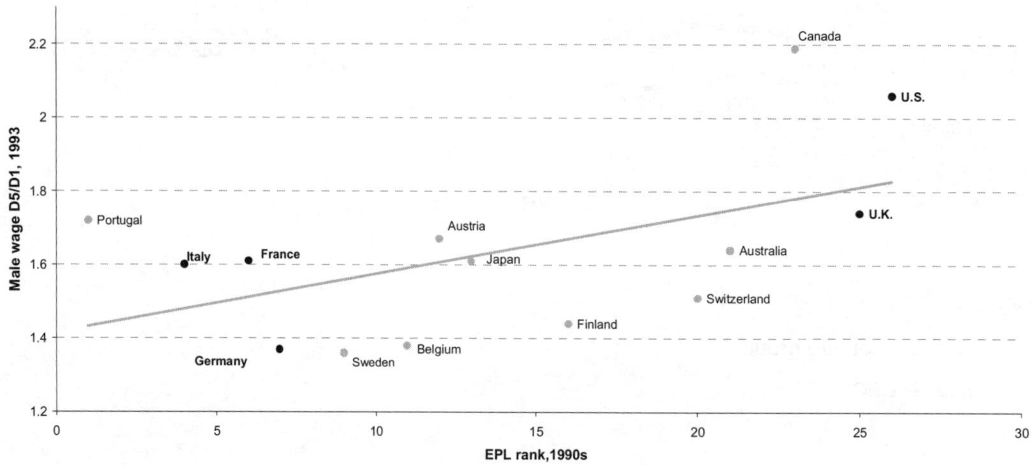

Chart 10.5. **Empirical relationship between wage stability (correlation of earnings over a 5-year period for full-time employees) and employment protection stringency indicator**

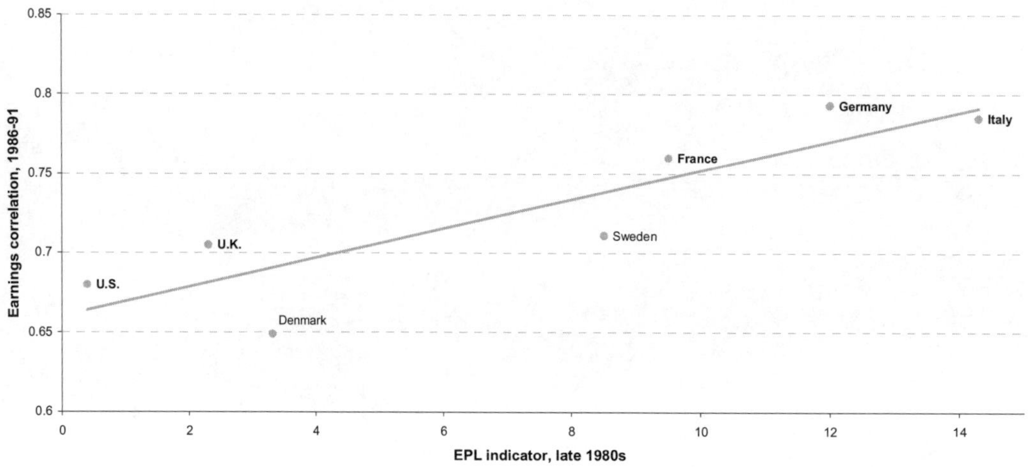

Source: OECD.

Chart 10.6. **Earnings inequality and unemployment**

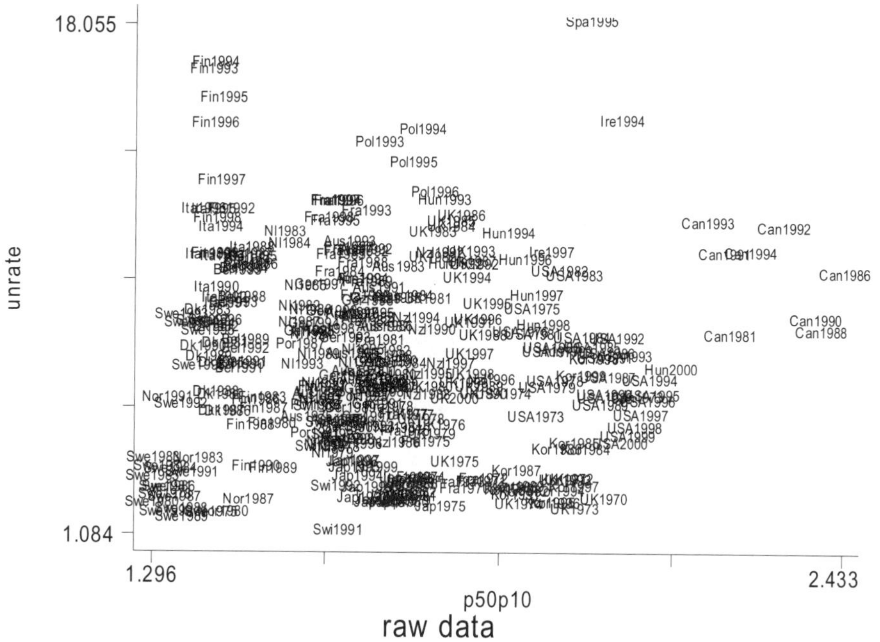

Note: Vertical axis: unemployment rate, OECD Economic Outlook definitions; horizontal axis: earnings dispersion in the low portion of their distribution.

Source: OECD.

Chart 10.7. **Earnings inequality and employment**

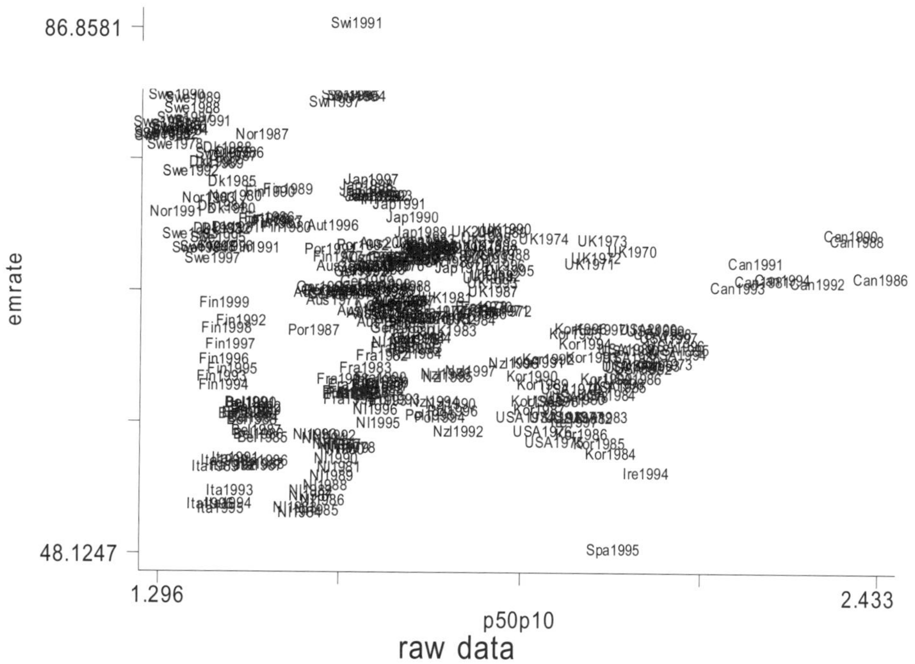

Note: Vertical axis: unemployment rate, OECD Economic Outlook definitions; horizontal axis: earnings dispersion in the low portion of their distribution.

Source: OECD.

Chart 10.8. **Residual wage inequalities and unemployment**

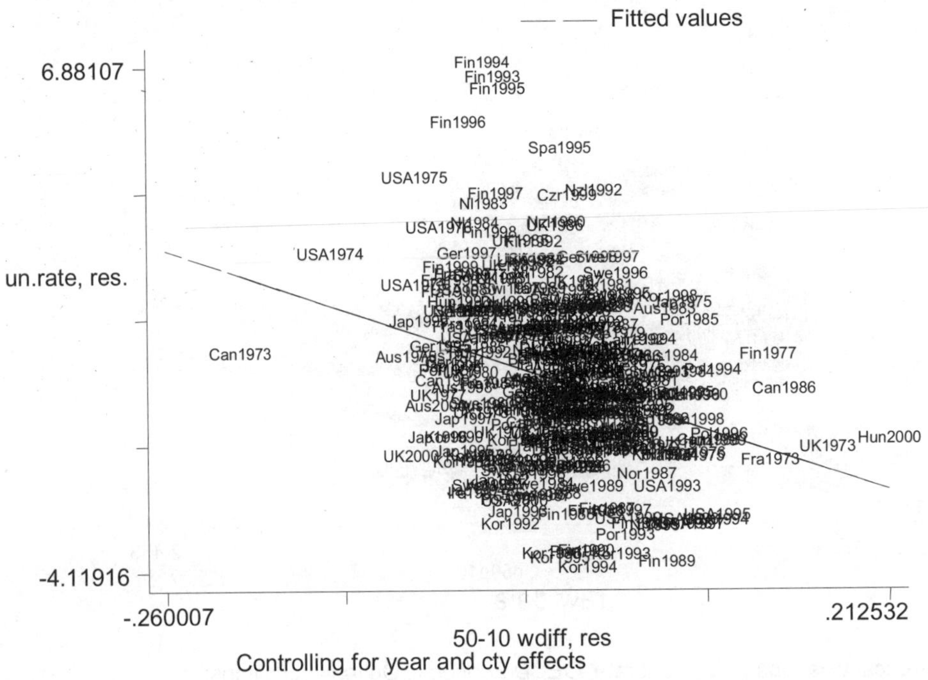

Note: Vertical axis: unemployment rate (as in Chart 10.6) after removing country and year effects; horizontal axis: earnings dispersion in the low portion of their distribution (as in Chart 10.6) after removing country and year effects. Data points are plotted along with OLS unweighted regression line.

Source: OECD.

Chart 10.9. **Residual wage inequalities and employment**

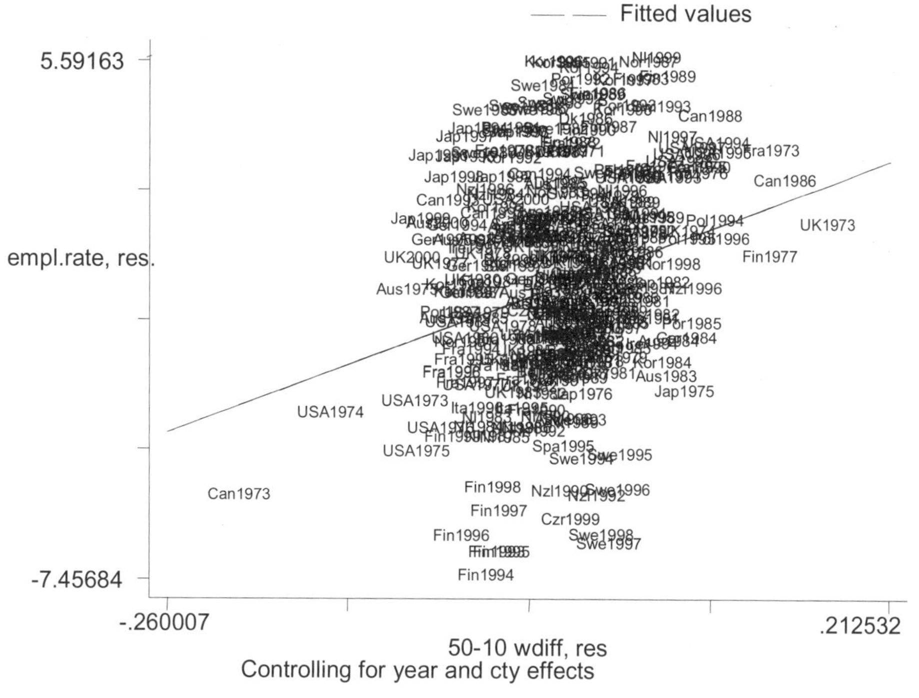

Note: Vertical axis: unemployment rate, OECD Economic Outlook definitions; horizontal axis: earnings dispersion in the low portion of their distribution.

Source: OECD. Data points are plotted along with OLS unweighted regression line.

Chapter 11

MEASURING REGIONAL ECONOMIES IN OECD COUNTRIES

by
Vincenzo Spiezia,

Head, Territorial Statistics and Indicators Unit,
Public Governance and Territorial Development Directorate, OECD

In recent years, regional development issues have returned to the policy agenda of many OECD countries. There are at least three reasons for this. First, increased integration driven by both institutional processes, *e.g.* the European Union (EU), the World Trade Organization (WTO), and economic trends, *i.e.* globalisation, are eroding traditional national borders and creating competition along regional lines in the world market. Second, the persistence of significant regional disparities within OECD countries challenges their capacity to promote economic growth while ensuring social cohesion. Finally, and no less important, economic growth appears more and more to be driven by the higher productivity of firms and workers concentrated around a small number of regional poles. The renewed interest in regional issues has generated a new demand for statistical indicators at the sub-national level. Policy makers are more and more interested in assessing the differences in economic performances between regions, or the concentration of economic activities in certain areas of their countries. The rationale for these developments does not always yield a straight answer. This is why for some years the OECD has been carrying out statistical work on the measurement of regional economies.[1]

How to make meaningful comparisons among very different regions

The main problem with economic analysis at the sub-national level is the very unit of analysis, *i.e.* the region. The definition of the word "region" varies so widely both within and between countries that it can mean very different things. For instance, the smallest OECD region (Concepcion de Buenos Aires in Mexico) has an area of less than 10 km^2; the area of the largest region (Nunavut in Canada) is over 2 million km^2. Similarly, population in OECD regions ranges from about 300 inhabitants in Balance, ACT, Australia, to more than 47 million in Kanto, Japan.

In order to address this issue, the OECD has established a classification of regions within each member country (OECD, 2001). The classification is based on two territorial levels. The higher level (Territorial Level 2) consists of about 300 macro-regions while the lower level (Territorial Level 3) is

1. The work is led by the OECD Working Party on Territorial Indicators, composed of international experts from the statistical offices of member countries.

composed of more than 2 300 micro-regions.[2] This classification – which, for European countries, is largely consistent with the classification elaborated by EUROSTAT[3] – facilitates greater comparability between regions belonging to the same territorial level. Indeed, these two territorial levels, which are officially established and relatively stable in all member countries, are used by many of them as a framework for implementing regional policies. A second issue is related to the different "geography" of each region. For instance, in the United Kingdom, the relevance of comparing the highly urbanised area of London to the rural region of the Shetland Islands could be questioned, despite the fact that both regions belong to the same territorial level. To take account of these differences, the OECD has established a Regional Typology according to which regions have been classified as Predominantly Urban, Predominantly Rural and Intermediate (OECD, 1995). This typology, based on the percentage of regional population living in rural or urban communities, enables meaningful comparisons between regions belonging to the same type (Box 11.1). Although these two classifications – territorial levels and regional typology – provide a useful tool for comparing regions both within and across countries, further problems arise in relation to specific issues of analysis. In particular, recent work undertaken by the OECD has focused on two measurement issues: territorial disparities and geographic concentration.

Box 11.1. **The OECD regional typology**

The OECD regional typology is based on two criteria:

1) The first identifies rural communities according to their population density. A community is defined as rural if its population density is below 150 inhabitants per square kilometre (500 inhabitants for Japan, to account for the fact that its national population density exceeds 300 inhabitants per square kilometre).

2) The second classifies regions according to the percentage of population living in rural communities. Thus, a region is classified as:

- *Predominantly rural*, if more than 50% of its population lives in rural communities.
- *Predominantly urban*, if less than 15% of the population lives in rural communities.
- *Intermediate*, if the percentage of population living in rural communities is between 15% and 50%.

How to measure territorial disparities?

Regional policies are often assessed against their effects on regional disparities. In theory, inequality indexes – such as the Gini coefficient – provide an appropriate measure of territorial disparities. There are, however, a number of problems arising from the application of inequality indexes to the issue of territorial disparity. First, inequality indexes are constructed for the analysis of income inequality between individuals, whereas this chapter deals with disparities between regions. While it is relatively straightforward to compare personal income among individuals, it is more difficult to measure disparities in, for example, GDP per capita among regions. In fact, there are at least three possible measures of territorial disparity.

The first measure simply considers the differences in GDP per capita among regions, *i.e.* each region is considered as an "individual". This implies giving the same importance to all regions. In

2. Level 0 indicates the territory of the whole country, while Level 1 denotes groups of macro-regions.

3. http://europa.eu.int/comm/eurostat/ramon/nuts/splash_regions.html

practice, however, policy makers may be more concerned by low GDP per capita in a very populous region, rather than in a region with only a few inhabitants. The second possibility is therefore to weight regions by their population. This method is not without drawbacks, because it does not take into account the "geography" of regions. For instance, since rural regions are less populated than urban regions, an index weighted by population would systematically underrate disparities between rural and urban areas. A third possibility is therefore to weight regions by their area (ideally considering only inhabitable areas, *i.e.* excluding desert, glaciers, etc., but this information is not available for all regions).

In general, these three different indicators of regional disparities give quite different results. For instance, the ranking of OECD countries varies significantly according to whether the regional disparity index – the Gini coefficient – is weighted by population or by area (Chart 11.1). In particular, regional disparities in the United States appear to be much higher when the index is weighted by area rather than population, while the opposite is true for Poland. This result suggests caution when assessing regional disparity in a country, or making comparisons between different countries. As it is difficult to choose "the best" index of regional disparity, the measure employed should vary according to the purpose of the analysis. A second problem arises from the fact that disparity indexes are very sensitive to the level of geographic aggregation. One reason is that, as the size of regions increases, territorial differences tend to be averaged out and disparities to decrease. A second reason is that, because of the way the index is constructed, it tends to underestimate territorial disparities when regions are large. In order to minimise the "error" due to different regional sizes, the OECD has therefore elaborated an ajusted territorial Gini index (Box 11.2).

The adjusted Gini index provides a correction for different levels of geographic aggregation. However, it cannot completely eliminate the differences arising from the use of different territorial levels. The reason is simply that, when data are available only for macro-regions, differences between micro-regions are unknown. This problem is illustrated in Chart 11.3, which compares the ranking of selected OECD countries based on disparities in GDP per capita in macro- and micro-regions, respectively. For a number of countries (Denmark, Greece, Hungary, Ireland, Italy and the Slovak Republic), the territorial level seems to have little or no impact on regional disparity. However, in most countries, the measurement of disparities is significantly affected by the level of geographic aggregation. For instance, regional disparities in Portugal appear to be much higher for micro-regions than for macro-regions, whereas the opposite is true for the Czech Republic.

As regions are defined by administrative boundaries, it may not be possible to use the preferred territorial level. A possible solution would be to use "functional regions" as defined by the patterns of workers' commuting (OECD, 2002a). Since data based on functional regions are not available for all member countries, the OECD has estimated the impact of commuting on regional disparity in GDP per capita. If workers live in one region and work in another, GDP per capita will be overestimated in those regions with a net inflow of commuting workers and underestimated in those regions with a net outflow. Chart 11.4 provides an estimate of the percentage of regional differences in GDP per capita due to commuting. In quite a number of countries, the impact of commuting is considerable.

A final issue is how to evaluate the observed regional disparities. Differences between regions may be due to a number of causes, each having different policy implications. For instance, low GDP per capita in a region should be evaluated differently, depending on whether it is due to a low level of infrastructure or to a high unemployment rate. In order to make this distinction, territorial disparity in GDP per capita can be explained as the result of underlying disparities in three components: average labour productivity, employment rates and activity rates. Each of these components can be regarded as an indicator of the determinants of territorial disparity in GDP per capita. Average labour productivity is a proxy for the productivity of the regional production system; employment rate is an indicator of the effective functioning of the local labour market; activity rate summarises the characteristics of the regional labour force. Chart 11.4 reports the contribution of each of these components, as well as commuting, to territorial disparities in GDP per capita in 18 OECD countries.[4]

Box 11.2. **The adjusted territorial Gini index**

The measurement of territorial disparity raises problems that are similar to those encountered in the analysis of income inequality with grouped data. First, the level of aggregation is crucial. This point can be illustrated with reference to a common measure of inequality, the Gini index. In the example presented in Chart 11.2, the cumulative regional distribution of GDP has been plotted against the corresponding distribution of population. The curve defined by these two distributions is called the "concentration curve". If there were no disparity, GDP per capita would be the same in all regions, so that the concentration curve would be a straight line. Therefore, the larger the distance between the straight (*i.e.* no disparity) and the actual concentration curve, the higher the degree of concentration. The Gini index is based on this idea and measures inequality as the area between the straight line and the actual concentration curve. Chart 11.2 depicts the concentration curve associated to the *same* regional distribution of GDP and population when data are available for macro-regions (dotted line) or micro-regions (dark line). It is clear that the area defined by the concentration curve based on macro-region is smaller than the corresponding area for micro-regions, so that the Gini index based on macro-regions systematically underestimates the degree of territorial disparity. This observation implies that the index is not suitable for international comparisons when the geographic level of regional data differs significantly between countries.

Two strategies seem appropriate to minimise the downward bias due to grouped data. The first is obviously to use data at the lowest level of aggregation available, *i.e.* territorial level 3 or micro-regions. The second strategy is to construct the concentration curve as if the variable analysed were continuous and to assume a uniform distribution within each region (Lerman and Yitzhaki, 1989).

A second problem is that, while the Gini index based on individual data ranges between zero and one, the index is always below one when the data are grouped. In particular, its maximum value tends to be lower, the larger the size of regions. Therefore, as the size of regions varies between countries, the Gini index is not suitable for international comparisons

The adjusted territorial Gini index corrects for this bias by dividing the Gini coefficient by its maximum value in each country. The index resulting from this correction has two properties (Deltas, 2003); the bias is very small and its direction cannot be signed (*i.e.* disparities are not systematically underestimated).

On average, disparities in labour productivity seem to be the main determinant and explain about 54% of the disparity in GDP per capita. Territorial differences in commuting and activity rates account for 19% and 17%, respectively, while the remaining 10% of the disparity in per capita GDP is due to differences in employment rates.[5] These findings suggest that a decrease in regional differences in productivity should be a primary objective of any policy aimed at reducing disparities in GDP per capita.

How to measure geographic concentration?

Concentration is probably the most striking feature of the geography of economic activity. In all OECD countries, production tends to be concentrated around a small number of urban areas, industries are localised in highly specialised poles and unemployment is often concentrated in a few regions. Although much research has been devoted to this issue, there seems to be little agreement on which

4. The methodology for this decomposition is detailed in OECD (2003a).

5. In the United States, the impact of commuting is none, as US regions are defined by workers' commuting patterns.

statistical indicator best measures geographic concentration. Furthermore, from the OECD perspective, the issue is complicated by the problem that the available indexes are not well suited to international comparisons. A widely used measure of geographic concentration is the concentration ratio, *i.e.* the ratio between the economic weight of a region and its geographic weight. Taking unemployment as an example, the concentration ratio is calculated by ranking regions by their level of unemployment and dividing the share of national unemployment of the first "*n*" regions by their share of national territory, *i.e.* their area as a percentage of the total area of the country. The larger this ratio, the higher is the geographic concentration.

This method, however, is unsuitable for international comparison because the measure of geographic concentration crucially depends on "*n*", the number of regions arbitrarily chosen for the comparison. As an example, consider the geographic distribution of unemployment in two countries as reported in Table 11.1. If the concentration ratio is measured according to the first region, unemployment appears more concentrated in country 1 than in country 2. However, if the concentration ration is based on two regions, then unemployment in country 1 turns out to be as concentrated as in country 2. Finally, the ranking is reversed when the concentration ratio is based on three regions.To overcome the limitations of the concentration ratio, the OECD has developed a new indicator, the adjusted geographic concentration index (AGC) (Box 11.3) (Spezia, 2002). The AGC compares the economic weight and the geographic weight over all regions in a given country and is constructed so as to account for both within and between-country differences in the size of regions. Chart 11.5 shows that unemployment is fairly concentrated in OECD countries. On average, the concentration index equals 0.39, but there appear to be large differences between countries, with the index going from 0.67 in Korea (the highest rank) to 0.08 in the Slovak Republic (the lowest rank).

Concentration of unemployment is the result of two factors: concentration of the labour force and regional differences in unemployment rates. To appreciate this point, assume that the unemployment rate is the same in all regions. In this case, the geographic concentration of unemployment would simply reflect the geographic concentration of the labour force. On the contrary, if the labour force density (*i.e.* labour force/area) were the same in each region, then the geographic concentration would be entirely due to regional differences in unemployment rates. Chart 11.6 shows the percentage of geographic concentration of unemployment due to regional differences in unemployment rates. The impact of territorial disparity appears considerable: in half of the countries, over 25% of geographic concentration of unemployment is due to territorial disparities in unemployment rates. This chart is above 30% in the Czech Republic, Korea and Spain, and reaches 49% in Belgium and 63% in Italy.

Identifying the determinants of regional performances

Territorial policy includes all development policies undertaken by public authorities – the central state as well as regional and local governments – with the aim of promoting a more efficient use of resources within specific geographical areas. As different regions have different resources, Territorial policy needs therefore to identify the comparative advantages of each region and assess whether its resources are fully exploited. The tool for acquiring this information is territorial benchmarking, which consists in comparing economic performances between regions and assessing the scope for a better use of their resources.

Economic performances can be measured as the difference between the level of GDP per capita in a region and the national average. From-the-average differences in GDP per capita can be decomposed into four major components (a detailed explanation of this methodology is reported in Box 11.4): average labour productivity; employment rates; activity rates; and commuting rates. Each of these components can be interpreted as an indicator of the determinants of economic performances at the regional level.

Box 11.3. **The adjusted geographic concentration index (AGC)**

A common measure of concentration is the Herfindahl index (H), which is defined as:

$$[1]\ H = \sum_{i=1}^{N} y_i^2$$

where y_i is the production share of region *i* and N stands for the number of regions. The index lies between 1/N (all regions have the same production share, *i.e.* there is no concentration) and 1 (all production is concentrated in one region, *i.e.* maximum concentration). In the example depicted in Chart 11.1, where all regions have the same area, the Herfindahl index equals 0.127 in Country 1 and 0.135 in Country 2, so that production is more concentrated in Country 2 than in Country 1.

In general, however, regions have different areas so that a correct measure of geographic concentration has to compare the production share of each region with its share in the national territory. An index that takes into account regional differences is the one proposed by Ellison and Glaeser (1997):

$$[2]\ EG = \sum_{i=1}^{N} (y_i - a_i)^2$$

where a_i is the area of region *i* as a percentage of the country area. If the production share of each region equals its relative area, then there is no concentration and EG equals 0. Therefore, the bigger the value of EG, the higher geographic concentration.

A major drawback of the EG index is that it is not suitable for international comparisons because it is very sensitive to the level of aggregation of regional data. This feature is due to the fact that the differences between the production share and relative area of each region are squared. To correct for this aggregation bias, the EG index can be reformulated into the following index of geographic concentration (GC):

$$[3]\ GC = \sum_{i=1}^{N} \left| y_i - a_i \right|$$

where | | indicates the absolute value. It can be proved (Spiezia, 2002) that in the aggregation bias would be smaller for the GC index than for the EG index.

International comparability of the GC index can be increased further by noticing that the index reaches its maximum when all production is concentrated in the region with the smallest area. The maximum value of the GC index is the equal to:

$$[4]\ CG^{MAX} = \sum_{i \neq \min} a_i + 1 - a_{\min} = 1 + 1 - 2a_{\min} = 2(1 - a_{\min})$$

where $a_{\min}$ is the relative area of the smallest region.

The GC index, therefore, is not internationally comparable if the size of regions differ systematically between countries. This would be the case, for instance, if one compared a country in which regions are classified at the Territorial Level 2 with a country where regional data are available at the Territorial Level 3.

A natural correction for this second aggregation bias is provided by the adjusted geographic concentration index (AGC), defined as

$$[5]\ AGC = GC / GC^{MAX}\ .$$

As the AGC index lies between 0 (no concentration) and 1 (maximum concentration) in all countries, it is suitable for international comparisons of geographic concentration.

Source: Spezia (2002).

Average labour productivity is a proxy for the productivity of the regional production system; employment rates is a measure of the efficient functioning of the local labour market; activity rates summarise the characteristics of the regional labour force; and commuting rates are a proxy for the effects of geographic location. These four components can be explained as the result of two types of resources: natural endowments and untapped resources. Natural endowments refer to the characteristics of a region that cannot be changed or can be changed only in the long run, *e.g.* geographic location, natural resources, urban or rural type and demographics. Untapped resources indicate all resources that could be more efficiently used and allocated to generate a higher level of GDP per capita: *e.g.* transportation, general infrastructures, tourism-oriented facilities, labour market institutions and regulation, human and social capital. The difference between the level of GDP per capita of each region and the country average can be therefore explained according to the methodology illustrated in Table 11.1.

This methodology is useful to establish a territorial typology based on the main determinants of economic performance. As an example, in Chart 11.7, from-the-average differences in regional GDP per capita in Belgium have been decomposed into the six components discussed above: sectoral specialisation, average labour productivity, employment rates, age of population, activity rates and commuting rates. The left side of the figures shows the effects of those factors that reduce the economic performance of a region, and on the right side, the effects of factors contributing to increase regional economic performances. The sum of both positive and negative effects due to all components gives the percentage difference between regional and national GDP per capita. For instance, in the region of Brussels, Belgium, low activity rates tend to reduce GDP per capita by about 3% (as compared to the national average). Commuting, productivity, employment rate and sectoral specialisation tend to increase GDP per capita by, respectively, 79%, 20%, 2% and 1%. The effect of population age is none. In summing up the effects of all components, the result is that GDP per capita in Brussels is 99% higher than the national average.

On the basis of this decomposition, each region can be classified according to the component that explains the largest proportion of the difference in GDP per capita. Table 11.3 summarises the main results for 19 OECD countries.[6] For a large majority of regions (68% of the sample), differences in productivity appear to be the main determinant of regional differences in economic performance. Activity rates and commuting rates account for the largest proportion of regional differences in, respectively, 15% and 11% of the sample. In only 3% of the regions are differences in GDP per capita mainly explained by differences in employment rates and sectoral specialisation. Age does not appear to be a major determinant of economic performances in any region. The results obtained so far provide answers to some of the questions raised in this study. In particular, they point out the major factors underlying the economic performances of each region. Although these results cannot be directly translated into policy recommendations, nonetheless they highlight the specific issues that policies should address in each region.

---

6. The full set of results is available in OECD (2003b).

Box 11.4. **Decomposition of GDP per capita**

GDP per capita (in logarithms) in region i can be written as:

[1] $$\frac{GDP_i}{P_i} = \frac{GDP_i}{EW_i} + \frac{EW_i}{LFW_i} + \frac{LFW_i}{LFR_i} + \frac{LFR_i}{P_i}$$

where P, EW, LFW and LFR stand, respectively, for population, employment at the workplace, labour force at the workplace and labour force at the place of residence.

Labour force at the workplace is defined as:

[2] $$LFW_i = LFR_i + NC_i$$

where NCi indicates net commuting to region i.

In theory, net commuting is equal to the difference between employment at the workplace and employment at the place of residence. In practice, however, data drawn from two different sources (regional accounts for employment at the workplace and labour force survey for employment at the place of residence) will be affected by their different sampling. This sampling error is revealed by the large difference existing between national employment at the workplace and national employment at the place of residence: in fact, assuming that international commuting is negligible, national employment at the workplace should equal national employment at the place of residence. At the level of each region, therefore, the difference between employment at the workplace and employment at the place of residence will measure net commuting plus the sampling error due to the use of different sources.

In order to correct for the sampling error, net commuting has been computed in the following way. Let define E(S), E(A) and E as employment measured by labour force survey, employment measured by regional account and the true value of employment. Denoting EW as employment at the workplace and ER as employment at the place of residence, we obtain:

[3] $$\frac{EW(A)_i}{EW(A)} = \frac{EW_i}{E} \quad \text{and} \quad \frac{ER(S)_i}{ER(S)} = \frac{ER_i}{E}$$

where the absence of a subscript indicates total national employment. Subtracting equation 4 from 3, we obtain:

[4] $$\frac{EW(A)_i}{EW(A)} - \frac{ER(S)_i}{ER(S)} = \frac{EW_i}{E} - \frac{ER_i}{E} = \frac{NC_i}{E}$$

Equation 5 provides therefore a correction for the sampling error. It follows that:

[5] $$\frac{LFW(A)_i}{EW(A)} = \frac{LFW_i}{E} = \frac{LFR(S)_i}{ER(S)} + \frac{EW(A)_i}{EW(A)} - \frac{ER(S)_i}{ER(S)} = \frac{LFR_i}{E} - \frac{NC_i}{E}$$

so that equation 1 can be computed as:

[6] $$\frac{GDP_i}{P_i} = \frac{GDP_i}{EW_i} + \frac{EW_i / E}{LFW_i / E} + \frac{LFW_i / E}{LFR_i / E} + \frac{LFR_i}{P_i}$$

or, equivalently

GDP per capita = Productivity + Employment rate + Commuting rate + Activity rate

Therefore, the difference in GDP per capita (in logarithms) between a give region and the country average is equal to the difference in each of these components.

Decomposition of differences in productivity

Average labour productivity in region i is equal to a weighted average of sectoral productivity:

$$\frac{GDP_i}{E_i} = \sum_j \frac{E_{ij}}{E_i} * \frac{GDP_{ij}}{E_{ij}} \quad [7]$$

where j indicates the sector.

From-the-average difference in productivity can be decomposed as:

$$\left(\frac{GDP_i}{E_i} - \frac{GDP}{E}\right) = \sum_j \left(\frac{E_{ij}}{E_i} - \frac{E_j}{E}\right) * \frac{GDP_j}{E_j} + \sum_j \frac{E_{ij}}{E_i} * \left(\frac{GDP_{ij}}{E_{ij}} - \frac{GDP_j}{E_j}\right) \quad [8]$$

The first term on the right-hand of the equation measures the proportion of the difference in productivity due to regional specialisation.

Decomposition of differences in employment rates

Employment rate in region i is equal to a weighted average of employment rates by educational attainments:

$$\frac{E_i}{LF_i} = \sum_j \frac{LF_{ij}}{LF_i} * \frac{E_{ij}}{LF_{ij}} \quad [9]$$

where j indicates educational attainments.

From-the-average difference in employment rates can be decomposed as:

$$\left(\frac{E_i}{LF_i} - \frac{E}{LF}\right) = \sum_j \left(\frac{LF_{ij}}{LF_i} - \frac{LF_j}{LF}\right) * \frac{E_j}{LF_j} + \sum_j \frac{LF_{ij}}{LF_i} * \left(\frac{E_{ij}}{LF_{ij}} - \frac{E_j}{LF_j}\right) \quad [9]$$

The first term on the right-hand of the equation measures the proportion of the difference in employment rates due to the skill-profile of the regional labour force.

Decomposition of differences in activity rates

Activity rate in region i is equal to a weighted average of activity rates by age groups:

$$\frac{LF_i}{P_i} = \sum_j \frac{P_{ij}}{P_i} * \frac{LF_{ij}}{P_{ij}}$$

where j indicates the age group.

From-the-average difference in activity rates can be decomposed as:

$$\left(\frac{LF_i}{P_i} - \frac{LF}{P}\right) = \sum_j \left(\frac{P_{ij}}{P_i} - \frac{P_j}{P}\right) * \frac{LF_j}{P_j} + \sum_j \frac{P_{ij}}{P_i} * \left(\frac{LF_{ij}}{P_{ij}} - \frac{LF_j}{P_j}\right)$$

The first term on the right-hand of the equation measures the proportion of the difference in activity rates due to the age-profile of the regional population

The way forward

The increasing relevance of regional issues has generated a new demand for statistical indicators at the sub-national level. However, measurement of regional economies is a difficult and delicate matter. Erroneous interpretations of indicators of regional disparities or geographic concentration may result in misleading policy recommendations to national and local governments. In order to have meaningful results, a clear view should be taken of the hypotheses and the limits of different indicators, with an awareness that regional boundaries vary significantly both within and between countries. The work carried out by the OECD represents a significant contribution in this direction. Its territorial classification and regional typology establish a common framework for the international comparisons of regions. However, the choice of "the best" measure of regional economies depends very much on the purpose of the investigation. In this respect, the comparative approach of the OECD represents a unique asset in that it permits the statistical measurement of regional economies to be matched with the demand from policy makers.

The ongoing work is focused on the development of the analysis of the determinants of regional performances in two directions. on the one hand, by taking into account the territorial typology on rural, urban and intermediate regions in explaining the specific assets of each region; and on the other, by enlarging the set of competitive factors to skills, physical infrastructure, innovation, social capital and environmental resources.

Access to key regional indicators from the Territorial Database as well as to ongoing work by the OECD Working Party on Territorial Indicators is provided through the website *www.oecd.org/gov/territorialindicators*.

BIBLIOGRAPHY

Deltas, G. (2003), “The Small Sample Bias of the Gini Coefficient: Results and Implications for Empirical Research”, *The Review of Economics and Statistics*, Vol. 85, No. 1, February, pp. 226-234.

Lerman, R. and S. Yitzhaki (1989), “Improving the Accuracy of Estimates of Gini Coefficients”, *Journal of Econometrics*, Vol. 42, No. 1, September, pp. 43-47.

OECD (1995), *Creating Employment for Rural Development: New Policy Approaches*, OECD, Paris.

OECD (2001), *OECD Territorial Outlook*, OECD, Paris.

OECD (2002a), *Redefining Territories: The Functional Regions*, OECD, Paris.

OECD (2002b), *Alternative Measures of Territorial Disparities*, OECD, Paris.

OECD (2002c), *Territorial Indicators and Socio-Economic Patterns and Dynamics*, OECD, Paris.

OECD (2003a), *Geographic Concentration and Territorial Disparity in OECD Countries*, OECD, Paris.

OECD (2003b), *Identifying the Determinants of Regional Performances*, OECD, Paris.

OECD (2003c), *Territorial Benchmarking for Competitiveness Policy*, OECD, Paris.

OECD (2003d), *Regional Indicators for Territorial Competitiveness Policies*, OECD, Paris.

Spiezia, V. (2002), “Geographic Concentration of Production and Unemployment in OECD Countries”, *Cities and Regions*, OECD, Paris.

Table 11.1. **Concentration ratios**

Region	Country 1			Country 2		
	Unemployment (as % of total)	**Area (as % of total)**	**Concentration ratio**	**Unemployment (as % of total)**	**Area (as % of total)**	**Concentration ratio**
1	40	20	2.0	30	20	1.5
2	20	20	1.5	30	20	1.5
3	20	40	1.0	30	20	1.5
4	20	20	1.0	10	40	1.0

Source: OECD.

Table 11.2. **Decomposition of the from-the-average differences in GDP per capita**

From-the-average difference in GDP per capita due to:	**Natural endowments**	**Untapped resources**
Average labour productivity	Sectoral specialisation	Technology + Infrastructures
Employment rate		Skill-profile of the labour force + Labour market efficiency
Activity rate	Age-profile of the population	Labour market participation
Commuting rate	Geographic location/history	

Source: OECD.

Table 11.3. **Main determinants of regional economic performances in selected OECD member countries**

	High Performance	Specialisation	Productivity	Employment rate	Commuting	Age	Activity rate	Low Performance	Specialisation	Productivity	Employment rate	Commuting	Age	Activity rate	Total
Australia	**5**	0	4	0	0	0	1	**3**	0	3	0	0	0	0	**8**
Austria	**10**	0	4	0	5	0	1	**25**	0	12	0	10	0	3	**35**
Belgium	**2**	0	1	0	1	0	0	**9**	0	6	0	3	0	0	**11**
Czech Republic	**1**	0	1	0	0	0	0	**13**	0	12	1	0	0	0	**14**
Denmark	**3**	0	1	0	1	0	1	**12**	0	7	0	5	0	0	**49**
Finland	**3**	1	1	0	1	0	0	**17**	0	9	1	1	0	6	**20**
France	**13**	0	4	0	8	0	1	**83**	2	59	0	13	0	9	**52**
Germany	**12**	0	10	1	0	0	1	**37**	1	21	1	0	0	14	**20**
Hungary	**4**	0	2	0	1	0	1	**15**	0	0	0	13	0	2	**96**
Ireland	**2**	0	1	0	1	0	0	**6**	0	4	0	2	0	0	**19**
Italy	**55**	4	12	10	2	0	27	**48**	0	19	9	9	0	11	**8**
Korea	**8**	n/a	7	0	1	n.a.	0	**8**	n.a.	6		1	n.a	1	**103**
Netherlands	**4**	0	2	0	2	0	0	**8**	0	4	0	4	0	0	**16**
Norway	**2**	1	0	0	1	0	0	**17**	1	13	0	2	0	1	**12**
Poland	**10**	2	8	0	0	0	0	**34**	17	3	4	0	0	10	**19**
Spain	**18**	0	9	7	0	0	2	**34**	1	15	7	0	0	11	**44**
Sweden	**3**	0	0	1	1	0	1	**18**	0	7	1	3	0	7	**21**
United Kingdom	**44**	0	13	1	19	0	11	**89**	0	32	1	41	0	15	**133**
United States	**88**	0	53	0	0	0	35	**677**	13	616	1	0	0	47	**765**

n/a = not available.
Source: OECD Territorial Database.

Chart 11.1. **Ranking of OECD countries based on regional disparities (micro-regions)**

Weighted by population and by area, 2000

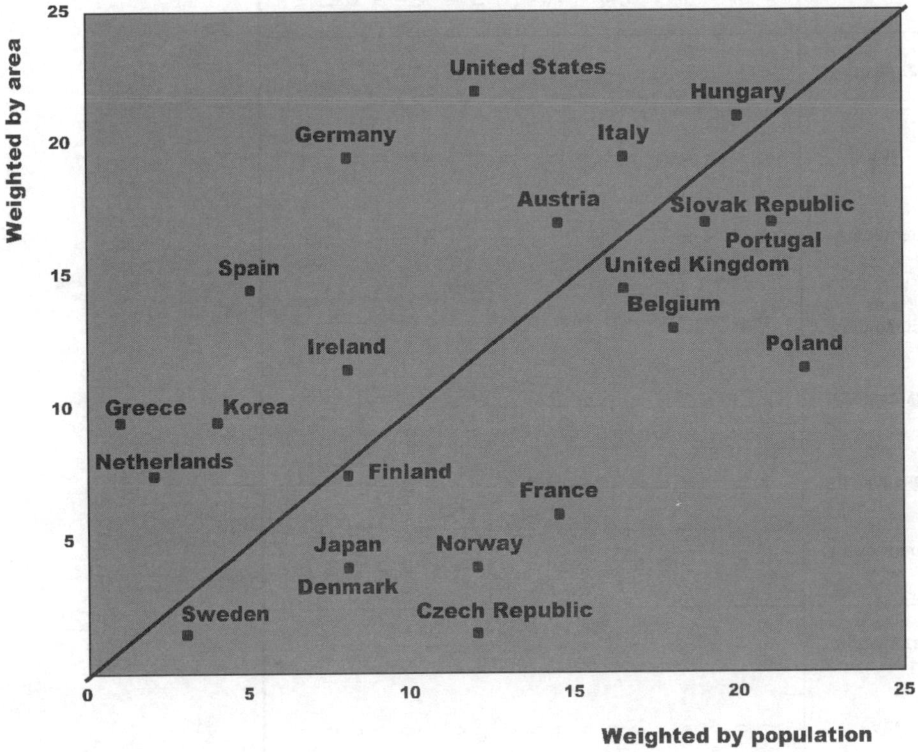

Source: OECD Territorial Database.

Chart 11.2. **Regional disparities in macro- and micro-regions**

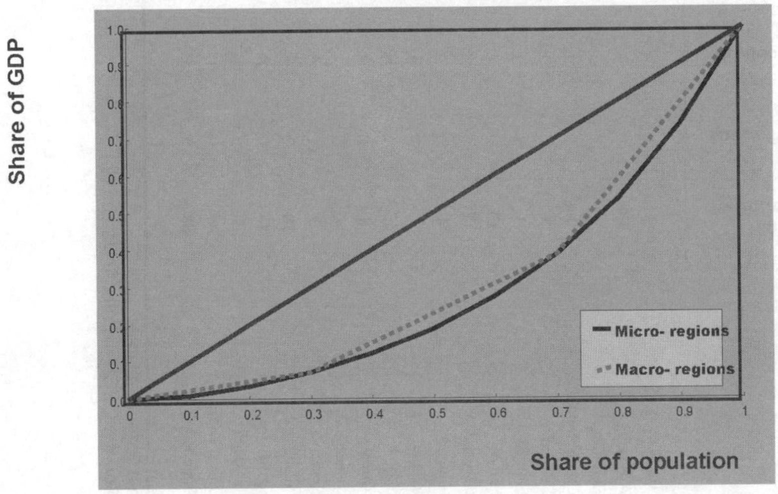

Source: OECD Territorial Database.

Chart 11.3. **Ranking of OECD countries based on regional disparities, macro- and micro-regions, 2000**

Weighted by population

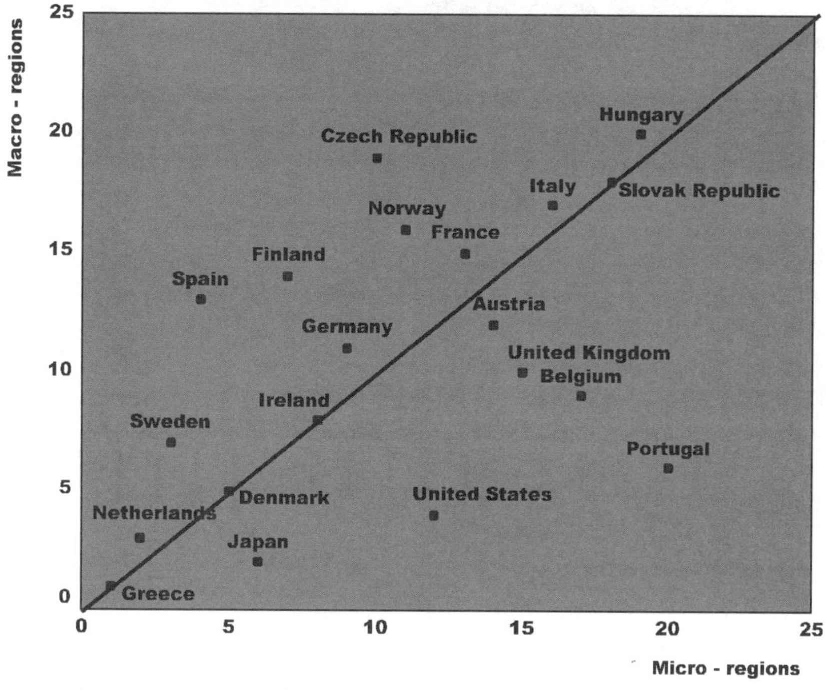

Source: OECD Territorial Database.

Chart 11.4. **Percentage of territorial disparity in GDP per capita due to disparity in productivity, commuting, employment and activity rates, 2000**

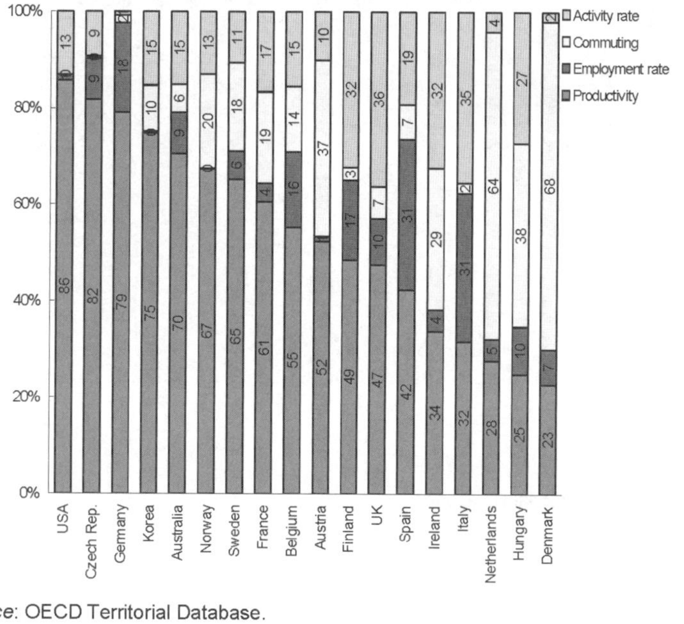

Source: OECD Territorial Database.

Chart 11.5. **Geographic concentration of unemployment, 2000**

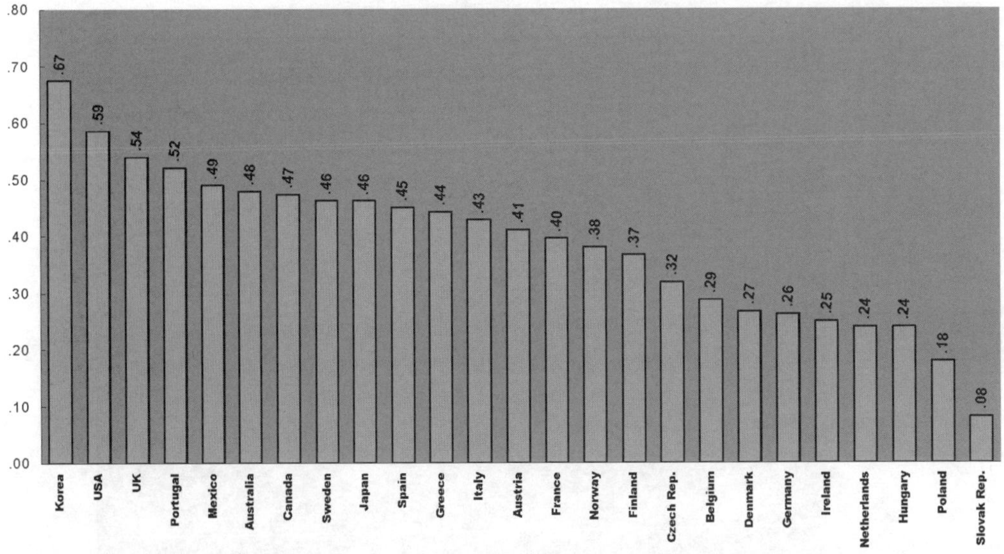

Source: OECD Territorial Database.

Chart 11.6. **Percentage of geographic concentration in unemployment due to regional differences in unemployment rates, 2000**

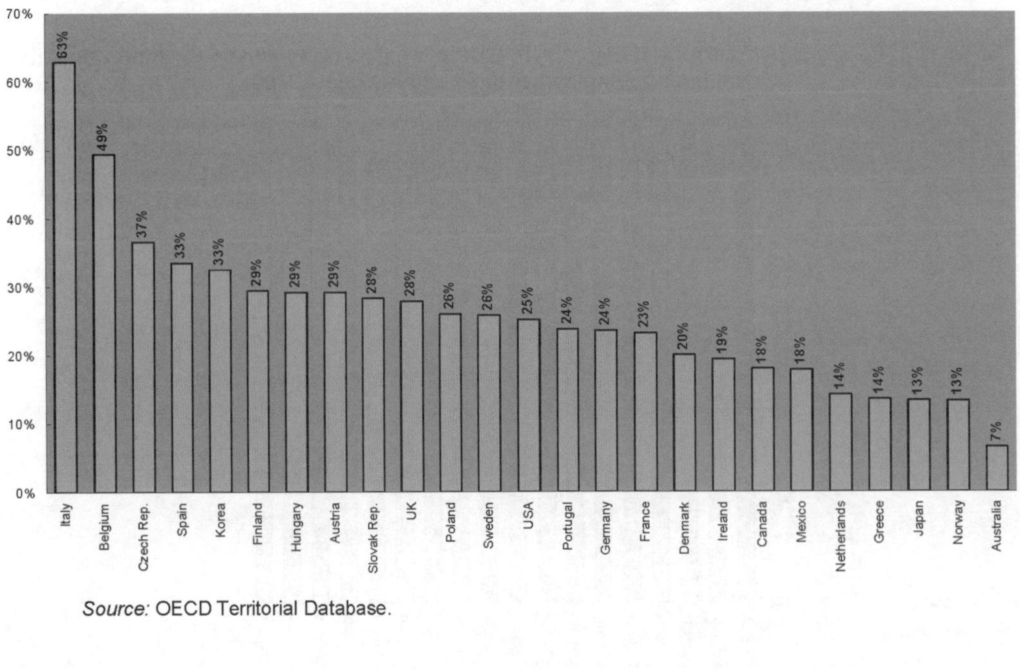

Source: OECD Territorial Database.

Chart 11.7. **Determinants of regional performances in Belgium, 2000**

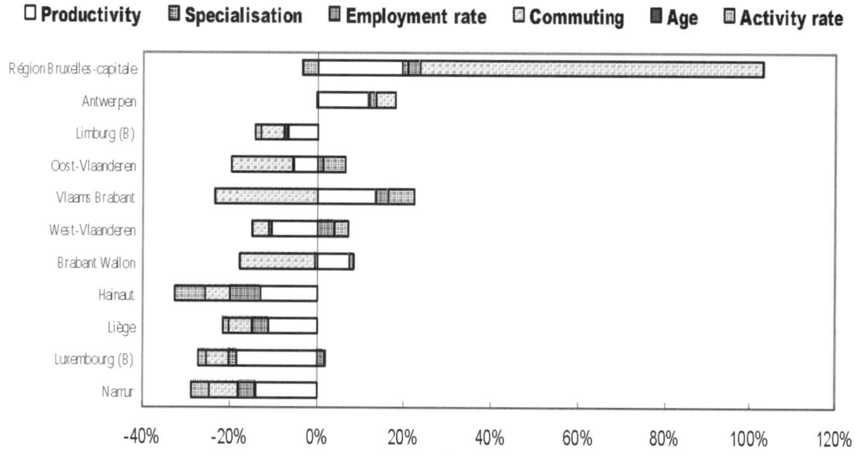

Source: OECD Territorial Database.

Chapter 12

THE DISTRIBUTION OF INCOME IN DIFFERENT REGIONS OF THE EUROPEAN UNION

by
Michael Förster,

Administrator,
Directorate for Employment, Labour and Social Affairs, OECD

Introduction[1]

This chapter is about regional differences in household living standards (expressed in incomes) in the 15 OECD member countries which formed the European Union (EU) prior to May 2004. Issues of regional coherence have received increased attention from policy makers, in particular in the framework of EU policies aiming towards economic and social convergence across Europe's regions. The EU's first progress report on cohesion (EC, 2002), for instance, reports a reduction in regional disparities at the level of the 15 EU member states but notes that the process of catching-up of the weakest regions will remain "a long-term objective". In the more general framework of OECD countries, the *OECD Territorial Outlook* (2001) reports that reduction in territorial disparities is becoming a priority for most OECD countries, as "convergence is slow and wide disparities remain across states and across regions within states".

To assess regional differences in material well-being, these and most similar studies make use of macro-economic indicators, in particular regional GDP per capita. While the GDP measure has the advantage of being available and robust at a fairly detailed regional level, it has two main short-comings for the analysis of material well-being disparities at household level:

- First, GDP measures the economic potential, rather than household living standards. Regional GDP measures regional production but does not necessarily mirror regional living standards, as GDP is a gross measure and does not take account of the impact of taxes and transfers.

- Second, regional GDP per capita is an average value. In that, it tells about disparities between different regions but nothing with regard to disparities within those regions.

1. This chapter builds on micro data analyses and detailed comments provided by Marton Medgyesi and Géza Tarcali, Social Economic Research Institute (TARKI), Budapest.

This exploratory chapter therefore uses survey data to look at regional disparities in disposable household incomes.[2] This is a fairly different perspective from that of GDP per capita, but one in which social policy makers are particularly interested. Findings based on these two different perspectives do not necessarily need to result in similar country patterns of regional disparities – precisely because of the impact of taxes and social transfers but also, because commuting patterns are taken into account differently.[3] Although still relatively unexplored, such a perspective of looking at regional inequality and poverty patterns from "below", *i.e.* on the basis of household incomes, has recently been analysed in a growing number of studies (*e.g.* Beblo and Knaus, 2000; Stewart, 2002; Förster *et al.,* 2002; Jesuit *et al.;* 2003; or Ravishankar, 2003).

This chapter aims to provide elements to answer the following questions:

- What are the differences in household income levels across EU member states and regions, and how have they developed over the later 1990s?
- Which countries display the highest and lowest regional disparities in household incomes in the EU, and can certain clusters be detected?
- Within each EU country, what is the main contributor to overall income inequality: inequality *between* its regions, or inequality *within* its regions?
- Looking at the EU as a whole, which are the countries' respective contributions to overall European income inequality, and to what extent is overall inequality driven by disparities between and within its member states?

Regional disparities are analysed in three steps, following the logic of inequality decomposition by population subgroups: first, differences between average household incomes of EU member states and regions are considered. In a second step, income dispersion within regions is analysed and disentangled by the roles of "between-regional" and "within-regional" dispersion in shaping overall inequalities in each country. Finally, results are provided of inequality decomposition for the EU, as a whole and separate, within and between member states inequality to explain overall EU disparities.

Due to data availability, this paper focuses on regions at a rather high aggregated level, the so-called European "NUTS-1" and "NUTS-2" levels. According to EU recommendations (EC, 2003a), NUTS-1 regions should lie between 3 and 7 million people and NUTS-2 regions between 800 000 and 3 million people. For three EU member states, no regional household income data were reported (Denmark, Luxembourg and the Netherlands). For four countries, NUTS-2 level regions are reported in the database and sample sizes are sufficient to analyse disparities at this level (Finland, Ireland, Portugal and Sweden). For the remaining countries, NUTS-1 level regions are reported. There are 81 such regions distinguished.

---

2. The survey data analysed stem from the European Community Household Panel Users' Database (ECHP UDB), December 2002. The income concept is that of equivalised disposable household income per person, as used and described in other OECD studies on income inequality, *e.g.* OECD (2002).

3. Commuting to high-density areas leads to overestimating regional disparities based on GDP data. In contrast, household income data are based on resident households.

Income disparities across countries and regions of the European Union

Differences in average incomes across EU member states

According to the EC Cohesion Reports, significant economic convergence has taken place in the European Union over the 1990s, and differences in GDP per capita between member states have diminished (EC, 1996, 2001 and 2003b). This sub-section analyses whether such a trend could be observed also in terms of household incomes, by investigating differences and changes in average disposable household incomes of EU countries. Table 12.1 shows average disposable household incomes in European purchasing power parities (PPPs) units in 1993 and 1998.[4] In the most recent year, the average income of an EU household per equivalent household member was equal to 13 766 in European PPP units. There were considerable differences across countries. Average incomes in Luxembourg were some two-thirds higher than the European average, while they were one-third below this average in Portugal. Also, Greece and Spain have below-average incomes (69% and 77% of the EU average, respectively) while incomes in Belgium and Denmark were 20% higher. All other EU countries have average incomes within a 15% range around the EU mean.

For 12 of the 15 EU countries,[5] changes between the early and later 1990s can be analysed. Between 1993 and 1998, real average household income per equivalent household member has increased by one-fifth in the European Union. A certain convergence across member countries has occurred, as all lower-income countries recorded above-average increases in income, while the lowest increase (+10%) was recorded in the highest-income country, Luxembourg. The largest increase was recorded in Ireland, where average incomes increased by 38% between the early and later 1990s. Large increases (26% to 30%) also occurred in Denmark, Greece, the Netherlands and Portugal.

Average values hide the underlying dispersion, and they can be the result of quite different income distributions. In order to get a better picture of how member countries income distributions are related to the European distribution, Chart 12.1 presents density curves for four "typical" countries, together with the density curve of the overall EU income distribution.[6] It can be seen that income distribution in France is similar to the overall EU income distribution, not only in its mean but also regarding its shape and dispersion. Such an "average shape" can also be found in Belgium. In Portugal, the modal income is significantly lower than for the European distribution and the frequency of modal incomes is also much higher. This is a distribution that is more unequal than the European one, which is illustrated by the longer right tail. The other three southern European countries, as well as Ireland, show a similar albeit less pronounced pattern. Denmark, on the other hand, not only has a mode which is higher than the European one (*i.e.* to the right in the chart) but the frequency of values close to the mode is also higher, while the right tail is less long. This is a distribution which is more equal than the overall European one. A similar pattern (higher modal incomes coupled with lower inequality) can be found also in Austria and the Netherlands, but much less pronounced. The density function of the fourth country in Chart 12.1, Luxembourg, shows a mode much higher than the European but also more dispersion around the mode, while the right tail is thicker than for the European distribution, which means that the frequency of above mean values is higher. Summary inequality indicators for EU countries are discussed in more detail below (see p. 202).

---

4. These are the earliest and latest available years in the underlying micro data.

5. Austria, Finland and Sweden joined the EU in 1995, and no earlier micro data are available.

6. The overall EU income distribution is based on population weighted incomes and, therefore, represents a "pan-EU income distribution".

Income differences between regions of EU member states

Chart 12.2 shows average income levels across 81 European regions (NUTS-1 or NUTS-2 level) for the year 1998.[7] These charts also report 95% confidence intervals in form of "cat's whiskers" around estimated averages. These whiskers illustrate that in many cases the sample sizes of regions are too small to be 95% confident that one region has higher incomes than its neighbouring region.[8] To take France as an example, it is (nearly) certain that the region Nord-Pas-de-Calais has the lowest average household incomes in France, the Ouest aside, and that the region Ile-de-France has the highest. In all other French regions, whiskers overlap.

Looking at the distance between the poorest and richest regions in each country, it appears that there are large disparities in the three southern European countries Italy, Portugal and Spain, where household incomes in the richest regions are at least three-quarters higher than in the poorest ones. The lowest differences between richest and poorest regions exist in Austria and Belgium (less than one-fifth). Examining the charts further, one can see three typical patterns of regional disparities emerging. In one group of countries, regional differences in average incomes are relatively moderate, except that there is one region (generally the region around the capital) which has an outstanding income position compared to most other regions of the country. This is the case in Finland, Greece, the United Kingdom, and to some extent France. In a second group of countries, regions cluster into three or more relatively well discernible groups with respect to average income. This is the case in Germany, Italy, Spain, and to some extent Portugal. In the remaining three countries – Austria, Belgium and Sweden – regional disparities seem to be generally more modest.

Countries with one particularly rich region. In France, the region of Greater Paris (Ile-de-France) has an outstanding income position. Other French regions lag far behind. While Ile-de-France, which is the second richest European region after Luxembourg, has an average income of over 20 000 European PPPs, the next richest region, Bassin Parisien, stands at around 15 000. The region with the lowest average income is the Nord-Pas de Calais, while eastern regions are somewhat better off than western ones. In Greece, the region of Attiki, containing the capital Athens, has an average income well above the other three regions. In Finland, the richest region is Uusimaa containing Helsinki, but there is no north-east divide. In the United Kingdom, all regions lag far behind the south-east containing London, and one can discern a north-south divide. Also in Ireland, the region around Dublin has incomes one-third higher than in the rest of the country, but unfortunately there are no further regional distinctions.

Countries with three or more clustering regions. Italy displays a strong south-north divide, with three distinctive clusters: the four southern regions have the lowest incomes, the two central regions (including Rome) medium incomes, and the northern regions by far the highest ones, especially Emilia Romagna and Lombardia. Three clusters can also be discerned in Spain, but here it is the capital Madrid which displays the highest incomes, while the southern, north-western and central regions have the lowest average incomes. But there is clearly a third, intermediate group of regions composed of the eastern and north-eastern regions (Catalonia and the Basque country). It is much more difficult

---

7. When interpreting different income levels, it should be noted that inter-country differences in non-measured, in-kind benefits (*e.g.* services provided by public education or public healthcare) are not taken into account. Furthermore, national PPPs do not capture regional differences in purchasing power.

8. The whiskers are, in fact, more restrictive than that, as they present independent 95% intervals for each region, rather than joint pair-wise significance tests.

to distinguish regional clusters in Germany, but there is clearly a certain east-west divide. The eastern regions of the "new *Länder*", especially Thüringen, have the lowest average incomes, while most of the western regions are clearly better off. The exceptions are the region composed of Rheinland-Pfalz and Saarland and the region of Niedersachsen. As in the case of Italy, the capital of Germany, Berlin, seems to take an intermediate position. Also in Portugal, it is less straightforward to distinguish clear clusters. Nevertheless, the capital, Lisbon, has clearly the highest incomes, followed by the north and the region neighbouring Lisbon. Incomes are lower in the centre and the south, and lowest in the islands.

Countries with lower regional disparities. In Austria,[9] Belgium and Sweden, the regions around the respective capital have above average incomes, but the distances to other parts of the countries seem lower. Whereas in both Austria and Sweden, the confidence intervals for the capitals do not overlap with those of other regions, this is not the case of Belgium, where incomes in Brussels can only be said to be higher than in Wallonia.

In terms of rankings, the patterns of below and above average income levels across EU regions seem to reflect broadly the picture drawn from findings derived by GDP per capita estimates (OECD, 2001; EC, 2002). Stewart (2002) shows for five EU countries consistency in regional performance across the two indicators, GDP per capita and average household income. However, as demonstrated by the same author, absolute differences in levels tend to be significantly lower for household incomes than for GDP, as average income is more evenly distributed than GDP. The extent of regional inequality is therefore much less pronounced when based on household incomes. The issue of summary indicators for income inequality between and within European regions is investigated in the next section.

Regional inequalities within EU member states

Inequalities between regions

The findings above suggested considerable differences in regional income disparities between EU member states. In order to quantify these differences, a number of summary inequality indicators can be used. The following analysis uses the Theil inequality index because of its decomposability feature (Annex 12.A1). Chart 12.3 shows the levels of income inequality between regions for the 12 EU countries for which regional income data are available, for the early and later 1990s. It can be seen that at the end of the 1990s, inter-regional income differences were very low in Austria, Belgium, Germany and Sweden, and very high in Italy and Spain, which displays the greatest value of between-regions income inequality at both the beginning and at the end of the 1990s. Significant inter-regional inequality also exists in France, Greece and Portugal, basically confirming the picture drawn above. Developments were not the same across countries: while both France and Germany managed to significantly reduce the level of inter-regional income inequality, Italy, Greece and, in particular, Spain, witnessed considerable increases.

Inequalities within regions

Household income distributions can further be analysed on a level within regions. Are specific regions, for instance, richer, more homogeneous, in terms of income distribution than others? Intra-

9. The pattern in Austria is somewhat understated, as the region Ostösterreich includes Vienna but also the poorest Austrian province, Burgenland. It can be seen in Table 10.2 that this region displays the highest within-regional inequality indicators in Austria.

regional income inequality can be expressed with different summary indicators. This is done in Table 12.2, which shows Gini coefficients of income concentration, Theil (1) inequality indices and P90/P10 decile ratios for the 81 European regions, as well as for the countries on the whole.

There is no generalised country pattern. In a range of countries, richer regions tend to have higher internal inequalities. This is the case in Austria, Belgium, France, Germany, Portugal and Sweden. In these six countries, inequality indicators are highest in regions with the highest average household incomes. On the contrary, in Italy and Greece, lower-income regions tend to have the highest inequality indicators (the Pearson correlation coefficient is negative). For the remaining countries, no consistent patterns can be found. Across the European Union, the lowest levels of inequalities (Gini coefficients below 0.2) are found in some of the eastern regions of Germany (the new *Länder*), and in some of the Swedish regions. The highest inequality levels are recorded in Lisbon, southern Portugal and in Voreia in Greece (Gini coefficients above 0.35).

Decomposition of country inequalities into "within" and "between" region components

Putting the two pieces of the preceding sections together, this section seeks to answer the question whether income inequalities between regions or inequalities within regions are the driving factor for overall inequality in EU countries. The last step of the decomposition exercise therefore analyses the part of inequality explained by inter-regional versus intra-regional income differences, and whether this has changed over the early to later 1990s. Chart 12.4 shows the results. It displays the percentage contribution of inter-regional income inequality to overall inequality in 12 EU countries, the remaining part adding up to 100% being due to intra-regional income inequality. The decomposition uses the Theil (1)-index.

A first conclusion is that inter-regional inequalities explain only a small if not negligible part of overall inequality in European countries, but there are significant country differences. In most countries, the contributions of "between" regional income disparities is less than 7% (and less than 2% in Belgium and Austria). Only in Spain and, in particular, in Italy, is this contribution somewhat higher, reaching almost 16% in the latter country. It is noteworthy that in all countries except Germany the part of inequality due to inter-regional income differences was on the rise in the 1990s, particularly in Italy and Spain. In that sense, and using this particular indicator and method of inequality decomposition, no trend towards greater regional convergence within EU member states during the 1990s can be confirmed. Nevertheless, the main bulk of inequality in EU member states continues to be explained by income disparities within and not between its regions.

Contribution of "between" and "within" EU member states' disparities to overall EU income inequality

The preceding sections discussed the features of income inequality within EU member states and regions. This section looks at the overall EU income distribution by pooling all its citizens' household incomes together. The question addressed is to what extent inequality at the EU level is explained by income disparities within or between its member states. In that sense, the EU is regarded as one single space and its member countries as "regions". Each citizen in this space is counted as one. Table 12.3 presents population and income shares, and commonly used inequality measures for the EU and its member states. The four largest countries (France, Germany, Italy and the United Kingdom) add up to more than two-thirds of the EU population, while the four smallest countries (Denmark, Finland, Ireland and Luxembourg) represent less than 5% of EU citizens. The household income share of member states from total EU income reflects national income levels besides population size: countries having an average income level above the EU average "contribute" proportionally more to the overall EU income stock than their population share. Germany, for instance, represents a bit less than 22% of the EU population but their households have 24.3% of the EU's household income. On the other hand, the income share of countries below EU average income is smaller than their population share: Portugal has 1.8% of total EU income, while it accounts for 2.7% of EU population. This is also important to note, because the Theil-index which is used below to decompose EU overall inequality is weighted by the income share of the subgroups (which are countries in the present exercise).

Examining the different inequality indicators across the 15 member states of the EU draws a fairly consistent picture for 1998. According to all measures, Portugal displays the most unequal income distribution, followed by Greece, while the Nordic countries Denmark, Finland and Sweden, have the least unequal distribution of household income. As for the remaining intermediate countries different inequality measures produce slightly different orders of magnitude, but in general countries in continental Europe (Austria, Belgium, France, Germany, Luxembourg, and the Netherlands) have below average values for income inequality measures, while southern European countries such as Italy and Spain, and the Anglo-Saxon countries Ireland and the United Kingdom, have higher values for most inequality indicators than the EU as a whole.

Changes in inequality measures between 1993 and 1998 for those 12 EU countries where this is available are also reported in Table 12.3. During this period, income inequality decreased in the EU – for the unweighted EU average, and even more for the overall European income distribution as a whole – according to all alternative inequality indicators. The economic distance between the top and lowest deciles (P90/P10 ratio) decreased by 15% from 4.8 to 4. The decrease in income concentration measures (s90/s10 and s80/s20) is even more considerable. For instance, the income share of the richest decile with regard to the share of the lowest decile fell from a ratio of 11.6:1 to 8.4:1. Similar declines occurred for the Gini coefficient and the Theil-index. The development of inequality in member states follows a more differentiated pattern: in some countries inequality decreased more than on average, *e.g.* in France and Germany. Less of a change or even a slight increase in inequality (depending on the indicator) occurred in Denmark, Ireland and the Netherlands.

In the above (p. 202), individual countries' inequality levels were decomposed into inter-regional and intra-regional components. Following the same logic and using the same method and index (Theil-index), overall EU inequality is decomposed in the following into inequality within and between subgroups, in this case member states. The results are shown in Table 12.4. The last column of this table displays the contribution of each member state's internal inequality to overall EU inequality in 1998. If a specific country's individual Theil-index is higher than the overall EU inequality index, this means that the contribution to the overall inequality will be consequently higher than the country's income share in EU income stock, and *vice versa*. The four largest member states thus contribute 61% to overall EU income inequality, while these countries' incomes add up to some 71% of EU household income. Countries with the lowest income inequalities (Denmark and Sweden) produce a proportionally lower contribution to EU disparities than their economic weight. Income inequalities within the member states explain as much as 93% of overall EU inequality, the remaining 7% being attributed to inequalities between EU countries, as shown in the last row of the table. This level of contribution is somewhat higher than the contribution of inter-regional inequalities to overall inequalities in the different member states described above. Nevertheless, the contribution of inter-state inequality to overall EU inequality remains at a relatively low level.

Looking at changes over time for the EU12 space, it can be seen that the contribution of inter-state inequality did not change significantly from 1993 to 1998: it decreased slightly from 7.7% to 7.4%. At the same time, overall inequality in the EU12 decreased due to significant changes in some of the larger member states.

Summary and conclusions

This exploratory chapter complements analyses of regional disparities in material well-being derived from macro-economic indicators such as GDP per capita with estimates for regional inequality in disposable household incomes in the European Union. In most EU member states, average household incomes lie within 15% around the EU mean (13 800 European PPPs per equivalised person). Average incomes in Luxembourg were some two-thirds higher than the European average, while they were one-third below this average in Portugal. Average household income has increased by one-fifth between 1993 and 1998. A certain convergence across member states has occurred, as all lower-income countries recorded above-average increases in income. The largest increase took place in Ireland.

In a number of countries, regional differences in average incomes are relatively moderate except that there is one region (generally the region around the capital) which has an outstanding income position compared to most other regions of the country. This is the case in the Finland, Greece and the United Kingdom, and to some extent France. In a second group of countries, regions cluster into three or more relatively well-discernible groups with respect to average income. This is the case in Germany, Italy, Spain, and to some extent Portugal. In Austria, Belgium and Sweden, regional disparities seem to be generally more modest.

Overall, the highest inter-regional disparities have been found in Italy and Spain and the lowest in Austria, Belgium, Germany and Sweden. However, inter-regional inequality explains only a small if not negligible part of overall inequality in European countries: in most countries, the contribution of "between" regional income disparities is less than 8%. Only in Spain and, in particular, in Italy, is this contribution somewhat higher, reaching almost 16% in the latter country. The large remaining part of income inequality in European countries is attributable to intra-regional inequality. It is, however, noteworthy that in all countries except Germany the part of inequality due to inter-regional income differences was on the rise in the 1990s, particularly in Italy and Spain.

Income inequality can be looked at an overall EU household income distribution level, and decomposed by between-state and within-state disparities. It has been found that the four largest member states together contribute 61% to overall EU income inequality, while these countries' incomes add up to some 71% of EU household income. Countries with the lowest income inequalities (Denmark and Sweden) produce proportionally lower contributions to EU disparities than their economic weights. Income inequalities within the member states explain as much as 93% of overall EU inequality, the remaining 7% being attributed to inequalities between EU countries. This level of contribution is somewhat higher than the contribution of inter-regional inequalities to overall inequalities in the different member states, described above, but was falling slightly during the 1990s.

ANNEX 12.A1. METHODOLOGY AND DATA

Regions can be defined at different levels of the EU: one may look at regional inequalities *within member states*, as has been done in the first sections of this paper. But a similar exercise can be performed at EU level, by analysing an overall European income distribution and calculating "regional" disparities as disparities between member states of the EU. The last section of the present paper looks at the European Union as a whole and constructs indicators derived from a EU-wide income distribution, thus treating the 15 EU member states as one single economic space with its countries as "regions".

The paper analyses survey data from the European Community Household Panel Users' Database (ECHP UDB), version of December 2002.[10] For the baseline calculation, the most recent available data wave 1999 (wave 6 of ECHP) has been used, which refers to incomes from the year 1998. The paper also presents changes in income and inequality measures over the longest available time period, *i.e.* between 1993 and 1998. For this purpose, only 12 EU member states are analysed, since three countries joined the EU in 1995 (Austria, Finland and Sweden).

The income concept used in the analysis is equivalent household disposable income, *i.e.* gross income from earnings, and capital income plus transfers, minus income taxes and social security contributions. The unit of analysis is the individual; the equivalent household income is assigned to each member of the household using the so-called "modified OECD equivalence scale".[11] Comparability of household incomes across countries and regions is ensured by converting them into a standard monetary unit using purchasing power parities provided by EUROSTAT. These take into account differences in price levels across EU member states (but not regions). For more details on constructing comparable household income and inequality indicators, see Förster and Pellizzari (2000).

Regional disparities within member states are considered at EU defined "territorial units for statistics" (NUTS), more precisely at NUTS-1 and NUTS-2 levels. In the case of Germany, sample sizes were too small for the regions of Hamburg and Bremen. Following Stewart (2002) the city-state of Hamburg has been combined with the region of Schleswig-Holstein, while Bremen has been merged with Niedersachsen. In the cases of Finland, Ireland, Portugal, and Sweden, NUTS2-level regions are reported in the database and sample sizes are sufficient to analyse disparities at this level.[12] The ECHP dataset does not contain information on the regional position of households in Denmark,

---

10. Data for Spain are provisional, as the Spanish Statistical Institute is updating the weighting of Spanish data at the time of writing.

11. Weight of 1 for the first adult, 0.5 for each subsequent adult and 0.3 for children aged below 14 years of age. The equivalence elasticity implied by this scale is very similar to the equivalence elasticity used in Chapter 8 in this volume.

12. The fact to make use of different levels of aggregation of territorial units in the analysis of inter- (but not intra) regional disparities is not without problems. Spezia (Chapter 11) demonstrates that disparity indexes can be very sensitive to the level of geographic aggregation in some, but not all countries.

Netherlands and Luxembourg; consequently it is not possible to analyse regional income differences in these countries.

Inequality estimates are decomposed above (see p. 201) with the help of the Theil (1)-index, which is a special case of a Generalized Entropy (GE) class index (for detailed description of decomposition of Generalized Entropy class indices see Deutsch and Silber, 1999). This index can be decomposed into two parts. One measures the part of overall inequality which is due to income dispersion *within* subgroups (countries, regions) and another, which measures inequality due to inequality *between* those subgroups. Within-group inequality is a weighted sum of Theil (1)-indices of the subgroups, where weights are income shares of the subgroups. Between-group inequality is the value of the Theil (1)-index of a hypothetical income distribution where every household has the average income of the subgroup to which it belongs. It equals the weighted sum of the logarithm of relative means of subgroups (relative to the overall mean), where the weights are income shares of subgroups.

BIBLIOGRAPHY

Beblo, M. and T. Knaus (2000), "Measuring Income Inequality in Euroland", IRISS Working Paper, No. 2000/10, CEPS, Luxembourg.

Deutsch, J. and J. Silber, (1999), "Inequality Decomposition by Population Subgroups and the Analysis of Interdistributional Inequality", in J. Silber (ed.), *Handbook on Income Inequality Measurement*, Kluwer Academic Publishers.

EC (European Commission) (1996), *First Report on Economic and Social Cohesion*, EC, Luxembourg.

EC (2001), *Second Report on Economic and Social Cohesion*, EC, Luxembourg.

EC (2002), *First Progress Report on Cohesion*, EC, Brussels.

EC (2003a), "Common Position with Regard to Establishment of a Common Classification of Territorial Units for Statistics (NUTS)", *Official Journal of the European Union*, 11 February 2003, First Report on Economic and Social Cohesion, EC, Luxembourg.

EC (2003b), *Second Progress Report on Economic and Social Cohesion*, EC, Brussels.

Förster, M., D. Jesuit and T. Smeeding (2002), "Regional Poverty and Income Inequality in Central and Eastern Europe: Evidence from the Luxembourg Income Study", Luxembourg Income Survey (LIS) Working Paper, No. 324, Luxembourg.

Förster, M. and M. Pellizzari (2000), "Trends and Driving Factors in Income Inequality and Poverty in the OECD Area", *OECD Labour Market and Social Policy Occasional Paper,* No. 42, OECD, Paris.

Jesuit, D., L. Rainwater and T. Smeeding (2003),"Regional Poverty Within the Rich Countries", LIS Working Paper, No. 318, Luxembourg.

OECD (2001), *OECD Territorial Outlook*, OECD, Paris.

OECD (2002), *Society at a Glance – OECD Social Indicators*, OECD, Paris.

Ravishankar, N. (2003), "Regional Redistribution: Applying Data from Household Income Data", LIS Working Paper, No. 347, Luxembourg.

Stewart, K. (2002), "Measuring Well-Being and Exclusion in Europe's Regions", CASE Paper, No. 53, London.

Table 12.1. **Average disposable incomes in EU member states, 1993 and 1998**

	1993		1998		
	Average income	**% of EU-average**	**Average income**	**% of EU-average**	**% change 1993-1998**
Belgium	14 148	122	16 621	121	17
Denmark	12 852	111	16 680	121	30
Germany	13 434	116	15 374	112	14
Greece	7 460	64	9 483	69	27
Spain	8 858	77	10 604	77	20
France	13 087	113	15 152	110	16
Ireland	9 512	82	13 149	96	38
Italy	9 749	84	11 719	85	20
Luxembourg	21 670	187	23 893	174	10
Netherlands	12 038	104	15 218	111	26
Austria			15 006	109	
Portugal	7 226	62	9 129	66	26
Finland			12 733	92	
Sweden			12 418	90	
UK	11 982	104	14 796	107	23
EU12	**11 573**	**100**	**13 786**		**19**
EU15			**13 766**	**100**	

Note: Incomes defined as disposable household incomes per equivalent person. Incomes expressed in European PPPs (purchasing power parities). EU averages are weighted averages.

Source: European Community Household Panel, UDB 6th wave.

Table 12.2. **Inequality measures for different regions in the EU, 1998**

	Average income	Theil	Gini	P90/P10	N	Population
Brux.	18 552	0,213	0,309	3,7	353	1 019 373
Fland.	16 754	0,219	0,297	3,1	1 098	5 894 760
Wallo.	15 737	0,132	0,268	3,1	1 229	3 269 099
Belgium	**16 607**	**0,193**	**0,290**	**3,1**	**2 680**	**10 183 231**
Ile Fr.	20 169	0,267	0,329	3,9	824	10 385 227
Bas.P.	14 934	0,245	0,308	3,2	1 024	10 186 486
Nord	12 419	0,110	0,259	3,1	352	3 890 120
Est	14 334	0,085	0,229	2,9	514	5 003 158
Ouest	13 344	0,109	0,254	3,3	861	7 333 632
S-Oue	13 570	0,114	0,263	3,3	655	5 782 830
Ctr-Est	14 286	0,116	0,259	3,1	620	6 857 535
Médit.	14 315	0,117	0,266	3,3	663	7 070 316
France	**15 168**	**0,185**	**0,292**	**3,5**	**3 927**	**56 509 304**
N-Ov	14 029	0,114	0,261	3,2	597	6 008 637
Lomb	14 635	0,121	0,259	2,9	666	8 443 690
N-Est	13 490	0,117	0,251	3,0	731	6 352 897
Em-Ro	14 691	0,117	0,250	3,2	356	3 603 414
Centr	12 859	0,117	0,249	2,8	701	5 888 274
Lazio	11 074	0,133	0,283	3,8	407	5 522 656
Abr-Mol	10 531	0,089	0,233	2,9	389	1 714 062
Campa	8 553	0,154	0,305	4,8	583	5 882 617
Sud	8 675	0,175	0,316	4,4	887	6 438 266
Sic	8 532	0,175	0,321	5,3	522	5 223 908
Sard	8 117	0,184	0,329	5,6	401	1 731 494
Italy	**11 727**	**0,155**	**0,299**	**4,1**	**6 240**	**56 809 915**
Voreia	8 021	0,235	0,358	5,3	1 367	3 161 051
Kentri	8 176	0,195	0,341	5,3	1 044	2 130 031
Attiki	11 453	0,180	0,312	3,9	952	3 888 814
Aig, Krit	8 719	0,163	0,313	4,4	532	987 740
Greece	**9 434**	**0,210**	**0,343**	**4,9**	**3 895**	**10 167 635**
N.-oest	9 391	0,142	0,284	3,7	741	4 934 143
N.-est	12 001	0,144	0,289	3,7	789	3 921 804
Madrid	14 587	0,182	0,334	5,5	476	4 968 949
Centro	8 402	0,182	0,321	4,5	875	5 302 636
Este	11 984	0,154	0,303	4,1	1,101	10 168 049
Sur	8 272	0,183	0,323	4,4	957	7 997 451
Canar.	8 079	0,165	0,313	4,3	322	1 557 101
Spain	**10 580**	**0,186**	**0,330**	**4,6**	**5 261**	**38 850 134**
Ostöst.	16 047	0,144	0,280	3,3	1,214	3 380 127
Südöst.	14 056	0,135	0,251	2,7	656	1 716 590
Westö.	14 339	0,100	0,235	2,8	920	2 796 766
Austria	**15 009**	**0,129**	**0,261**	**3,0**	**2 790**	**7 893 483**

Table 12.2. **Inequality measures for different regions in the EU, 1998** (contd.)

	Average income	Theil	Gini	P90/P10	N	Population
Würt	15 548	0,097	0,241	3,3	735	10 740 265
Bayern	16 394	0,105	0,245	3,1	747	11 784 464
Berlin	15 895	0,110	0,260	3,4	241	3 162 827
Br.burg	13 562	0,061	0,187	2,3	269	2 497 325
Hessen	17 160	0,137	0,281	3,6	395	5 853 093
Meckl	14 046	0,109	0,249	3,0	179	1 736 600
N.sachs	14 713	0,104	0,244	3,1	479	8 419 357
Nr.-Westf	16 112	0,131	0,267	3,1	1 140	17 733 156
Sachs	13 402	0,090	0,218	2,3	486	4 511 696
Sa-Anh	13 705	0,063	0,196	2,6	344	2 603 491
Sch-Hol	15 562	0,102	0,236	2,6	194	4 399 438
Thür	12 488	0,065	0,199	2,8	307	2 433 252
Rhein	14 096	0,084	0,218	2,5	329	5 330 035
Germany	**15 374**	**0,110**	**0,249**	**3,0**	**5 845**	**81 205 000**
North	14 037	0,141	0,292	4,0	297	3 366 360
Yorksh.	12 821	0,141	0,290	3,9	472	5 641 926
Ea.Midl.	13 540	0,180	0,308	3,9	429	4 775 857
Ea.Angl.	14 235	0,147	0,295	3,7	216	2 413 773
S.East	17 052	0,216	0,329	4,1	1 377	17 886 013
S.West	14 304	0,159	0,298	3,9	437	4 925 162
W.Midl.	13 668	0,174	0,319	4,3	426	5 407 126
N.West	14 639	0,180	0,320	4,5	512	6 271 526
Wales	13 736	0,165	0,300	3,6	267	3 206 969
Scotl.	13 428	0,152	0,300	3,6	455	4 629 959
UK	**14 796**	**0,187**	**0,317**	**4,1**	**4 888**	**58 524 671**
Irel.	11 858	0,167	0,297	3,8	1 689	2 447 158
Dublin	15 465	0,219	0,327	4,0	475	1 057 264
Ireland	**12 946**	**0,194**	**0,314**	**4,0**	**2 164**	**3 504 422**
Norte	8 717	0,197	0,332	4,6	846	3 498 382
Centro	7 402	0,186	0,324	4,3	966	1 704 786
Lisboa	11 277	0,257	0,382	6,1	509	3 311 672
Alentejo	7 885	0,183	0,323	3,7	453	523 564
Algarve	7 301	0,227	0,362	5,3	610	331 759
Acores	7 143	0,223	0,349	4,2	618	216 522
Madeira	6 487	0,152	0,299	4,2	566	251 866
Portugal	**9 167**	**0,235**	**0,363**	**5,1**	**4 568**	**9 838 550**
Uusim	14 901	0,115	0,252	2,9	913	1 370 116
Etela	12 529	0,107	0,238	2,8	1 393	1 793 531
Ita	11 269	0,111	0,237	2,6	618	669 388
Vali	11 400	0,088	0,215	2,5	565	686 059
Pohjois	11 516	0,091	0,226	2,7	325	575 777
Finland	**12 735**	**0,112**	**0,246**	**2,8**	**3,814**	**5 094 871**

Table 12.2. **Inequality measures for different regions in the EU, 1998** (contd)

	Average income	Theil	Gini	P90/P10	N	Population
Stockh.	14 336	0,118	0,253	3,0	935	1 680 718
Ö. Mellans.	12 050	0,091	0,213	2,5	919	1 470 911
Sydsv.	12 471	0,145	0,245	2,6	702	1 186 198
N. Mellans.	11 869	0,071	0,203	2,5	519	819 254
Mellerst.	11 886	0,067	0,202	2,4	248	371 931
Övre N.	11 539	0,065	0,194	2,5	310	525 363
Smal	11 213	0,072	0,205	2,4	489	809 784
Vastsv.	12 051	0,080	0,213	2,6	1 043	1 808 955
Sweden	**12 418**	**0,100**	**0,227**	**2,6**	**12 421**	**8 673 114**

Note: Incomes defined as disposable household incomes per equivalent person. Average incomes expressed in European PPPs (purchasing power parities). P90/P10 decile ratio defined as the ratio of the upper bound value of the ninth income decile to the upper bound value of the first income decile. Gini coefficient and Theil index are summary inequality measures. Results may differ from those presented in Tables 12.3 and 12.4, because calculations for this table exclude observations with missing region variable.

Source: European Community Household Panel, UDB 6th wave.

Table 12.3. **Basic indicators and inequality measures in the EU, 1998 and changes 1993-1998**

	Population share 1998 (%)	**Income share 1998 (%)**	**P90/P10 decile ratio 1998**	**P90/P10 change (%)**	**S80/S20 quintile share 1998**	**S80/S20 change (%)**	**Gini coefficient**	**Gini change (%)**
Belgium	2.8	3.3	3.1	*-13.6*	4.3	*-8.4*	0.291	*-2.7*
Denmark	1.4	1.7	2.7	*1.3*	3.2	*0.0*	0.225	*-1.5*
Germany	21.8	24.3	3.0	*-18.2*	3.6	*-24.6*	0.249	*-14.3*
Greece	2.8	1.9	4.9	*-17.8*	6.2	*-18.0*	0.344	*-6.3*
Spain	10.6	8.1	4.6	*-4.6*	5.7	*-6.0*	0.331	*-3.5*
France	15.5	17.0	3.5	*-10.1*	4.4	*-23.9*	0.292	*-15.3*
Ireland	1.0	1.0	4.0	*3.0*	4.9	*3.4*	0.319	*-0.5*
Italy	15.5	13.2	4.1	*-15.7*	4.9	*-19.7*	0.299	*-10.0*
Luxembourg	0.1	0.2	3.3	*-12.8*	3.9	*-22.5*	0.271	*-12.7*
Netherlands	4.2	4.6	3.0	*-3.0*	3.7	*-1.2*	0.260	*-1.1*
Austria	2.2	2.3	3.0		3.8		0.260	
Portugal	2.7	1.8	5.1	*-19.1*	6.4	*-22.1*	0.363	*-6.2*
Finland	1.4	1.3	2.8		3.5		0.246	
Sweden	2.3	2.1	2.6		3.2		0.227	
United Kingdom	15.8	17.0	4.1	*-12.3*	5.2	*-9.3*	0.317	*-0.6*
EU12 avg.	-	-	3.8	*-10.2*	4.7	*-12.7*	0.297	*-6.2*
EU15 avg.	-	-	3.6	-	4.5	-	0.286	-
EU12	-	-	**4.1**	***-15.4***	**5.1**	***-18.2***	**0.307**	***-8.7***
EU15	-	-	**3.9**	-	**4.9**	-	**0.302**	-

Note: Incomes defined as disposable household incomes per equivalent person. EU12 and EU15 averages refer to unweighted country averages, EU12 and EU15 to overall EU income distribution indicators. P90/P10 defined as the ratio of the upper bound value of the ninth income decile to the upper bound value of the first income decile. S80/S20 defined as the total income share going to the top quintile divided by the total income share going to the bottom quintile. Gini coefficient and Theil index are summary inequality measures.

Source: European Community Household Panel, UDB 6th wave.

Table 12.4. **Theil inequality indexes for EU countries and decomposition of overall EU inequality in within- and between-member states inequality**

	Theil (1)		Income share (%)		Contribution to EU inequality (%)	
	1993	**1998**	**1998**	**1993**	**1998 (EU12)**	**1998 (EU15)**
Belgium	0.175	0.193	3.3	3.0	3.9	3.8
Denmark	0.100	0.100	1.7	0.8	1.0	1.0
Germany	0.150	0.110	24.3	19.9	16.5	15.8
Greece	0.246	0.211	1.9	2.3	2.5	2.4
Spain	0.202	0.187	8.1	8.6	9.4	9.0
France	0.268	0.184	17.0	24.2	19.3	18.6
Ireland	0.192	0.210	1.0	0.8	1.3	1.2
Italy	0.193	0.155	13.2	13.0	12.5	12.1
Luxembourg	0.170	0.128	0.2	0.2	0.2	0.2
Netherlands	0.121	0.133	4.6	2.7	3.8	3.7
Austria		0.129	2.3			1.8
Portugal	0.262	0.235	1.8	2.3	2.6	2.5
Finland		0.112	1.3			0.8
Sweden		0.100	2.1			1.2
UK	0.171	0.187	17.0	14.5	19.5	18.7
Between countries EU12		-	-	**7.7**	**7.4**	-
Between countries EU15		-	-	-	-	**7.3**
EU12	**0.205**	**0.177**	**94.3**	**100.0**		**100.0**
EU15	-	**0.169**	**100.0**	-		**100.0**

Note: Incomes defined as disposable household incomes per equivalent person. EU12 and EU15 refer to overall EU income distribution indicators. P90/P10 defined ass the ratio of the upper bound value of the ninth income decile to the upper bound value of the first income decile. S80/S20 defined as the total income share going to the top quintile divided by the total income share going to the bottom quintile. Gini coefficient and Theil index are summary inequality measures.

Source: European Community Household Panel, UDB 6th wave.

Chart 12.1. **Income distribution of selected EU member states, 1998**

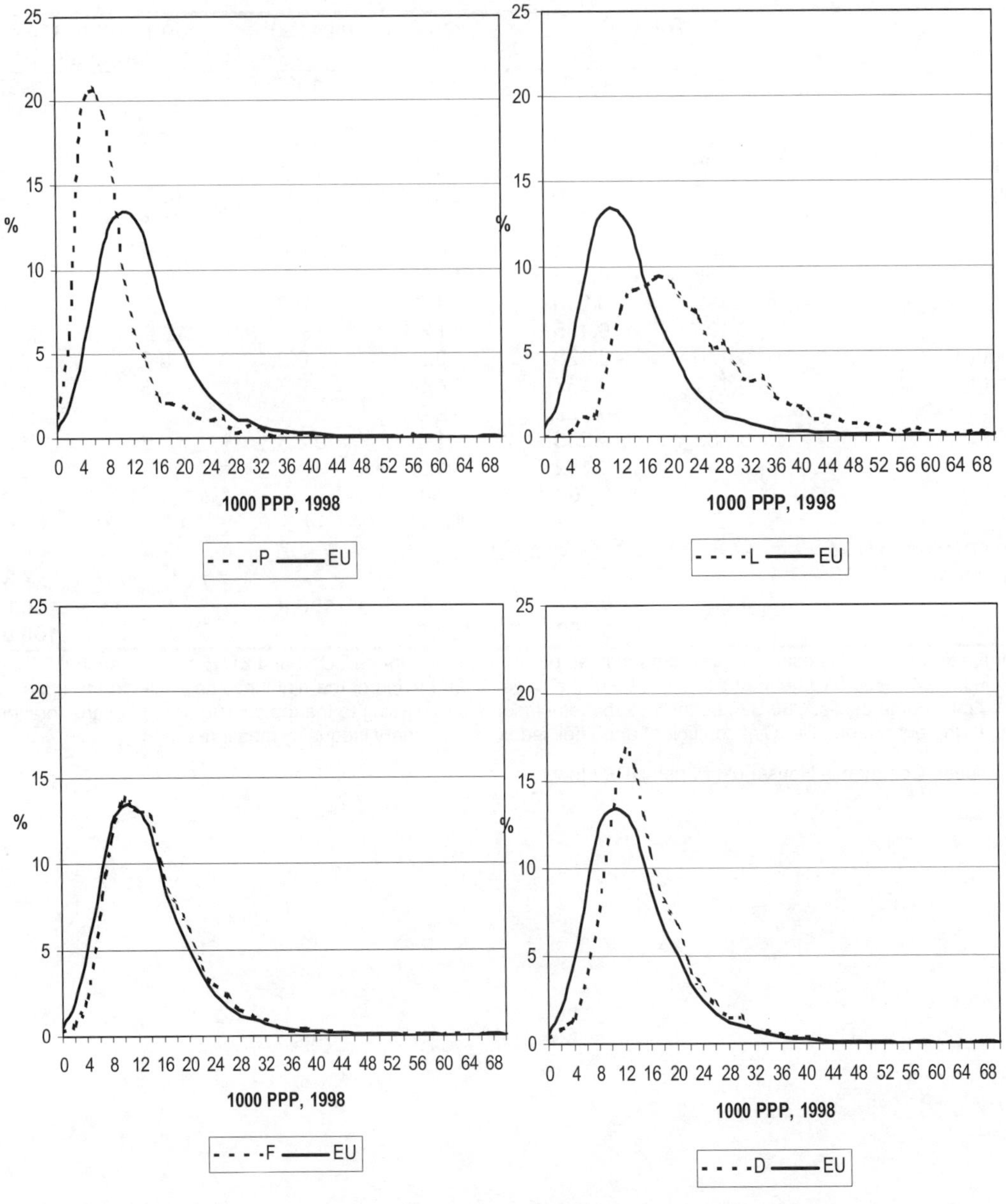

Note: incomes defined as disposable household incomes per equivalent person. Incomes expressed in European PPPs (purchasing power parities). EU average is population weighted.

Source: European Community Household Panel, UDB 6th wave.

Chart 12.2. **Average regional incomes in European PPPs, 1998**

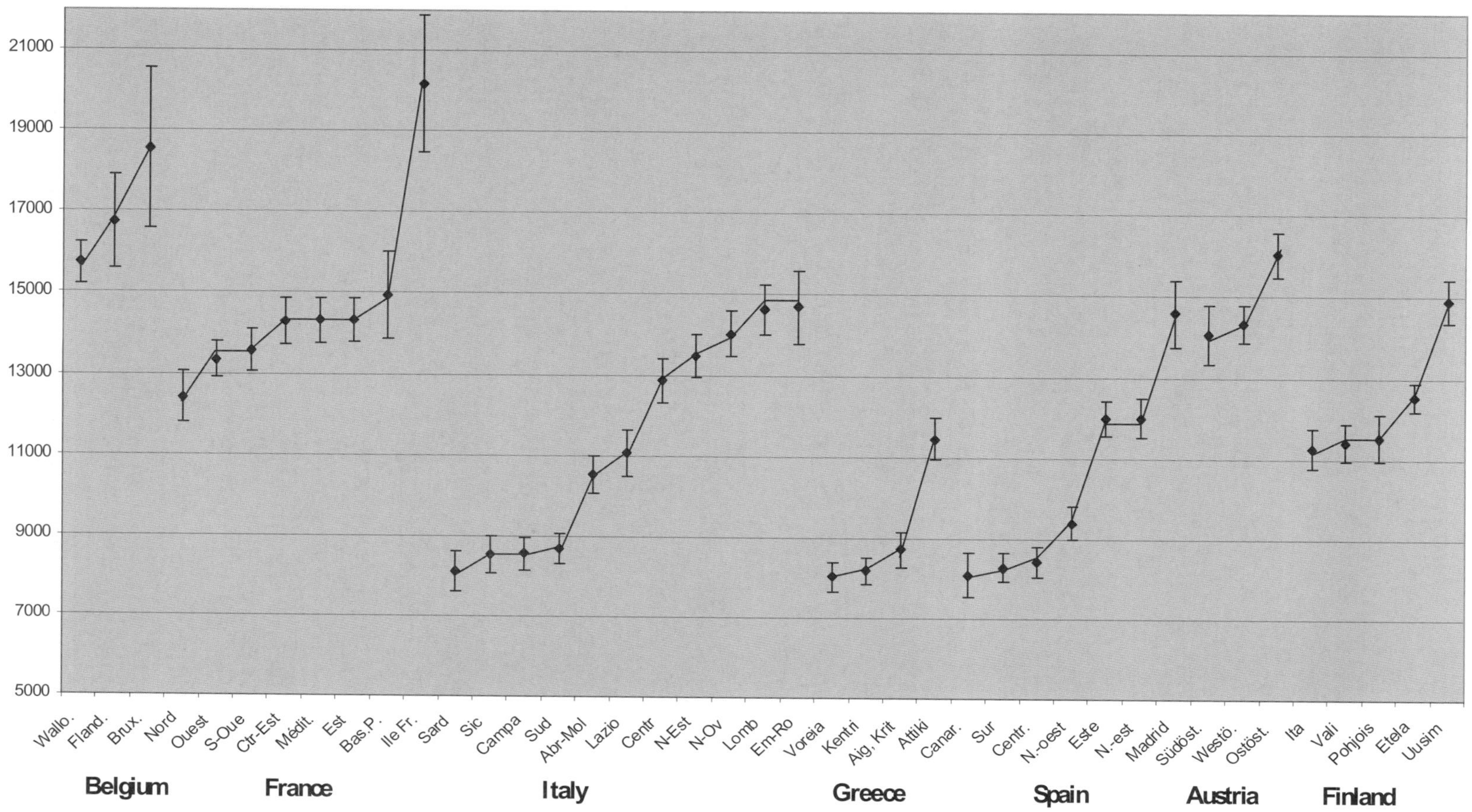

Chart 12.2. **Average regional incomes in European PPPs, 1998** (cont.)

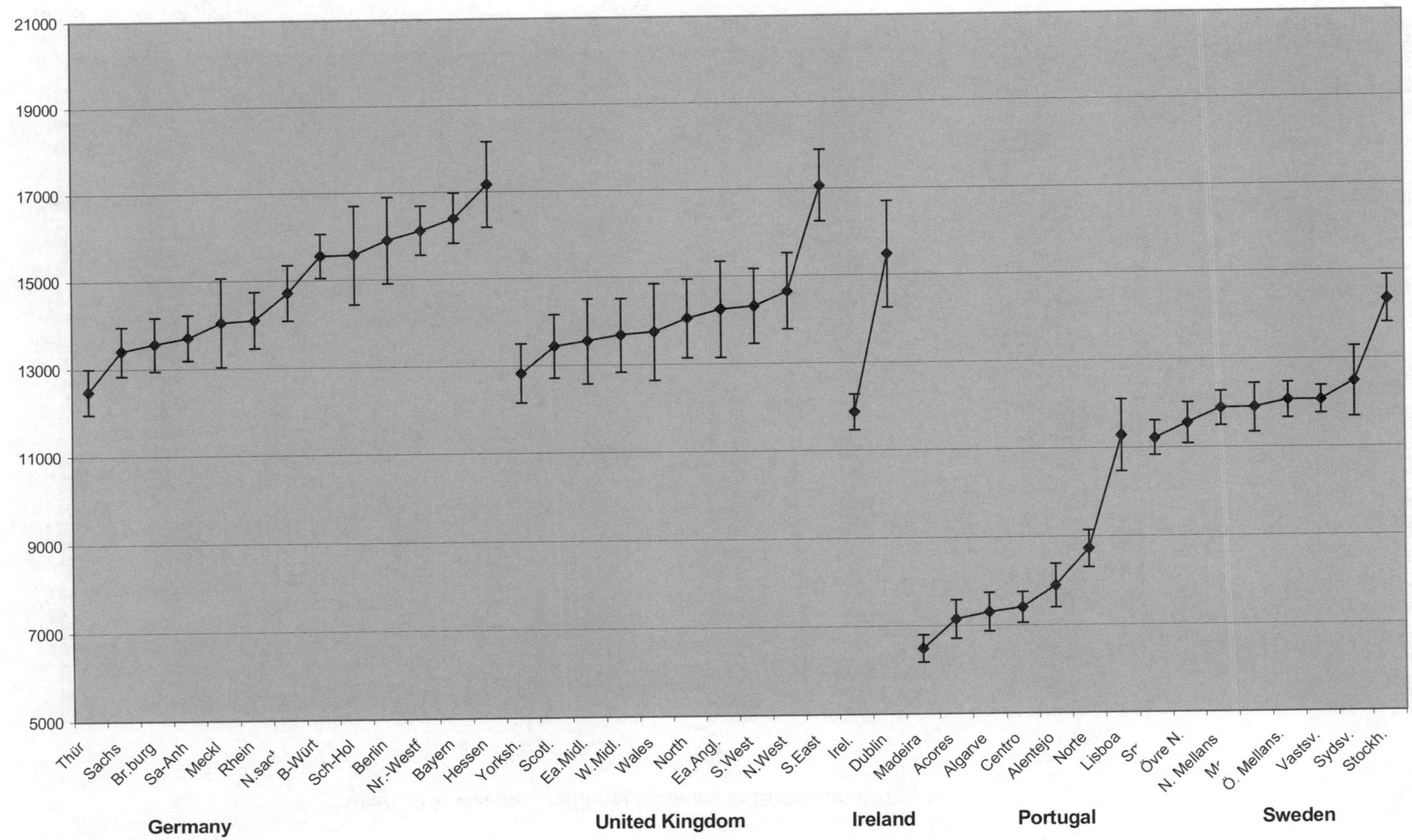

Chart 12.3. **Between-regions inequality in12 EU countries as measured by the Theil-index** (100*Theil)

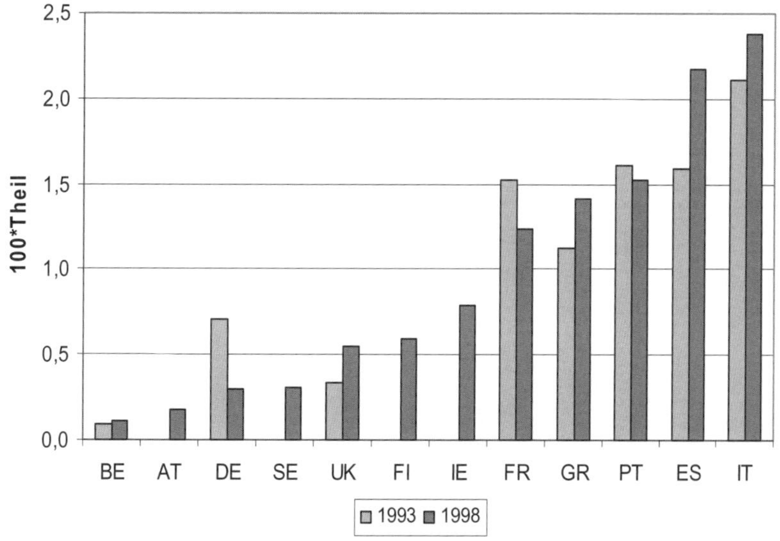

Chart 12.4. **Contribution of "between-regional" inequality to overall inequality in EU countries, as measured by Theil-index**

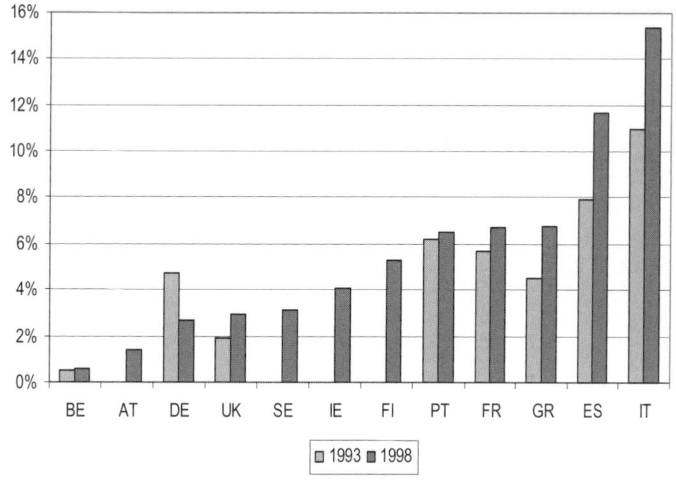

Note: Overall income inequality (100%) is decomposed into "between-regional" and "within-regional" inequality in each country.

Source: European Community Household Panel, UDB 6th wave.

GLOSSARY

CASS	Chinese Academy of Social Sciences
CNY	Yuan renminbi (Chinese monetary unit)
COE	Collectively-owned enterprise
CPC	Consumption per capita
CPI	Consumer price index
Danwei	Work unit
EPL	Employment protection legislation
FDI	Foreign direct investment
HH	Household
HHI	Household income
HHS	Household surveys
Hukou	Household registration system
INSEE	*Institut National de la Statistique et des Études Économiques*
MLG	Minimum living guarantee
NAWRU	Non-accelerating wage rate of unemployment
NBS	National Bureau of Statistics
PCGDP	Per capita GDP
PCI	Per capita Income
PPP	Purchasing power parity units
PRC	People's Republic of China
RHHS	Rural household survey
SEZ	Special economic zones
SOE	State-owned enterprise
SSB	State Statistical Bureau
RHHI	Rural household income
RHHS	Rural household survey
RPCI	Rural per capita Income
TVE	Township and village enterprise
UHHI	Urban household income
UHHS	Urban household survey
UI	Unemployment insurance
UPCI	Urban per capita Income
VAT	Value added tax
WB	World Bank
WTO	World Trade Organization

LIST OF PARTICIPANTS

CHINA

Mr. Han Wenxiu
Deputy Director General
Department of National Economy
National Development and Reform Commission (NDRC)

Mr. Nian Yong
Division Director
Department of National Economy
National Development and Reform Commission (NDRC)

Mr. Yin Yanlin
Director of Division of Income Distribution
National Development and Reform Commission (NDRC)

Mr. Feng Jianlin
Programme Officer
Department of National Economy
National Development and Reform Commission (NDRC)

Ms. Zhao Kun
Programme Officer
Department of National Economy
National Development and Reform Commission (NDRC)

EXPERTS

Mr. Yuko Arayama
School of Economics
Nagoya University
Japan

M. Claude Aubert
Directeur de Recherche
INRA-ESR
Paris

Mr. Giuseppe Bertola
Dipartimento di Economia
C.so Mediterraneo 136
University of Turin

Ms. Gudrun Biffl
Austrian Institute of Economic Research
WIFO

Mr. Francois Gipouloux
Senior Research Fellow, CNRS.
Centre d'études sur la Chine moderne et contemporaine
Ecole des Hautes Etudes en Sciences Sociales

Mr. Björn Gustafsson
Department of Social Work
Göteborg University

Mr. Pascal Mazodier
INSEE
France

Ms. Laila Porras
University of Paris 7

Ms. Mary-Françoise Renard
CERDI/IDREC
Université d'Auvergne
Clermont-Ferrand

Ms. Dipa Singh Bagai
World Bank

OECD

Mr. Eric Burgeat
Director
Centre for Co-operation with Non-Members (CCNM)

Mr. Frédéric Langer
Head of Unit
Asia and China Programmes Unit (CCNM)

Mr. Sean Dougherty
Administrator
Asia and China Programmes Unit (CCNM)

Mr. Jean-Pierre Garson
Head of Division,
DELSA, Non-member Economies and International Migration Division (NEIM)

Mr. Georges Lemaître
Principal Administrator, DELSA/NEIM

Mr. Anders Reutersward
Principal Administrator, DELSA/NEIM

Mr. Peter Whiteford
Principal Administrator, DELSA/Employment Analysis and Policy Division (EAP)

Mr. Michael Förster
Administrator, DELSA/NEIM

Ms. Marie-Ange Maurice
Consultant, DELSA/NEIM

Mr. Andrzej Kwiecinski
Administrator
Agricultural Policies in Non-member Economies (AGR/NME)

Mr. Vicenzo Spiezia
Administrator
Territorial Statistics and Indicators Unit/Public Governance and Territorial Development Directorate (TSI/GOV)

Mr. Kenneth Davies
Principal Administrator
Investment in China
Directorate for Financial, Fiscal and Enterprise Affairs

Mr. Hiroko Uchimura
Administrator
Development Centre

OECD PUBLICATIONS, 2, rue André-Pascal, 75775 PARIS CEDEX 16
PRINTED IN FRANCE
(14 2004 11 1 P) ISBN 92-64-01720-8 – No. 53675 2004